FRIENDS

In this enlightening book, Sreeram Chaulia charts yet new territory in India's foreign, security and economic policies. His case studies of India's friends encompass what Abraham Lincoln said about destroying enemies when you make friends with them, and John Lennon's getting by with a little help from one's friends. A must-read work for anyone interested in India's ascent to the highest rung in the international order.

—Lakshmi Puri
Former UN Assistant Secretary-General and former Indian Ambassador to Hungary and Bosnia and Herzegovina

Chaulia meticulously ties together India's rise as a responsible and inclusive power with the need to engage with like-minded partners. The book makes for a compelling read for afficionados of geopolitics who want to understand the current state of play and India's role within it. A timely and essential addition to the field of International Relations.

—Ram Madhav
President, India Foundation, and author of *The Indian Reality: Changing Narratives, Shifting Perceptions*

India's relationships can bamboozle the West—like aligning with the USA while reassuring Russia, and working with the Quad while remaining in the BRICS. Sreeram Chaulia's book is a must-read guide to understanding these intricacies and how they have helped establish India's global influence and rise as the next superpower.

—Justin Bassi
Executive Director, Australian Strategic Policy Institute, and former National Security Adviser to Australian Prime Minister Malcolm Turnbull

No one in the world can ignore India. However, many are unaware of India's way and approach in foreign policy. This book fills the gap via detailed case studies of India's relations with both great powers and middle powers. It is one of the best works to explain the essence of Indian diplomacy and statecraft.

—Satoru Nagao
Non-Resident Fellow, Hudson Institute, and scholar on India's military strategy and Japan-USA-India security cooperation

Chaulia has written an insightful survey of India's most important bilateral relationships in the age of great power competition. Guiding the reader through the history and dynamics of each partnership, he explains India's strategy of multi-alignment and points to its likely role in shaping a future global order.

—Lisa Curtis
Director of Indo-Pacific Security, Center for a New American Security, former US Deputy Assistant to the President, and former US National Security Council Senior Director for South and Central Asia

FRIENDS

INDIA'S
Closest Strategic Partners

SREERAM CHAULIA

RUPA

Published by
Rupa Publications India Pvt. Ltd 2024
7/16, Ansari Road, Daryaganj
New Delhi 110002

Sales centres:
Bengaluru Chennai Hyderabad
Jaipur Kathmandu Kolkata
Mumbai Prayagraj

P-ISBN: 978-93-6156-987-6
E-ISBN: 978-93-6156-830-5

First impression 2024

10 9 8 7 6 5 4 3 2 1

The moral right of the author has been asserted.

Printed in India

*To the wisdom of ancient Indian statecraft,
which spelt out the art and science of making friends
for countering enemies and accumulating power.*

∿

CONTENTS

INTRODUCTION:
A WORLD OF FRIENDS

In front of the conqueror and close to his enemy, there happen to be situated kings such as the conqueror's friend, next to him, the enemy's friend, and next to the last, the conqueror's friend's friend, and next, the enemy's friend's friend.[1]

—Kautilya, Indian strategist, 4th century BCE

It was 9 September 2023. Early on day one of the 18th G20 (Group of Twenty) summit of major world economies, I was nervously pacing about in the cavernous International Media Centre of the majestic Bharat Mandapam, the summit venue in New Delhi. Representing India's national broadcaster Doordarshan, and mingling with hundreds of foreign media persons who had gathered there to cover the summit, I could feel the uncertainty in the air. The million-dollar question in the mind of every observer at the most anticipated global diplomatic event of the year was—would India succeed in getting all the G20 member countries to agree on a final joint communiqué?

Given that the G20 meetings India had hosted in the lead-up to the main summit, involving finance ministers, central bank governors, foreign ministers, and trade and investment

---

[1]Shamasastry, Rudrapatna, *Kautilya's Arthashastra* (Translated), 2019, Global Vision Publishing House, New Delhi, p. 363.

ministers, had all yielded only chair summaries rather than full consensus-based joint statements[2], there was considerable angst about the grand finale in New Delhi.

The 2023 summit was attended by heads of government and heads of delegations of 29 countries (India also invited nine non-G20 member nations) and 14 international organizations. As they arrived at the Bharat Mandapam that day, there was apprehension about whether we would witness more international deadlock without the much-touted leaders' declaration. The declaration holds unique significance as it sets goals and priorities for the world's most important economies on matters that are critical to global governance. Since the commencement in Washington, D.C., in 2008, of this form of inclusive multilateral diplomacy to bring together advanced and emerging economies to combat global crises, all prior G20 summits had produced joint declarations. As one British news outlet put it, at the 2023 summit, 'India faces the very real prospect of presiding over the first G20 ever to fail to agree on a leaders' communique.'[3]

The prospect of a G20 summit ending without a deal, at a time when confidence in multilateralism had reached its lowest point since the end of the Cold War, was disturbing. Amid polycrises involving simultaneous ill-effects of 'interrelated environmental, geopolitical and socio-economic risks'[4], had the New Delhi G20 summit succumbed to the trend of intensifying international division and mistrust, the signal it would have conveyed was of a new world disorder, with no hope for any

[2]Mohan, Geeta, 'G20 Joint Communiqué Elusive Even After 19 Meets Amid China, Russia Opposition', *India Today*, 4 September 2023, https://tinyurl.com/4sbs7s3x. Accessed on 29 May 2024.
[3]Sharma, Shweta, 'Will India's G20 Summit be a "Stunning" Success—or an Embarrassment?' *The Independent*, 8 September 2023, https://tinyurl.com/3hyk8sbx. Accessed on 29 May 2024.
[4]WEF, *The Global Risks Report 2023*, World Economic Forum, Geneva, 2023, p. 9.

collective action, cooperation or leadership. Notwithstanding the lofty unifying motto of India's G20 presidency—'One Earth, One Family, One Future'—the possibility of the world sliding back into what English political theorist Thomas Hobbes termed in the 17th century as a savage state of nature marked by *'bellum omnium contra omnes'* (war of everyone against everyone)[5], seemed terrifyingly real. History bears witness that when multilateral institutions collapse or become ineffective, the guardrails fall, giving rise to violent and destructive outcomes. Nothing less than the future of the world and of planet earth was at stake on that fateful day in New Delhi.

BRINGING THE BILATERALS BACK IN

For the host nation India, and its ambitious Prime Minister Narendra Modi, international prestige as a rising power that can constructively build bridges between the Global South and the Global North, and between the geopolitical West and the geopolitical East, was at stake. Prime Minister Narendra Modi had left no stone unturned in making India's G20 presidency a milestone in the country's diplomatic history, amply reflected in India conducting 'over 220 meetings in 60 cities across all 28 states and 8 union territories', receiving 'more than 1 lakh [a hundred thousand] participants from approximately 125 nationalities' and ensuring that '1.5 crore [15 million] individuals in our country have been involved in these programmes or have been exposed to various aspects of them.'[6] Dubbed as 'the country's coming-out party, on a

[5]Hobbes, Thomas, *Leviathan*, 2009, Cosimo Books, New York, p. 72.
[6]MC, 'India's Growth is Good for the World', *Moneycontrol*, 6 September 2023, https://tinyurl.com/dhzh39en. Accessed on 17 June 2024.

par with China's 2008 Olympics,[7] the idea was to showcase through the G20 presidency that India had finally arrived on the world stage as the number one problem solver, and as what Modi had popularized—a *Vishwaguru* (mentor/teacher to the world).

The 2023 G20 summit was conceptualized at a grand scale for it to be remembered as the inflection point from where India surged to the fore and was universally acknowledged as the next big player in world politics. One needed no better example of how a rising power could utilize multilateralism to enhance its influence and leave its stamp of authority on international affairs, than the New Delhi G20 summit.

Cognizant of the magnitude of that moment, we were all astounded at the Bharat Mandapam to learn within a few hours of the summit's first day that India had pulled off the miracle. Defying the sceptics and the doomsayers, and contrary to expectations that hard-nosed haggling and bargaining among the G20 members over the draft final communiqué would agonizingly stretch into the 11th hour of the second and final day, Prime Minister Modi confidently announced the 'good news'—consensus had been reached due to the 'hard work of our teams'—and banged the gavel on the desk thrice to indicate that the New Delhi Leaders' Declaration had been adopted unanimously.[8] The icing on the cake was that this joint communiqué had not even a single dissenting footnote or chair summary—a surprisingly good result. We rushed to take position in front of our

---

[7]Bajpaee, Chietigj, 'Why India's G20 Triumph Means Much More than the Tangible Results', *South China Morning Post*, 19 September 2023, https://tinyurl.com/3dh27s4n. Accessed on 29 May 2024.

[8]Laskar, Rezaul, 'Consensus on G20 Summit Leaders' Declaration Achieved, Announces PM Modi', *Hindustan Times*, 9 September 2023, https://tinyurl.com/yh6vwxja. Accessed on 29 May 2024.

television cameras to explain the import of this diplomatic *coup* to audiences. The world breathed a sigh of relief and the delegates at the Bharat Mandapam seemed relaxed. Journalists who had been prepping readers and viewers to hunker down for a bitter battle, with no guarantee of a happy ending, could be seen throwing up their hands in wonder at this outcome!

Not privy at that time to what exactly Prime Minister Modi's foreign policy mandarins did behind the scenes to register the great international triumph, my intuitive guess was that the G20 success must have been the outcome of deft harnessing of a pivotal diplomatic treasure—India's array of key bilateral strategic partnerships. That multilateralism is built upon a web of robust bilateral linkages has been widely documented in the scholarly field of International Relations. Multilateralism need not be seen as distinct from or as contradictory to bilateral ties, but rather as an amalgamation and manifestation of a series of intersecting and cross-cutting bilateral relationships. International Relations scholar Alice Pannier's observations are cited below in some detail for the reader:

> [...] all multilateral negotiations (e.g. at the UN and the World Trade Organization—WTO) require pre-negotiations and coalition-building on a bilateral level [...] Bilateral partnerships may therefore affect negotiations at the multilateral level, and in return, strong bilateral relations tend to influence national strategies and stances in multilateral arenas. On the one hand, a bilateral relationship deemed highly important ("special relationships") may, in any given multilateral negotiation, lead a government to take a position that seems not to be in line with "national interests," with the aim of preserving that bilateral relationship. Conversely,

conflictual bilateral relations may have the effect of blocking multilateral relations.[9]

For the New Delhi G20 Leaders' Declaration, India teamed up with its multiple special partners to make it happen. Prime Minister Modi personally held more than 15 bilateral meetings and pull-asides on the sidelines of the summit, including with his counterparts from countries officially designated as India's strategic partners—Brazil, France, Germany, Italy, Japan, Saudi Arabia, South Korea, the United Kingdom (UK), the United States of America (USA), the United Arab Emirates (UAE), and the European Union (EU—a multilateral entity which has signed a bilateral strategic partnership with India on behalf of its 27 member countries).[10]

Just a day before the New Delhi G20 summit, Modi was in Jakarta to attend a summit with the ten-member Association of Southeast Asian Nations (ASEAN), which has a comprehensive strategic partnership with India. There, Modi also met President Joko Widodo of Indonesia, another strategic partner of India that hosted the G20 in 2022 and was part of the troika alongside India and the G20 host for 2024, Brazil.[11] Since Vladimir Putin, the President of Russia, had decided to skip the New Delhi G20 summit and sent his Foreign Minister Sergey Lavrov instead, so that the former could avoid tense in-person interactions with Western adversaries who were arming and financing Ukraine in its war

---

[9]Pannier, Alice, 'Bilateral Relations', in Balzacq, Thierry, Frédéric Charillon and Frédéric Ramel, eds., *Global Diplomacy: An Introduction to Theory and Practice*, 2020, Palgrave Macmillan, London, pp. 26–27.

[10]IT, 'PM-Biden Bilateral at his Residence, 14 Other Meetings on Sidelines of G20', *India Today*, 8 September 2023, https://tinyurl.com/pyenpx48. Accessed on 29 May 2024.

[11]NM, 'PM's Departure Statement Ahead of his Visit to Jakarta, Indonesia', Narendra Modi, 6 September 2023, https://tinyurl.com/sxndww6v. Accessed on 24 June 2024.

against Russia, Modi had a personal telephonic conversation with Putin a few weeks before the G20 summit in which he conveyed thanks to Russia for its 'consistent support to all initiatives under India's G20 Presidency'.[12]

Modi was aided and assisted by India's G20 core team of ministers and negotiating diplomats who assiduously networked with each and every strategic partner of India at different levels of official hierarchy to address specific concerns and objections, and to remind each country of the higher purpose which bound India to it through the strategic partnerships. The implicit generic messaging was that India had made its G20 presidency an event of supreme national pride, and that the G20 was the platform where real friends and strategic partners would be expected to stand up to be counted for India's honour. Had any of India's strategic partners stiffed it at the G20, the implication would have been deleterious for its bilateral relationship with India.

Such a threat may not have been explicitly issued, but the sheer seriousness and sense of responsibility that India demonstrated during its G20 presidency left little doubt that spoilsports at the summit would have to bear a cost for raining on India's parade. Pannier's point that the need for preservation of a special bilateral relationship can compel countries to climb down from their maximalist positions, and compromise in a multilateral setting, is well illustrated by what happened behind closed doors before and during the New Delhi G20 summit.

---

[12]BT, 'G20 Summit: PM Modi speaks to Putin; Lavrov to Represent Russia in India', *Business Today*, 28 August 2023, https://tinyurl.com/yc38enza. Accessed on 5 June, 2024.

THE POLITICS OF CONSENSUS

The principal sticking point which had raised fears of a washout at the New Delhi summit was the ongoing Russia-Ukraine War, and the stark polarization between two camps over it within the G20. Western powers wanted strong accusatory language in the Leaders' Declaration that would name and shame Russia for its invasion and occupation of large parts of Ukraine. The G20 joint communiqué was intended by the USA and its European allies to become one more instrument for applying concerted pressure on Russia so that it would look like the core of the international community had spoken with moral clarity, and delegitimized Moscow's behaviour. On the other side of the aisle was Russia itself, which publicly insisted that 'there will be no general declaration on behalf of all members if our position [on Ukraine] is not reflected.'[13] China, whose President Xi Jinping also preferred to not show up for the G20 summit owing to unfathomable motives, echoed the sentiment of its comprehensive strategic partner Russia, and refused to accept wording in the joint communiqué that would condemn Russia for aggression, and demand its complete and unconditional withdrawal from Ukrainian territory. Beijing and Moscow had conceded to such wording during the 2022 G20 summit in Bali, Indonesia, but hardened their lines and threatened to use their veto power by the time it was India's turn to host the G20 in 2023.[14]

This deadlock reflected much more than what Russia and China dubbed as misuse or politicization of the G20,

---

[13]Reuters, 'Russia to Block G20 Declaration if its Views are Ignored, Lavrov Says', 1 September 2023, https://tinyurl.com/e7r24anf. Accessed on 29 May 2024.

[14]PTI, 'Russia, China Isolated on Ukraine Crisis: EU Official Amid India's Efforts to Build Consensus on Draft G20 Leaders' Declaration', *The Times of India*, 7 September 2023, https://tinyurl.com/yc7zxv7d. Accessed on 29 May 2024.

whose mandate is supposed to be confined to global *economic* matters. In a profound way, it pointed to a full-blown crisis of multilateralism and the spread of what Prime Minister Modi lamented as 'global trust deficit'.[15] The story of how India overcame this trust deficit, at least in the G20, and pieced together the joint communiqué is laden with evidence about the centrality of bilateral strategic partnerships in today's conflict-prone and brittle world order. Based on insider accounts from multiple G20 countries, it came to light that India played the China threat card with the USA and the Europeans to convince them to water down the harsh anti-Russia language they were seeking. The host nation indicated that 'if the Indian presidency failed in the quest, not only did the summit risk being a failure, there was a bigger risk of China's efforts to carve out an alternative international power structure gaining traction.' Modi's mavens also dangled the carrot that 'the West and the Global South could nuance their positions about the implications of the [Ukraine] war,' provided the West showed flexibility on the anti-Russian wording. Consequently, the USA, which is knee-deep in strategic competition with China for global influence, realized how heavily it was invested in seeing the success of the Indian presidency, saw merit in the argument, and displayed unexpected flexibility to support New Delhi. The apparent conversion or softening of the American stand on the G20 joint communiqué due to the logic of enabling India's rise and checking China's power, was a game-changer that helped arrive at a consensus.

In dealing with the opposite camp, India assured Russia that it would not be put in the dock by being accused as an

---

[15]Sharma, Harikishan, 'G20 Summit: PM Flags "Global Trust Deficit", Calls for Human-Centric, Inclusive Approach', *The Indian Express*, 9 September 2023, https://tinyurl.com/3u6by88v. Accessed on 5 June, 2024.

aggressor. Moreover, the declaration would urge 'all states' to refrain from the 'threat or use of force' against territorial integrity as well as 'political independence' of any state, meaning that it could be interpreted as validating Russia's concerns about the eastward expansion of the USA-led North Atlantic Treaty Organization (NATO). In return, Moscow had to 'also convince its friend, Beijing, to play along.' If it did not take this offer, then 'it was for Moscow to understand how it would be perceived in India and the Global South.'[16] The combination of cajoling and threatening seemingly worked, because just as the USA was anxious to preserve its comprehensive global and strategic partnership with India at all costs, Russia could not afford to forsake its special and privileged strategic partnership with India.

Apart from bridging the geopolitical gap between the West and the East on the Russia-Ukraine War, India also succeeded in gaining recognition as the genuine 'Voice of the Global South' during its presidency. It was a happy coincidence that India had bilateral strategic partnerships with both Indonesia and Brazil, its co-passengers in the G20 troika, as well as with South Africa. This quartet of large emerging economies, whose national interests mostly converge, quite effectively pressurized G20 members that were holding out on one issue or the other and blocking consensus.

India's sherpa (Prime Minister Modi's senior representative to the G20) Amitabh Kant recalled after the New Delhi summit concluded that 'Indonesia, Brazil and South Africa supported us in strategy, process, and persuasion [...] We successfully built a coalition of emerging markets which began with members of the troika [...] and expanded to all emerging markets in

---

[16]Jha, Prashant, 'At G20, Skilful Diplomacy to Clear Messaging: How India Forged Consensus on the Declaration', *Hindustan Times*, 10 September 2023, https://tinyurl.com/25jmcah7. Accessed on 24 June 2024.

G20.'[17] Since these countries had their own respective bilateral strategic partnerships with China, Russia and the developed countries belonging to the G7 group, they also impressed upon all principal parties to find common ground. Like India, these emerging economies perceived their national identities as falling squarely on the side of the Global South, and emphasized their concerns that 'development issues are far more important than war issues.' Kant noted that ultimately, 'I think what helped were bilateral meets with each country [...] Important thing was to draw each nation's red lines.'[18]

The fact that India had formal strategic partnerships with 17 of the 20 G20 members (*see* Annexure, Table III), barring Canada, Mexico and Turkey, gave the host nation a leg up in ensuring the consensus. Of these 17, only the strategic partnership with China has become dysfunctional due to a metamorphosis in Chinese foreign policy since the advent of Xi Jinping. China is today undoubtedly India's main strategic adversary, and readers will see throughout this book how Chinese threat animates and imbues India's strategic partnerships with a core strategic intent. Here, the point being made is that the value of strategic partnerships cannot be overstated, not just in terms of mutual benefits that a bilateral dyad engenders for the two partners, but for the wider cause of global governance. Bilateral diplomacy has been, and will remain, the most basic and fundamental form of foreign relations, even as trilaterals, minilaterals, plurilaterals and multilaterals proliferate, with the goal of addressing a multitude of issues and problems. To use a culinary metaphor, bilaterals are the bread and butter for any country's foreign

---

[17]Kant, Amitabh, 'How India Scaled Mount G20', *The Times of India*, 13 September 2023, https://tinyurl.com/y56styb7. Accessed on 5 June 2024.
[18]Som, Vishnu, '"Negotiated With Russia, China, Only Last Night...": G20 Sherpa On Consensus', *NDTV*, 10 September 2023, https://tinyurl.com/3exk2h3m. Accessed on 5 June 2024.

policy, while the other extended forms of diplomacy add extra dishes and dessert on the dining table. Without a substantive portion of the bread and butter, the meal would be dissatisfying and leave everyone hungry.

Turning the focus on bilateral strategic partnerships is all the more necessary in contemporary times, especially because multilateralism is tottering and progressively proving to be less legitimate, feasible and fruitful. Notwithstanding India's successful presidency, the general state of multilateralism is in doldrums due to big structural changes. Large multilateral institutions like the United Nations (UN), the World Trade Organization (WTO), and the International Criminal Court (ICC) are proving less capable of serving their mandates today due to their lack of representative and performance legitimacy.[19] Senior UN official David Chikvaidze has argued that 'we no longer live in a bipolar [two great powers] or unipolar [a single great power] world; and not yet in a multipolar [more than two great powers] one, but, rather, in an unsettled world with multiple actors of different calibre, with clashing interests and often isolationist politics of fear and resentment.' He adds that 'multipolarity without strong and accepted multilateral instruments is inherently unstable, volatile, and dangerous,' and that as commonly accepted rules, institutions and regimes are disintegrating, 'There is a feeling of growing instability and hair-trigger tensions, which make everything far more unpredictable and uncontrollable, with a heightened risk of miscalculation.'[20] Forces of economic globalization and interdependence will still sustain demand for effective multilateralism, as we have seen through the

---

[19]IANS, 'India Warns UN May Face Oblivion Without Reforms to Make it Relevant', *Business Standard*, 23 August 2022, https://tinyurl.com/fum24bar. Accessed on 5 June 2024.
[20]Chikvaidze, David, 'Multilateralism: Its Past, Present and Future', *CADMUS*, Vol. 4, No. 2, 2020, pp. 130–131.

surging expectations from the G20. But even these underlying economic determinants which have been credited with fostering a spirit of broad pragmatic cooperation among countries, are progressively becoming shakier.[21]

The risks that arise during global power transitions from one order to another, and the erosion of stability and confidence in larger group-based diplomacy mean that countries have to fall back on orthodox and time-tested methods of attaining security and economic prosperity, i.e. bilateral strategic partnerships with small group extensions. No matter how volatile and unstable the international system is, a group of close friends willing to have your back because reciprocally, you will go out of your way to help them, is worth its weight in gold. From the perspective of a country's core national interests, there has never been a substitute for bilateral friendships. The shifting world order is reinforcing this truism and highlighting the salience of bilateral strategic partnerships.

A RISING POWER'S CHOICES

This book is about India's most consequential bilateral strategic partnerships, and the impact each of these friendships has had on India's rise as a leading power in the world.[22] Listed below are some questions it seeks to address:

What does India's choice of friends tell us about the kind of power that India is and the type of grand strategy it has adopted?

---

[21]Ripsman, Norrin, 'Globalization, Deglobalization and Great Power Politics', *International Affairs*, Vol. 97, No. 5, 2021, pp. 1317–1333.
[22]ANI, '"India's Quest to be a Leading Power Built on Investing in Relationships": Jaishankar at India International Centre', *The Economic Times*, 22 February 2023, https://tinyurl.com/uakk4rrf. Accessed on 5 June 2024.

How did each friend strengthen India's military might, its economic growth and its soft power, and what did that friend receive from India as a quid pro quo?

Why have these friendships become so thick and resilient that they are able to withstand periodic shocks and disruptions in the present transitory world order?

What explains the unique productivity and regional or global impact of a particular friendship?

Can India's friends be friends with India's enemies and still retain its trust and vice versa?

Can India carry on with its friendships, or will friendships have to one day yield to rigid marriages as a result of deteriorating global conditions?

Since it takes two to tango, the chapters that follow will reveal not only a view of India's friends from an Indian lens, but also a view of India from the vantage point of those friends. In fact, the aforementioned guiding questions could easily be transposed on to each of India's main friends. As seen in the case of the G20 coalition-building, each friend of India has its own friendships, and it is essential to move beyond navel gazing to depict how India's friends perceive it in comparison to others, what they expect from it, and to what extent India is catering to their needs. India's image and identity are not entirely self-made but codetermined by the outside world, particularly by its friends who happen to be powerful in both material and ideational realms. The old Spanish proverb, 'Tell me who your friends are, and I'll tell you who you are,'[23] will be a leitmotif in this book as we examine India's friendships, and shed light on the essence of

---

[23]Hays, Pamela, *Connecting Across Cultures: The Helper's Toolkit*, 2012, SAGE Publications, Thousand Oaks, p. 44.

India itself on the world stage.

The purpose and function of India's friendships can only be appreciated properly if we assess the kind of power India is in the present world order. A middle power is defined as 'a state with medium-range capabilities (material and immaterial) at its disposal to protect its core interests [...] endowed with regional impact [...] capable of revising specific elements of the systemic order [...] must identify itself as a middle power [...] and be recognised by others in this perceived role.'[24] As early as 1979, when India was a very poor low-income country with far lesser capabilities than is the case today, American thinker John Mellor christened it as a 'rising middle power' by virtue of being one of the most advanced Third World countries, with an independent foreign policy and a 'growing ability [...] to influence world events.'[25]

Over the decades, the label of 'middle power' has continued to be assigned to India, with some qualifying prefixes and suffixes. In 2003, International Relations scholar T.V. Paul called it a 'quasi-status quo middle power' that is 'not fully satisfied with the hierarchy of power in the international system, but is willing to accept many of the parameters of the international order.'[26]

In 2014, the Australian and Indian writers Rory Medcalf and C. Raja Mohan clubbed India along with Australia, Japan, South Korea, Indonesia, Vietnam, etc., and argued that they can all 'plausibly be defined as middle powers for the time

---

[24]Swielande, Tanguy Struye de, 'Middle Powers: A Comprehensive Definition and Typology', in Swielande, Tanguy Struye de, Dorothee Vandamme et al, eds., *Rethinking Middle Powers in the Asian Century*, 2019, Routledge, London, p. 23.
[25]Mellor, John W., ed., *India: A Rising Middle Power*, 1979, Westview Press, Boulder, p. 368.
[26]Paul, T.V., 'Systemic Conditions and Security Cooperation: Explaining the Persistence of the Nuclear Non-Proliferation Regime', *Cambridge Review of International Affairs*, Vol. 16, No. 1, 2003, p. 139.

being, given their internal challenges, and the limits of their capacity to shape the strategic environment unilaterally.'[27] Writing in 2023, Polish scholar Emilian Kavalski referred to the 'contested nature of India's standing—jostling between an aspiring great power, a regional South Asian hegemon, and a begrudging middle power.'[28]

Some observers have deemed India as having already become a great power in certain contexts. One scholar, Manjeet Pardesi, contended in 2015 that given the 'regionalization of world politics', India has emerged as an accepted great power in Southeast Asia, which falls outside its home region of South Asia.[29] British commentator Martin Wolf judged in 2023 that with rapid economic growth strides, India was 'a rising great power', and it was 'quite reasonable to assume' that it 'will become a great power'.[30]

Projections into the future about a fully formed multipolar world order list India as one of the great powers that will take its due place in the international power configuration. For example, Norwegian diplomat Jo Inge Bekkevold wrote in 2023 that 'in the long term, the world may indeed become multipolar, with India being the most obvious candidate to join the ranks of the USA and China. Nevertheless, that day is still far off. We will be living in a bipolar world for the foreseeable future—and strategy and policy should be designed

---

[27]Medcalf, Rory, and C. Raja Mohan, 'Responding to Indo-Pacific Rivalry: Australia, India and Middle Power Coalitions', The Lowy Institute, Sydney, p. 7.
[28]Kavalski, Emilian, 'India's Indo-Pacific Gambit: An Awkward Power Striving for Status?' *Teoria Polityki*, Vol. 6, 2022, p. 207.
[29]Pardesi, Manjeet, 'Is India a Great Power? Understanding Great Power Status in Contemporary International Relations', *Asian Security*, Vol. 11, No. 1, 2015, p. 1.
[30]Wolf, Martin, 'Western Leaders are Making a Sensible Bet on India', *Financial Times*, 18 July 2023, https://tinyurl.com/4ty34ysc. Accessed on 5 June 2024.

accordingly.'[31] Nationalistic Indians themselves often bristle at the tag of 'middle power', and tend to think and speak of their country as a great power or superpower.[32] But the weight of neutral assessments places India in the middle and rising categories, with the caveat that it may be considered a nascent great power or a global power-to-be.

Since the bulk of the discourse on India, as of 2024, prefers to affix the status of 'middle power' or 'rising power', it is useful to unpack the typical foreign policy behavioural characteristics of middle and rising powers to fully grasp India's approach to making and maintaining friends or strategic partners. Unlike great powers, which have a preponderance of military and economic resources, and which display natural tendencies to act unilaterally and coercively, middle powers are cognisant of their limitations and constraints.

The Canadian scholar Ronald Behringer's concept of 'middlepowermanship' contends that archetypal middle powers have three distinct characteristics. Firstly, since they cannot dabble in each and every matter in world affairs, they specialize in certain issue areas where they have competence and skills, and exercise effective leadership in those domains. Since great powers dominate the military and security landscape, middle powers choose to operate in 'economic and social realms'. Secondly, they 'use their entrepreneurial skills to build a coalition of the like-minded' which is made to look as if it represents 'humanitarian interests of the international community, rather than the narrow national interests of any particular state.' Thirdly, they channelize their energies into exercising soft power options such as 'diplomatic persuasion,

---

[31]Bekkevold, Jo Inge, 'No, the World is Not Multipolar', *Foreign Policy*, 22 September 2023, https://tinyurl.com/55wabj8d. Accessed on 5 June 2024.
[32]LM, 'PM Modi Transformed India from a Third-World Country into a Global Superpower in Just 8 Years: Harsh Vardhan', *Mint*, 7 June 2022, https://tinyurl.com/ykk54v6y. Accessed on 5 June 2024.

use of information and communications technologies, and their prestigious reputations as credible and reliable actors.'[33] The case studies of middle powers which Behringer cited to establish this schema of traits included Australia, Austria, Canada, Mexico, the Netherlands, Norway, Poland, Sweden and Switzerland.

Aspects of this rather benign and virtuous-sounding portrayal of middle powers do find some resonance in contemporary Indian foreign policy. The sincerity and commitment with which India took on the role of steering the G20 through a difficult phase for multilateralism, the stress India laid on being the 'Voice of the Global South' by consulting and mobilizing representatives from 125 developing countries[34], the constant Indian refrain that 'the path of diplomacy and dialogue should be the only viable option'[35] for resolving active wars and armed hostilities worldwide, and India carving out a niche for itself as a provider and promoter of digital public infrastructure (DPI) for the developing world[36]—all exemplify the middle-power playbook to the hilt.

Apart from the generic behavioural features identified by Behringer, middle powers have also been ascribed with distinct foreign policy inclinations vis-à-vis great powers. The Canadian writer Andrew Cooper notes that the 'first wave' of Western middle powers like Australia and Canada performed

---

[33]Behringer, Ronald, 'The Dynamics of Middlepowermanship', *Seton Hall Journal of Diplomacy and International Relations*, Vol. 36, No. 52, 2013, pp. 14, 16, 18.

[34]MEA, 'Voice of the Global South Summit 2023', Ministry of External Affairs, Government of India, 13 January 2023, https://tinyurl.com/mrps99sk. Accessed on 5 June 2024.

[35]PTI, 'Path of Diplomacy, Dialogue Should be the Only Viable Option: India on Ukraine Conflict', *The Hindu*, 7 May 2022, https://tinyurl.com/y443vjve. Accessed on 5 June 2024.

[36]Roy, Annapurna, 'India's Digital Public Infrastructure to Reach 50 Countries in Next 5 Years: Nilekani', *The Economic Times*, 27 August 2023, https://tinyurl.com/2m8yyucx. Accessed on 5 June 2024.

'followership' or 'system supporter' roles under the alliance system led by the USA during the Cold War era.[37] Occasionally, they would serve as a loyal opposition to the USA on specific issues, but were overall helpful in managing the global order that was designed by it.

In the post-Cold War era, a new set of countries joined Canada and Australia to populate the middle powers list as part of a 'second wave'. These later arrivals, such as Argentina, Indonesia, South Africa and South Korea, showed a burst of diplomatic activism in multilateral settings and undertook greater bargaining, but did not challenge the USA-led liberal order. Rather than being 'antagonistic to the global order as it stood', they 'wanted to stretch and refine that order' in a more ethical and moral direction.[38] These non-traditional middle powers had a reformist bent of mind, whereas traditional middle powers followed a path of appeasing, or sustaining the Western-led order. However, whatever reform the second-wave middle powers sought were within limits because they were not interested in making 'deep concessions to the interests of peripheral countries', i.e. the least developed nations.[39]

A 'third wave' of middle powers, including Mexico, Turkey and Saudi Arabia, all of whom rose to prominence after the 2008 global economic crisis through their inclusion in the G20, has been associated with more rebellious approaches. These nations 'seek fundamental revisions of or transformations in the post-WWII institutions in order to address the problems of the majority of the world's states,' and also have faith

---

[37]Cooper, Andrew, 'Testing Middle Powers' Collective Action in a World of Diffuse Power', *International Journal*, Vol. 71, No. 4, 2016, pp. 533, 536.
[38]Cooper, Andrew, and Emel Dal, 'Positioning the Third Wave of Middle Power Diplomacy', *The International Journal*, Vol. 71, No. 4, 2016, p. 518.
[39]Jordaan, Eduard, 'The Concept of a Middle Power in International Relations: Distinguishing Between Traditional and Emerging Middle Powers', *Politikon*, Vol. 30, No. 2, 2003, p. 176.

in regionalism for tackling rivalries posed by neighbouring powers or great powers.[40]

India's conduct in the contemporary era does not at all match the profile of a traditional Western middle power. It has shades of the non-traditional second-wave and third-wave middle powers, but it transcends the usual middle power bracketing due to two overwhelming factors. Firstly, as mentioned earlier in the present Introduction, India is widely viewed as the contender with the best chance from among a dozen or so middle powers to rise up the totem pole, and one day, take its seat as a great power. According to American scholar Randall Schweller, if getting in and moving out of middle-power status is seen as a dynamic journey or flow, then there are three routes.

> Developing middle powers with the requisite critical mass to become major powers eventually climb the ladder of power out of the category. Conversely, declining major powers fall to middle power status. And rising minor powers must pass through the middle power rank on their way up the hierarchy of power.[41]

India has a foot on the ladder and is ontologically different from Russia—a former great power on the decline—and also different from Israel and the UAE—small powers in a global sense, and at best, destined to be middle powers. Recognizing this unique position of India in an international order that is in rapid flux is key to comprehending the rationale and

---

[40]Neack, Laura, 'Pathways to Power: A Comparative Study of the Foreign Policy Ambitions of Turkey, Brazil, Canada and Australia', *Seton Hall Journal of Diplomacy and International Relations*, Vol. 14, No. 2, 2013, p. 63.

[41]Schweller, Randall, 'The Concept of Middle Power', in Cha, Victor, and Marie Dumond, eds., *The Korean Pivot: The Study of South Korea as a Global Power*, 2017, Center for Strategic and International Studies, Washington, D.C., p. 5.

workings of its friendships with other middle and great powers.

India is not the straightforward status quoist middle power that happily works to uphold the liberal international order, or maintain American hegemony with minor modifications and improvements. There are undoubtedly significant convergences of interests between India and the USA (*see* Chapter 3). At the same time, India is not comparable to middle powers which are formal American allies such as Australia, Canada, Germany, Saudi Arabia and Turkey, which may occasionally disagree with the USA, but in effect, operate within the parameters of the American alliance system.

India has a history of prizing strategic autonomy and an articulated vision of a multipolar order, with itself as one of the poles in a democratized international system that prevents hegemonic domination by any single country. Shyam Saran, former Foreign Secretary to the Government of India, harks back to India's cosmological texts to show that they do not assign centrality or superiority to *Bharatvarsha* (ancient Sanskritic term for India) but envision it as 'one among the lotus petals that make up our universe'. This Indian worldview is the exact converse of the Chinese historical vision 'which sees the Han core as the most advanced', and countries around and further away as 'barbaric and less civilised'.[42] Two millennia since the ancient Hindu mythological writings, the idea of a genuinely multipolar world, with India as one among many lotus petals remains an article of faith in the country. Throughout this book, the reader will come across this sentiment, and see how it has guided India's choice of friends, and the kinds of cooperation it engages in with them.

The second quality which sets India apart from other middle powers is that its geopolitical and strategic calculus

---

[42]Saran, Shyam, *How India Sees the World: Kautilya to the 21ˢᵗ Century,* 2017, Juggernaut Books, New Delhi, p. 16.

is informed by hotly contested land borders and maritime spaces, with a recently arisen aggressive great power, China, which props up Pakistan, a nuclear-armed state, to pin down India in South Asia. India cannot afford to be content with diplomacy meant to prove its credentials as a good global citizen, launching initiatives for world welfare in multilateral institutions, and promoting moral norms via soft power techniques. It has to deal with the ugly realities of power politics and practise hard realpolitik, manoeuvring through carefully organized bilateral strategic partnerships that have strong military components—a phenomenon not normally seen as the forte of middle powers. European security scholar Andriy Tyushka has questioned the stereotype of altruistic and restrained Good Samaritan middle powers, and observed that emerging middle powers have 'growingly forceful and strategic postures [...] which assert their rights, status, goals and roles in strategically cooperative and non-cooperative (confrontational) ways.' He cites Prime Minister Modi's comment: 'Those days are gone when India had to beg. Now we want our right,' as the best example of 'such a rising self-confidence and assertiveness drive of a "new middle".'[43]

As will be evident in the chapters that follow, combative diplomacy based on bilateral strategic partnerships which are squarely aimed at counterbalancing and pressurizing rivals, has become a tenet of India's friendships in the Modi era. Writing in 2011, three years before Modi became prime minister, the International Relations scholar Charalampos Efstathopoulos could justifiably make the case that 'India has achieved an across-the-board improvement of relations, but has yet refrained from forging solid strategic partnerships, especially if these are believed to produce an offensive stance towards

---

[43]Tyushka, Andriy, 'Middle Power Assertiveness as a Behavioural Model in Foreign Policy', in Swielande, Tanguy Struye de, et al, eds., op. cit., p. 122.

other powers.'[44] But since then, much water has flowed down the Ganges, and the reader will see from the chapters that follow how the 'strategic' content of India's friendships has grown by virtue of a transformation in India's strategic culture.

Since the straitjacket of a middle power, carrying a defined set of connotations, does not always aptly suit a country like India, there is merit in looking at India through the prism of a 'rising power'. The International Relations scholar Joan Deas argues that there is sufficient evidence to 'place rising power as an "intermediate" category between middle power and great power in the pyramid of power', and that rising powers fall above the middle-power category thanks to 'their willingness and capacity to change the status quo and affect, reform, spoil or circumvent the system to better represent their interests.'[45] A rising power is fundamentally distinct from a status quo-satisfied middle power by virtue of its 'goal to transform the international distribution of power into a more multipolar system', and its proclivity to engage in 'soft balancing' against at least one hegemonic great power.[46]

To fulfil a rising power's ambition to be a great power, it is important to establish or consolidate its regional preponderance in its extended neighbourhood. British writer Andrew Hurrell, who drew attention to rising powers with the phrase 'would-be great powers', avers that these countries lay claim to being the legitimate representatives of their regions, try to form regional coalitions to bargain from a position

---

[44]Efstathopoulos, Charalampos, 'Reinterpreting India's Rise through the Middle Power Prism', *Asian Journal of Political Science*, Vol. 19, No. 1, 2011, p. 84.

[45]Deas, Joan, 'Too Big to Fit? Locating "Rising Powers" Regarding the Middle Power Category', in Swielande, Tanguy Struye de, et al, eds., op. cit., p. 96.

[46]Stephen, Matthew, 'The Concept and Role of Middle Powers During Global Rebalancing', *Seton Hall Journal of Diplomacy and International Relations*, Vol. 14, No. 2, 2013, p. 48.

of strength with outside players, adopt an assertive role in regional crisis management, and attempt to fulfil a 'managerial or order-producing role' within their regions to ward off extra-regional competitors.[47] As the reader will learn throughout this book, India's closest friendships reflect its need to preserve regional leadership against hegemonic China, not only in its conventional backyard of South Asia but also in the wider Indo-Pacific. No country which challenges or denies India's regional ascendance can be its strategic partner. This simple fact explains why China, which did sign a 'Strategic and Cooperative Partnership for Peace and Prosperity' with India way back in 2005 (*see* Annexure, Table III), is today on the other side of the equation—India's number one strategic opponent.

When Western analysts appraise rising powers, their principal concern is about what the new kids on the block might do vis-à-vis the USA and the liberal international order. One popular line is to paint alarmist scenarios of rising powers outrightly rejecting and overturning liberal norms and principles like democracy, human rights, free market capitalism, free trade and respect for territorial integrity of states, which are said to have been painstakingly embossed into the world's DNA by the USA through its decades-long liberal stewardship. This is a defensive line of reasoning wherein rising powers are described as 'a major strategic challenge for the USA in the coming decades' since they refuse to be co-opted or integrated 'to embrace Western principles, norms and rules', and are instead, 'altering existing rules, not adopting them hook, line, and sinker.' Since Washington cannot control the choices of these countries, it has been argued that 'there is

---

[47]Hurrell, Andrew, 'Hegemony, Liberalism and Global Order: What Space for Would-Be Great Powers?' *International Affairs*, Vol. 82, No. 1, 2006, p. 8.

no guarantee that the world's rising powers will become the USA's strategic partners.'[48]

This only goes to underscore that discomfort about the advent of a multipolar world order, and fear that non-Western rising powers will alter the parameters of global governance by moving the world in a dystopian illiberal direction, are deeply ingrained in Western policymaking and intellectual circles. This is especially so because, as seen with the usage of the notion of 'middle powers', the concept of 'rising powers' has not been unpacked. When a think tank or an academician sitting in New York or London surveys rising powers as a combined whole, and passes judgement on them as a category, there is less room for nuanced understanding about a singular and unique rising power like India. If India is clubbed together with Brazil, China, Russia and South Africa, as is often the case when rising powers are evaluated under the umbrella term of BRICS, then the distinctness of India as a unique rising power is lost. Treating India as a *sui generis* rising power is all the more relevant today, when it has distanced itself from China, and is offering an antithesis to the Chinese model of hegemonic behaviour while staying inside BRICS.[49]

A contrasting perspective to the Western alarmists comes from reassurers who insist there is little to be frightened about rising powers, as not all of them are uniformly aiming to upset the apple cart that the USA put together after 1945 and elevated to the pinnacle during its unipolar heyday of the 1990s. For instance, in 2017, International Relations scholars Cameron Thies and Mark Nieman evaluated all five BRICS member countries in terms of whether they became more

---

[48]Patrick, Stewart, 'Irresponsible Stakeholders? The Difficulty of Integrating Rising Powers', *Foreign Affairs*, Vol. 89, No. 6, 2010, pp. 44, 47, 50.
[49]Chaulia, Sreeram, 'BRICS Shows its Usefulness, Despite Clear Limitations', *Nikkei Asia*, 23 June 2022, https://tinyurl.com/52d6ekc2. Accessed on 5 June 2024.

revisionist and conflict-prone in their economic and military behaviour as they accumulated greater material power over the decades. They found 'little evidence in words or deeds, identity, or militarized and economic conflict to lend credence to the notion of an overly assertive or aggressive Brazil as it emerges into potential great power status.'[50] In the case of Russia, since it is a declining power that seeks to regain its lost glory, they expected that it 'will continue to see itself as a great power that balances the interests of the USA and EU, frequently involving itself in militarized disputes, especially in its home region.'[51] With India, which sees itself as an emerging global power, the authors observe 'an increasing emphasis on military power and the emulation of previous great powers,' but they 'do not foresee any dramatic shift in foreign policy orientation or conflict behaviour.'[52] As to China, the authors conclude that it perceives itself as a responsible great power and will not risk direct confrontation with the USA, but they add the caveat that 'this does not preclude conflict, as great powers engage in a significant percentage of all conflict,' and 'it would be unusual for a great power not to manage the affairs of its home region, including through the use of periodic militarized conflict.'[53] For South Africa, a middle power that is not a candidate for great power status, 'it is unlikely that we will see much in the way of militarized or economic conflict' even though Pretoria routinely criticizes the economic iniquities of the Western liberal order.[54]

---

[50]Thies, Cameron, and Mark Nieman, *Rising Powers and Foreign Policy Revisionism: Understanding BRICS Identity and Behavior Through Time*, 2017 University of Michigan Press, Ann Arbor, p. 62.

[51]Ibid., p. 98.

[52]Ibid., p. 115.

[53]Ibid., p. 133.

[54]Ibid., p. 157.

With China and Russia breaking the shackles and resorting to territorial expansionism and even all-out war against neighbouring countries in recent years, optimism about them getting socialized into the liberal international order and becoming responsible stakeholders has gone out of the window in Western capitals. The official designations of these two countries as a 'pacing challenge' and an 'acute threat' by the USA[55], and as a 'systemic rival' and a 'prime military danger' by Europe[56], mean that the battle lines are being drawn between status quo powers and revisionist powers. It is in this context, dubbed popularly as a 'new Cold War', that the peculiar place of India stands out. Even before the sharp deterioration of relations between the West on one side, and China and Russia on the other, India had an intermediate estimation in the minds of many. Writing in 2013, the scholars Brian Schmidt and Nabarun Roy contrasted China with India and argued, 'Given that the USA's disagreements on security issues are fewer and less severe with India than with China, and in light of India's traditional status as a "moderately revisionist" power [...], one understands why Delhi is being courted by the USA.'[57]

The differential treatment by the West towards China and India is not just because the power gap between China and the USA is much smaller than that between India and the USA. There is also a values-based calculation here. China is an authoritarian dictatorship, while India is the most successful democracy among developing countries. Anxiety

---

[55]Pentagon, 'National Defense Strategy of the United States of America', 27 October 2022, U.S. Department of Defense, Washington, D.C., p. 2.
[56]Lau, Stuart, 'Russia Crisis Gives EU a Grim Sense of What's to Come with China', *Politico*, 1 April 2022, https://tinyurl.com/32s6d9sv. Accessed on 5 June 2024.
[57]Schmidt, Brian, and Nabarun Roy, 'Rising Powers: A Realist Analysis', in Friedman, Rebekka, et al, eds., *After Liberalism? The Future of Liberalism in International Relations*, 2013, Palgrave Macmillan, London, p. 81.

about the Chinese model of repression of human rights and non-transparent governance being exported globally through the Belt and Road Initiative (BRI), and fear that a 'Beijing consensus' will overrun and replace the 'Washington consensus'[58], have pushed Western powers to see India as a perfect antidote. The American political scientist Stacie Goddard uses historical examples to show that 'creators of an order may feel compelled to protect a dominant institution of rules and norms,' and that accordingly, they may decide to either block or enable a rising power, depending on whether it is a threat or a saviour of the dominant institution. She writes that 'the more institutionally vulnerable a great power, the more likely a rising power's appeals to dominant legitimating principles will resonate' as 'an opening to shore up the status quo'.[59] In the chapters that follow, the reader will see that not only a great power like the USA, but also middle powers such as Japan, Australia and France nurse deep forebodings about the institutions and values which might predominate if a Sino-centric world order is allowed to take shape. Their respective enduring friendships with India are cemented by admiration and respect for its democratic and non-expansionist credentials.

Still, it must be clarified that while the West considers India its best bet to sustain the liberal international status quo, India has a stubborn mind and personality of its own, and is not a pliant state that will bend to anyone's will. India has both liberal and illiberal friends, and its domestic and international words and deeds do not match the textbook definition of liberalism. Conceptually, it is helpful to break out of the moulds of both 'middle power' and 'rising power',

---

[58]Halper, Stefan, *The Beijing Consensus: How China's Authoritarian Model Will Dominate the Twenty-First Century*, 2010, Basic Books, New York.
[59]Goddard, Stacie, *When Right Makes Might: Rising Powers and World Order*, 2018, Cornell University Press, Ithaca, p. 34.

and see India for what it says it is—a 'leading power'—so that we get a better handle on its friendships around the world. The phrase is closely associated with Prime Minister Modi and External Affairs Minister Subrahmanyam Jaishankar. It is deliberately worded to present India as an exceptional state, and to steer clear of the mainstream Western lingo of 'great power', 'rising power' or 'middle power', which can discursively confine India's space to innovate and navigate its ascent in world politics.

In 2015, when Jaishankar was Foreign Secretary, he had proclaimed that India wanted to be 'a leading power than just a balancing power,' and that this ambition conveyed a 'willingness to shoulder greater global responsibilities.' He added that in the context of 'the growing reality of a multipolar world... [as well as] ...a multipolar Asia,' India wanted to 'build our bilateral relationships with all major players, confident that progress in one account opens up possibilities in others.'[60] India's vastly diverse range of bilateral strategic partnerships, sometimes at odds with Western preferences and demands, will be evident from the chapters that follow. It is not simply a case of India prizing its foreign policy freedom and choosing friends from various camps in international politics. Geopolitical compulsions as well as the grand strategy of a leading power make India's friends a heterogenous set of countries.

In India's domestic context of a multi-ethnic society, the motto 'Unity in Diversity' is often bandied about as a foundational principle and core ethos, holding the republic together. This same concept has an international angle in the way India has sought to string together a diverse set of

---

[60]MEA, 'IISS Fullerton Lecture by Dr. S. Jaishankar, Foreign Secretary in Singapore', Ministry of External Affairs, Government of India, 20 July 2015, https://tinyurl.com/2vb6ftu4. Accessed on 5 June 2024.

friends to attain its overarching foreign policy goals as a leading power. This is not to suggest that any other country which is a great power, rising power or middle power lacks diversity in its strategic partnerships. Rather, there is a distinct hue and purpose behind India's panoply of friends, which makes its case worthy of a deeper study in a comparative framework.

A MULTI-PARTNER WORLD

In July 2009, Hillary Clinton, the then Secretary of State of the USA, was addressing the mecca of American diplomacy, the Council on Foreign Relations, about the priorities of the newly incumbent administration of President Barack Obama. One part of her remarks stood out as reflective of a trend that was gaining universal traction—the penchant to enter into bilateral strategic partnerships with several countries across geographical and thematic areas. Clinton's remarks were the clearest articulation of how the USA, which at that time still enjoyed a clear lead over China in global power standing, envisaged going about making new friends, with the primary objective of sustaining the status quo.

> We'll use our power to convene, our ability to connect countries around the world, and sound foreign policy strategies to create partnerships aimed at solving problems. We believe this approach will advance our interests by uniting diverse partners around common concerns. It will make it more difficult for others to abdicate their responsibilities or abuse their power, but will offer a place at the table to any nation, group, or citizen willing to shoulder a fair share of the burden. In short, we will lead by inducing greater cooperation among a greater number of actors and reducing competition, tilting the

balance away from a multi-polar world and toward a multi-partner world.[61]

In hindsight, Clinton's liberal expectations that strategic competition could be reduced and replaced with cooperation, and that the transition to a multipolar world could be halted, proved illusory. Her 'special emphasis on encouraging major and emerging global powers—China, India, Russia and Brazil, as well as Turkey, Indonesia, and South Africa—to be full partners in tackling the global agenda'[62] suggested that Washington had misread China and Russia, which would turn out to be prime antagonists of the West a few years down the line. Nonetheless, the fact that the USA, which had a decades-long habit of entering into formal military alliances, stepped into the realm of loose and less binding strategic partnerships, was telling. Since many middle and rising powers Clinton referred to in that speech were unwilling to sacrifice their autonomy and freedom of action by binding themselves under formal alliances, Washington understood that it had to have skin in the geopolitical game by adapting to the trend of strategic partnerships, especially in Asia, as the centre of gravity in world affairs shifted from the Atlantic to the Pacific.

The flurry of strategic partnerships which the USA signed from 2010 was concentrated in the Indo-Pacific, a phrase that replaced Asia-Pacific in American diplomatese during Obama's presidency. These partnerships went hand-in-hand with the 'pivot' or 'rebalancing' of the American strategic posture towards Asia. Annexure, Table I demonstrates the Indo-Pacific focus in Washington's push to enter into strategic partnerships. While Washington did announce strategic partnerships in

---

[61]State Department, 'Foreign Policy Address at the Council on Foreign Relations', 15 July 2009, U.S. Department of State, Washington, D.C., https://tinyurl.com/48m83vnb. Accessed on 5 June 2024.
[62]Ibid.

West Asia/the Middle East, Eastern Europe, Africa and Latin America, one can notice most of them involve conflation of terminology between 'ally' and 'partner', with many formally designated NATO and non-NATO allies also being referred to as strategic partners in American diplomatic communications. Washington often does not strictly differentiate allies from strategic partners, leading to confusion. For our purpose, though, there is clarity in the pattern of American strategic partnerships being centred in the Indo-Pacific. India, Indonesia, Malaysia, Vietnam and Singapore are not allies of the USA, but all of them have signed strategic partnerships with it, and some have subsequently upgraded them with prefixes like 'comprehensive' and 'comprehensive global and strategic'.

From the listing in Annexure, Table I, the basic strategic motivations behind the USA's push for close bilateral partnerships in the Indo-Pacific are evident. Southeast Asia expert Prashanth Parameswaran has noted that the American objective is to 'create a more extensive network of partners in the region beyond traditional allies as part of a rebalancing strategy,' and to connect allies with partners to form 'webs' or 'networks' to keep China under check.[63] Since signing a 'constructive strategic partnership' with China in 1997, the USA has come a long way and transitioned from being optimistic to getting alarmed by the dragon in recent years. Pushing back against Beijing's expansionism explains the USA's befriending of countries like India, Indonesia, Malaysia and Vietnam.

Countering radical Islamist extremism and terrorism also figures as an American priority in bilateral strategic partnership agreements and was much more prominent

---

[63]Parameswaran, Prashanth, 'Explaining US Strategic Partnerships in the Asia-Pacific Region: Origins, Developments and Prospects', *Contemporary Southeast Asia*, Vol. 36, No. 2, 2014, p. 268.

when the Global War on Terrorism (GWOT) preoccupied the national security system of the USA. Since 2017, when President Donald Trump's administration reordered American priorities and named 'the revisionist powers of China and Russia' as the primary threats[64], there has been a refocusing of American attention to engage with friends in the Indo-Pacific, mainly with a view to counterbalance China. Geopolitics is the main consideration behind the USA's new bilateral strategic partnerships.

But Washington's attempts to stitch together a network or web of friends to constrain China are tempered by the reality that many of its strategic partners in Asia have signed parallel strategic partnerships or some variants of them with Beijing (*see* Annexure, Table II). In 2023, Jakarta and Beijing declared they were upgrading bilateral ties from a ten-years-long 'strategic partnership' to a 'comprehensive strategic partnership'.[65] Kuala Lumpur already had a 'comprehensive strategic partnership' with Beijing since 2013, and has expressed an intent to further enhance it.[66] In 2008, Hanoi signed a 'comprehensive strategic cooperative partnership' with Beijing, and it has since committed to keep deepening it.[67] In 2023, Singapore inked an 'all-round high-quality future-oriented partnership' with China, and stated a desire to continually

---

[64]TWH, 'National Security Strategy of the United States of America', December 2017, The White House, Washington, D.C., p. 25, https://tinyurl.com/2h8zxb2r. Accessed on 5 June 2024.
[65]MOFA, 'Joint Statement on Deepening Comprehensive Strategic Cooperation between the People's Republic of China and the Republic of Indonesia', 18 October 2023, Ministry of Foreign Affairs of the Republic of Indonesia, https://tinyurl.com/3y3ccwhk. Accessed on 5 June 2024.
[66]TS, 'Malaysia, China to Elevate Ties to a Higher Level', *The Star*, 29 March 2023, https://tinyurl.com/yc5kd4kj. Accessed on 5 June 2024.
[67]VL, 'Vietnam-China Comprehensive Strategic Cooperative Partnership', *Vietnam Law & Legal Forum*, 17 October 2023, https://tinyurl.com/yzys9h3y. Accessed on 5 June 2024.

expand bilateral cooperation.[68] All these Southeast Asian countries remain wary of incurring China's wrath by aligning too closely with the USA as part of any counterbalancing or containment. They treat strategic partnerships as part of a complex hedging strategy, wherein friendship with the USA prevents military domination by China, while friendship with China is essential for their economic growth and exports. Nagging doubts about the USA's commitment to their security and entrenched economic intertwinement with China add to the dual-faced or promiscuous nature of these strategic partnerships.[69]

As previously mentioned in the present Introduction, India too had signed a strategic partnership with China in 2005. Unlike the Southeast Asian strategic partners of the USA, India is one American friend which has progressively discarded the Chinese hand of friendship in light of heightened national security threats, and outbreak of physical clashes between Indian and Chinese troops in the disputed Himalayan borders. Even though there remains a sizeable Sino-Indian trade relationship, India is economically more integrated with the USA, and counts it as its number one trade partner and a top foreign investor. The dependence of some sectors of the Indian economy on China has been a cause of serious concern, but India's economic fortunes and rise are more closely tethered to the USA compared to the fortunes of

---

[68]Ting, Koh Wan, 'Singapore, China Elevate Bilateral Ties Following PM Lee Meeting with Xi Jinping', *Channel NewsAsia*, 31 March 2023, https://tinyurl.com/9jmxu9zp. Accessed on 5 June 2024.

[69]Harding, Brian, and Andreyka Natalegawa, 'Enhancing the U.S.-Indonesia Strategic Partnership', 9 July 2018, Center for Strategic and International Studies, Washington, D.C., https://tinyurl.com/39cnm5uz. Accessed on 5 June 2024; Tran, Bich, 'From "Rebalance to Asia" to "Free and Open Indo-Pacific": The Development of the U.S.-Vietnam Comprehensive Partnership', 20 November 2019, East-West Center, Honolulu, https://tinyurl.com/4ypa5a5z. Accessed on 5 June 2024.

Washington's other Asian strategic partners. From an overall standpoint, America's strategic partners are tenuous, less controllable and more fluid compared to its formal NATO and non-NATO allies over whom Washington has an upper hand, and who can be coaxed, cajoled or even coerced to fall in line at critical moments in world politics.

Still, with the drift towards a multipolar world, the USA has no option but to invest in strategic partnerships. The realization that formal allies alone will not suffice to pursue the USA's grand strategic goals was clear in American Secretary of State Antony Blinken's description of both alliances and partnerships as 'our greatest strategic asset' and his vow to work 'with purpose and urgency to deepen, broaden, and align our friends in new ways' for goals like handling 'a fierce and lasting strategic competition'.[70] According to the former Pentagon official Abraham Denmark, since most of the USA's allies and strategic partners in the Indo-Pacific are inclined to counterbalancing China rather than bandwagoning (submitting to its hegemony), this presents 'an opportunity for the United States'. Washington, he writes, must be realistic and 'not oppose efforts by any country to engage Beijing'. Instead, Washington should 'ensure that such engagement does not transform into a more general strategy of bandwagoning, and acquiescence to Beijing's coercion and suzerainty.'[71] Friendships in the Indo-Pacific are thus force multipliers for the USA, a great power, to throw spanners in the wheel of China, a rival great power, as it marches to supremacy in Asia.

---

[70]State Department, 'Secretary Antony J. Blinken Remarks to the Johns Hopkins School of Advanced International Studies (SAIS) "The Power and Purpose of American Diplomacy in a New Era"', 13 September 2023, U.S. Department of State, Washington, D.C., https://tinyurl.com/26c8j8vn. Accessed on 5 June 2024.
[71]Denmark, Abraham, *U.S. Strategy in the Asian Century: Empowering Allies and Partners*, 2020, Columbia University Press, New York, pp. 87, 102.

Compared to the USA, China has been a much more prolific player in the art of building bilateral strategic partnerships. Its intentions with regard to friendships also differ somewhat from those of the USA. When the Cold War ended in 1991, China used the collapse of the bipolar world order to restructure the way it interacted with other countries. It 'no longer focused on great powers alone, but tried to improve relations with a broader range of states' through a 'new diplomatic approach that has been termed "multidimensional diplomacy".' Bilateral strategic partnerships, which Beijing saw as 'win-win thinking while not targeting the partnership against a third party,' were pursued as vehicles to 'create a better environment for China's continuous rise.'[72]

China started with a 'long-term and stable strategic partnership' with Brazil in 1993, followed by a 'strategic partnership of equality, mutual confidence and mutual coordination' with Russia in 1996, and a 'collaborative partnership for the 21st century' with South Korea in 1998. There was even a 'constructive strategic partnership' that China struck with the USA in 1997[73], an event that seems incongruous and unbelievable from a present-day rear-view mirror, but which was part of a routine partnership-building spree that Beijing undertook at a time when it did not perceive the West as a strategic threat, and when the USA was under the impression that China could be socialized and integrated into the liberal international order. The 1998 'comprehensive partnership' between China and the EU, which was later upgraded to

---

[72]Zhongping, Feng, and Huang Jing, 'China's Strategic Partnership Diplomacy: Engaging with a Changing World', European Strategic Partnerships Observatory, Working Paper 8, June 2014, https://tinyurl.com/3dd2xmk2. Accessed on 5 June 2024, pp. 11, 13.
[73]Chinese Embassy, 'China-US Joint Statement (October 29, 1997)', Embassy of the People's Republic of China, Washington, D.C., https://tinyurl.com/48k2vusa. Accessed on 5 June 2024.

'comprehensive strategic partnership' in 2003, also belonged to that rose-tinted era when Europeans wanted to engage with China primarily for economic gains, and with the hope that they could politically liberalize its communist regime.

Apart from strategic partnerships, Beijing also launched several 'comprehensive partnership' agreements (the absence of the word 'strategic' in them meant they were a little lower down the hierarchy) with Canada, France and Mexico in 1997, and Italy and the UK in 1998, all of which were subsequently upgraded and renamed with the add-on 'strategic' in the following decades (*see* Annexure, Table II).

Besides prominent middle and rising powers, another category which China targeted for strategic partnerships were resource-rich small powers in the Global South, especially in Africa, Latin America and West Asia/the Middle East. Since there are no specific regional loci where China's strategic partnerships are clustered, Annexure, Table II, is sorted alphabetically. From Afghanistan to Zimbabwe, China's universe of strategic and other forms of partnerships is scattered, and traverses the entire planet. The twists and turns in terminology that China has invented to describe and customize its vast repository of partnerships, are also mindboggling. Wordings like 'win-win', 'equality', 'mutual benefit', 'permanent' and 'ever-lasting' are all taken out of China's diplomatic jargon, and are intended to project that, as a communist state with a long history of fighting Western imperialism, China treats its partners with greater respect than the way the USA handles its friends.

Since a large proportion of China's more than 80 strategic partnerships are with developing countries (middle to small powers), economic factors figure as a main motivator in Beijing's friendship spree. The American political scientist Evan Medeiros has argued that 'for China, strategic partnership has a different meaning from the Western connotation of the term. They are not treated as quasi-military alliances, which involve extensive security and military cooperation, as implied by the term 'strategic'. Rather, in the Chinese foreign policy lexicon, a partnership is strategic for two reasons: 1. It is comprehensive, including all aspects of bilateral relations (e.g. economic, cultural, political, and security), and 2. Both countries agree to make a long-term commitment to bilateral relations.'[74]

The primacy of economic objectives in China's strategic partnerships dovetails with the ruling Communist Party's 'non-alliance policy' since the 1980s, which is premised on the belief that by avoiding rigid formal alliances, China can preserve its foreign policy independence, and prevent the formation of a countervailing military alliance against it in Asia.[75] If all of China's strategic partnerships had strong security cooperation and military coordination angles, and if they were to transition into full-blown alliances, the orthodox Chinese view is that it would be counterproductive to Beijing's interests which are to convince the world that its rise is peaceful, and that it is a different kind of great power which will not repeat the behavioural pattern of Western great powers which used friendships for power politics and splitting the world into blocs.[76]

Signing bilateral strategic partnerships with a diverse range of countries, including allies of the USA, paved the way for China to expand its BRI connectivity project across multiple continents. China specialist Georg Strüver's quantitative study of a large data set of China's strategic partnerships shows that

[74]Medeiros, Evan, *China's International Behaviour: Activism, Opportunism and Diversification*, 2009, RAND Corporation, Santa Monica, p. 82.
[75]Ruonan, Liu, and Liu Feng, 'Contending Ideas on China's Non-Alliance Strategy', *The Chinese Journal of International Politics*, Vol. 10, No. 2, 2017, pp. 151–171.
[76]Xiaohui, Su, 'Major-Country Diplomacy with Chinese Characteristics', China Institute of International Studies, 14 March 2018, https://tinyurl.com/mr38j89y. Accessed on 5 June 2024.

Beijing's primary rationale is pragmatic rather than ideological camaraderie. Partner countries that offer economic market potential, access to natural resources, and have high regional influence are more likely to form partnerships with China. Countries which are more dependent on trade with China are also more likely to enter into strategic partnerships with it. Strüver does not find strong evidence of any ideological dividend based on shared socialist or communist legacies, and highlights the irony that 'Beijing is generally more inclined to establish cooperative ties with democracies than with authoritarian peers.'[77] From Latin America and Africa to Europe and West Asia/the Middle East, there is an observable link between the needs of China's economic modernization juggernaut and its numerous strategic partnerships.

However, it would be reductionist to treat China's friendships as devoid of any geopolitical competition with the USA. International Relations scholars Quan Li and Min Ye evaluated 24 different types of bilateral partnerships China formed worldwide, and concluded that 'facing the USA as the only super power in the post-Cold War era, China seeks to rely on its partners to counter US pressure. Such a motivation grows even stronger when the relative power of the USA over China increases. Instead of challenging the US primacy, it appears that China uses the partnership as a defensive mechanism to alleviate US pressure.'[78] The fact that some of the USA's closest friends have agreed to enter into strategic partnerships with China (*see* Annexure, Table II) lucidly

---

[77]Strüver, Georg, 'International Alignment Between Interests and Ideology: The Case of China's Partnership Diplomacy', German Institute for Global and Area Studies, Working Paper 283, March 2016, https://tinyurl.com/2p943jp2. Accessed on 5 June 2024, p. 19.
[78]Li, Quan, and Min Ye, 'China's Emerging Partnership Network: What, Who, Where, When and Why', *International Trade, Politics and Development*, Vol. 3, No. 2, 2019, p. 79.

shows the means by which Beijing seeks to compete hard with Washington for global influence.

American strategist Edward Luttwak has written that Beijing's plan is 'not to peel away U.S. allies and bring them over to China's side, but rather to diversity their interests, complicate their calculations, blur their loyalties, and set the stage for further erosion of what were once rock-solid, diplomatically monogamous relationships.'[79] True to the inheritance of the ancient Chinese strategist Sun Tzu (6th century BCE), who recommended that one must 'look into the matter of his [the enemy's] alliances and cause them to be severed and dissolved,'[80] the contemporary Chinese approach towards bilateral partnerships has a purpose of eroding the USA's influence not only in major power centres of Europe and Asia but throughout the Global South.

Since China and the USA are two great powers engaged in what President Joe Biden called 'extreme competition'[81], it is natural for both of them to have an instrumental view of friendships as weapons to push back against each other. The USA's conception of strategic partnerships is more direct, and has a bigger military component, carrying an intended hint of 'alliance lite' and raising for both the USA and its friends, the interesting question, 'Is strategic partnership a "light version" of military alliance or a more "popular version" of bandwagoning?'[82]

[79]Luttwak, Edward, *The Rise of China vs. the Logic of Strategy*, Harvard University Press, 2012, Cambridge, p. 175.

[80]Mcneilly, Mark, *Sun Tzu and the Art of Modern Warfare*, 2001, Oxford University Press, Oxford, p. 30.

[81]AP, 'Biden: China Should Expect Extreme Competition from US', *The Associated Press*, 7 February 2021, https://tinyurl.com/4jf2x5my. Accessed on 5 June 2024.

[82]Larionova, Mila, 'Conceptualizing Soft Balancing Beyond Cold War: What's Changed, What Remains the Same?' *Central European Journal of International and Security Studies*, Vol. 14, No. 3, 2020, p. 86.

The Chinese conception of strategic partnerships is softer, and has greater economic content and thrust, although its 'comprehensive strategic partnership of coordination' with Russia has a notable and growing security dimension. Lagging behind the USA in military capabilities, China has emphasized its comparative advantages in trade, economic aid and infrastructure-building as its main calling cards in bilateral friendships. But just because hard military counterbalancing is not a visible feature of China's strategic partnerships, they are not lacking in 'strategic' essence. As the American commentator Abraham Denmark lamented about the Indo-Pacific, China 'offers to the region [...] political acquiescence in exchange for economic development [which is] far more attractive than what many believe the United States offers: political acquiescence in exchange for no economic development.'[83]

If the USA's style of partnerships is geared towards 'offshore balancing' (to 'rely on local powers [friends within Asia] to contain China [...] coordinate their efforts and [...] throw its considerable weight behind them')[84], then China's style of partnerships matches what is called 'soft balancing'. Instead of forging rival military alliances or using China's own military might to directly provoke the USA, the strategy of soft balancing involves 'using international institutions, economic statecraft, and diplomatic arrangements' to 'delay, frustrate and undermine aggressive unilateral U.S. military policies'.[85]

China's soft balancing activity in Central Asia, West Asia/ the Middle East and Africa includes a heavy dose of loans and investments to partner countries in return for access to oil, gas

---

[83]Denmark, Abraham, op. cit., p. 62.
[84]Mearsheimer, John, and Stephen Walt, 'The Case for Offshore Balancing: A Superior U.S. Grand Strategy', *Foreign Affairs*, Vol. 95, No. 4, 2016, p. 81.
[85]Pape, Robert, 'Soft Balancing Against the United States', *International Security*, Vol. 30, No. 1, 2005, p. 10.

and other minerals, as well as creation of alternative regional institutions in coordination with strategic partners to reduce the USA's power and influence in those regions.[86] The BRI, a mega connectivity network weaving together dozens of China's strategic partners, has been interpreted as a means to achieve 'asymmetric economic interdependence', which 'enables Beijing to translate its economic power into political power, leverage its influence over Eurasian countries to its strategic interests, and undermine the US dominance.'[87] China's 'weaponization of interdependence' or 'predatory liberalism' to gain hegemonic control over partner countries and challenge the USA[88] is no less neo-colonial than the USA's military interventions for regime change. Contrary to Chinese propaganda that they are pursuing 'a new model of state-to-state relations featuring dialogue and partnership, not confrontation or alliance,'[89] the net effect of Beijing's strategic partnerships is to impose structural domination and dependence on its friends. The reader will appreciate the less-than-equal nature of China's friendships in the chapters that follow, where countries that signed strategic partnership agreements with China will appear eager to befriend alternatives like India in order to shake off the Chinese stranglehold.

---

[86]Gill, Stephan, 'China's Soft Balancing Strategy and the Role of Resource Investment', *Yonsei Journal of International Studies*, Vol. 2, No. 2, 2010, pp. 247–258.

[87]Zhou, Weifeng, and Mario Esteban, 'Beyond Balancing: China's Approach Towards the Belt and Road Initiative', *Journal of Contemporary China*, Vol. 27, No. 112, 2018, p. 494.

[88]Cha, Victor, 'Collective Resilience: Deterring China's Weaponization of Economic Interdependence', *International Security*, Vol. 48, No. 1, 2023, p. 91.

[89]Chinese Embassy, 'US Hegemony and its Perils', February 2023, Embassy of China in Samoa, https://tinyurl.com/2s4b6cxe. Accessed on 5 June 2024.

INDIA'S STRATEGIC FRIENDS

Having compared the models of bilateral strategic partnerships operated by the USA and China[90], the strategic partnerships of the central protagonist of this book, India, can be brought into sharp relief. As a rising power or a leading power, India is at a different historical juncture, with a set of needs that vary from the needs of great powers. Since the USA and China have already risen to the top of the pyramid in the global power structure, they see strategic partnerships as utilitarian tools for balancing each other, and for sustaining their respective geopolitical sway over critical regions. On the other hand, India is still rising and predicted to catch up with the great powers in the coming decades. India's friendships carry a visceral value for it to realize its destiny, and transform the present international order into a multipolar one. Bilateral strategic partnerships are imperatives for piloting India's upward ascent in a complex interdependent world with sharpening geopolitical fault lines. They are indispensable for India to preserve its sovereignty and security against the menacing challenge of China, blunt the threat of radical Islamist terrorism, turbocharge its economic growth engine, and spread its diplomatic and political wings beyond its immediate subcontinental backyard. The 'aspirational India' that its leaders herald[91] is as reliant on domestic reforms and innovations as on foreign policy deftness and astuteness, especially with regard to nurturing

---

[90]The European Union (EU) counts in its kitty around ten strategic partners, including India. But since the EU is not a sovereign state, but a multilateral regional institution, with a legal personality and outlook quite distinct from that of a single country, its model has not been utilized in this comparative analysis.

[91]PTI, 'This Amrit Kaal, Every Indian Aspiring to See Fast Progress of New India: PM Narendra Modi', *The Economic Times*, 15 August 2022, https://tinyurl.com/yr7mf99t. Accessed on 5 June 2024.

bilateral strategic partnerships and extracting maximum value from them. Lacking the deep pockets and the vast military arsenals of great powers, which often act unilaterally and in disregard of the interests of their friends, a leading power or a rising power has to act in respectful and consultative concert with its closest partners against shared threats, and in pursuit of common benefits. In other words, diplomacy with close strategic partners is a far more crucial and existential asset for a rising power or leading power than for a great power.

The Australia-based scholar Thomas Wilkins has defined strategic partnerships as a 'structured collaboration between states (or other 'actors') to take joint advantage of economic opportunities, or to respond to security challenges more effectively than could be achieved in isolation.'[92] The inevitable presence of an economic pillar and a security pillar (whether direct or indirect), and joint pursuit of common objectives in these two core areas, are more or less constant in each and every bilateral strategic partnership. The European foreign policy expert Anna Michalski echoes this line of thought by referring to strategic partnerships as 'vehicles for foreign policy goals set up to achieve specific material foreign policy goals of a strategic, economic or social nature' with friendly countries. But she enriches this barebones conceptualization with an additional function—strategic partnerships are 'role-enhancing arenas set up to respond to specific ambitions concerning the actor's position in the international system tied to non-material interests such as prestige, status and identity.'[93] Michalski contends that countries like India 'see

---

[92]Wilkins, Thomas, '"Alignment", not "Alliance"– The Shifting Paradigm of International Security Cooperation: Toward a Conceptual Taxonomy of Alignment', *Review of International Studies*, Vol. 38, No. 1, 2012, p. 67.
[93]Michalski, Anna, 'Diplomacy in a Changing World Order: The Role of Strategic Partnerships', The Swedish Institute for International Affairs, Paper No. 10, 2019, p. 7, https://tinyurl.com/y4supap2. Accessed on 5 June 2024.

strategic partnerships as a deliberate strategy for strengthening their position in a multipolar world order while at the same time retaining a high degree of strategic autonomy.'[94]

For a rising power like India, the intangible merits of strategic partnerships cannot be overestimated. In the chapters that follow, the reader will see how India's closest friends valorise its claim to being a leading power, and in return, also receive India's validation of their respective desired statuses in the world order. India's soft power, 'the ability to obtain preferred outcomes by attraction rather than coercion or payment,'[95] is also inextricably tied to its strategic partnerships with key countries who help consolidate India's image in international discourse as a responsible rising power that is a force for good in the world.

Triumphs in multilateral institutions like the G20 surely contribute to India's soft power as a provider of global public goods, and as a leading power that is a source of hope for the future of humanity.[96] But since chairmanship or membership of multilateral bodies is rotational and not permanent, it is not by itself sufficient to sustain India's soft power at a highly visible level on a continuous basis. Bilateral strategic partnerships have greater iterative power due to repeated annual or more frequent ministerial meetings, summits and joint activities such as military exercises. The affirmation that India receives through bilateral interactions from its closest friends is frequent and cumulative, helping generate positive sentiment not just in India and the partner nation but on a

---

[94]Ibid., p. 8.
[95]Nye, Joseph, 'Soft Power: The Origins and Political Progress of a Concept', *Palgrave Communications*, 21 February 2017, p. 2, https://tinyurl.com/4hbm4ywh. Accessed on 5 June 2024.
[96]Kumar, Mohan, 'India Transitions into a Leading Power', *Hindustan Times*, 11 September 2023, https://tinyurl.com/becktwbv. Accessed on 5 June 2024.

wider canvas. When partner X proclaims that India is its best friend or 'natural ally', it rubs off on friends of X who then also warm up to India and want to upgrade ties with India. It is a virtuous cycle of mutual backslapping that has positive spin-offs across a whole region. Each chapter illustrates how India's bilateral strategic partnership with a certain country enhanced its regional stature in that country's surroundings.

Bilateral strategic partnerships also boost India's soft power in terms of getting promoted as a role model from the angle of its domestic affairs. In a polarized ideological atmosphere where Western Left-wing activists, liberals and Islamists have attacked India under Prime Minister Modi for alleged backsliding on democracy and human rights of minorities, bilateral strategic partnerships can be helpful in neutralizing such negative portrayals and in presenting a different face of India to the world. For example, in Chapter 7, the reader will see how India's 'comprehensive strategic partnership' with the UAE came in handy to counter Islamist critiques of India over treatment of its Muslim citizens, and management of its only Muslim-majority territory of Jammu and Kashmir. The more a strategic partner gets concrete material gains in economic, military and geopolitical domains through its friendship with India, the likelier it is to promote the Indian narrative about its internal developments to international audiences.

India's bilateral strategic partnerships also accumulate tremendous goodwill for India as a dependable and trusted actor that is a safe haven in a turmoil-ridden world. The repeated emphasis Indian leaders have placed on how their country enjoys 'trust' of strategic partners[97] amid fragmentation and heightened recriminations among global power centres is a leitmotif in this book. Every close friend of India has

---

[97]PTI, 'World Sees India as a Trustworthy and Promising Partner', *NDTV*, 4 December 2020, https://tinyurl.com/39fvtwef. Accessed on 5 June 2024.

gone further than usual for India's sake, thanks to this trust and reliability factor. India's increasing economic and military capabilities, and its willingness to shoulder more regional and global responsibilities, such as a net security provider in the Indian Ocean Region (IOR) or as the vaccine capital of the world, have elevated its trustworthiness. An India stepping up to the plate with more diplomatic vigour and vim will automatically be more magnetic as other nations see it as a giver rather than a taker. Like human beings, countries also want friends who are not going to be burdensome or parasitic. The attraction of having a friend like India lies in its international image as an asset rather than a liability. As Prime Minister Modi asserted, India has 'carved a place for itself as *Vishwa Mitra* [friend to the world] and the entire world is seeing a friend in India' because of 'our *sanskaar*s [positive qualities]'.[98]

While most members of the international community want to form strategic partnerships with a progressively better endowed and proactive India, a rising power with finite resources and geographically less spread-out core interests has to be judicious and systematic in choosing its friends so as not to get entangled or bogged down by unproductive or counterproductive friends. Compared to the USA's combined tally of strategic partners and formal allies, or to China's voluminous list of strategic partners, India has been parsimonious and selective in signing formal strategic partnerships. Annexure, Table III, lists around three dozen countries and institutions sorted by region with whom India has signed strategic partnerships. It is informative that the largest cluster of India's special friendships is in the Indo-

---

[98]ANI, 'During G20, India Emerged as a "Vishwa Mitra": PM Modi', *The Times of India*, 21 September 2023, https://tinyurl.com/495bfcv5. Accessed on 5 June 2024.

Pacific (11 entities), followed by Europe (9 entities), West Asia/the Middle East (6 countries) and Central/South Asia (4 countries). As mentioned before, the strategic partnership with China is the only one in the Indo-Pacific which can be considered to have lapsed amid India's growing rivalry and competition with it.

Since 2021, when Afghanistan was captured by the historically anti-India and pro-Pakistan Taliban, New Delhi refused to recognize the new Islamist regime and, *ipso facto*, the 'strategic partnership' of 2011 with Afghanistan was terminated. On the eastern flank, it was not unreasonable to consider Bangladesh, India's next-door neighbour with whom bilateral ties grew by leaps and bounds after 2009, as 'deeper than any other strategic partnership'.[99] But the overthrow of Prime Minister Sheikh Hasina's regime in 2024 through alleged meddling by China and Pakistan[100] left in its wake anxieties in New Delhi about sustaining the gains of the previous fifteen years.

All in all, there is a discernible Asia concentration in India's strategic partnerships, indicating how a rising or leading power looks to primarily consolidate its influence and make a mark in its extended neighbourhood through special friendships. In the following chapters, the reader will appreciate how India's most relevant strategic partnerships in West Asia/the Middle East, Europe and with the USA are also related to its home turf of the Indo-Pacific. Friends whose mainland territories are thousands of miles away from India's immediate surroundings, but which are capable of projecting power over

---

[99]PTI, 'India-Bangladesh Ties Deeper than any Other Strategic Partnership: Harsh Vardhan Shringla', *The Times of India*, 23 October 2021, https://tinyurl.com/mw96nthb. Accessed on 5 June 2024.
[100]Shekhar, Raj, 'China, ISI Orchestrated Trouble to Install a Regime Inimical to India', *The Times of India*, 6 August 2024, https://tinyurl.com/yv6ca4jm Accessed on 9 August 2024.

long distances and coordinating with India to be present in the Indo-Pacific and shape it, are priceless for a rising or leading power seeking to stretch the ambit of its geopolitical influence and mitigate the national security threats it faces from hostile neighbours—China and Pakistan. The axiom that physical distance is not always a barrier in friendship holds true in the case of India's high-impact strategic partnerships.

Strategic partnerships were by no means India's inventions. They became de rigueur in global diplomatic praxis after the end of the Cold War. With no bipolar division of the world into two rival blocs of East and West, it made no sense for any country to limit its relationships to any single power centre. The exclusive nature of alliances, where a country could belong to only a single camp, held appeal as long as there was a serious threat of war, invasion or subjugation by a great power. In the post-1991 era, lessened likelihood of great power confrontation and major inter-state wars, as well as the integration of the whole world into a single capitalist order under the rubric of economic globalization, created an environment for what the International Relations scholar Vidya Nadkarni calls 'omni-directional strategic partnerships' which provide 'maximum diplomatic, political, and economic flexibility and minimum commitments from involved parties.'[101] Loose partnerships which could be formed irrespective of the prospective friend's other friendships were also rational choices for countries at that time due to the preponderance of the USA's power and the need for all players, including China and Russia, to pursue beneficial relations with it.

In December 1998, although the then Russian Prime Minister Yevgeny Primakov proposed forming a new 'strategic triangle' or alliance-like formation among Russia, China and

---

[101]Nadkarni, Vidya, *Strategic Partnerships in Asia: Balancing Without Alliances*, 2010, Routledge, New York, p. 17.

India to counter unilateral and illegal American military interventions, the idea never really took off. A trilateral dialogue forum of these three—RIC—was initiated in 2003, with the goal of canvassing for a multipolar world and resisting the USA's dominance. It later got enmeshed into BRICS, but separate RIC ministerial meetings have continued to take place. Yet, given the internal differences and suspicions among the RIC members, as well as the separate bilateral strategic partnerships China and India had signed with the USA (*see* Annexure, Tables I, II and III), the RIC trio proved to be 'not an alliance [...] but just a *ménage à trois* of intermittent "one-night stands" [...] taking common positions on selected, but not the most important, issues.'[102] So, instead of a simple bifurcated matchup of RIC versus the USA, with the EU either tagging along with Washington or seeking to be an intermediary between two blocs, what emerged was a spider's web of strategic partnerships of each country with every other country and no bilateral friendship being a pairing aimed explicitly at a third country. The fuzziness of this opening period of strategic partnerships can be gleaned from the fact that India's earliest such agreements were with a heterogenous set of countries, some of whom were traditionally antagonists towards each other—South Africa (1997), France (1998), Russia (2000), Germany (2001), Iran (2003), the UK (2004), the USA (2004) and China (2005). India's dualistic self-perception as a leading member of the Global South and as a rising power that needed deeper economic interaction with the Global North were both reflected in the choice of these friends.

At the level of foreign policy doctrine, India's strategic partnerships can be explained by the adoption of 'multi-

---

[102]Kemenade, Willem van, *Détente Between China and India: The Delicate Balance of Geopolitics in Asia*, 2008, Clingendael Institute, Wassenaar, p. 140.

alignment' or 'interest-based alignment' as opposed to its signature Cold War-era 'non-alignment' posture. Indian scholar Rahul Mishra deems multi-alignment as a mindset 'to engage as many international stakeholders and partners as possible, based on India's own politico-strategic and economic calculations.' The logic behind this approach is that, while inching closer to the USA for economic and geopolitical reasons, India wishes to preserve its long-cherished strategic autonomy and avoid being seen as 'subservient to the US interests' or as succumbing to the pressure of any other power centre.[103] Strategic partnerships are ideally suited in such circumstances. Through them, India can aspire to eat the American pie, have the Russian cake, bite the Indo-Pacific puddings, savour the European icing, and relish the West Asian/Middle Eastern desserts. Minister of External Affairs Subrahmanyam Jaishankar's declaration in 2020 that 'this is a time to engage America, manage China, cultivate Europe, reassure Russia, bring Japan into play,'[104] summarizes why India has taken to strategic partnerships as talismans for steering it to 'leading-power' status. To reiterate, unlike a traditional middle power which might be content to uphold the status quo by hitching its wagon to one great power benefactor, India is a would-be great power and, hence, needs thick bonds of friendship on a wide canvas with several players all at once. The reader will find an in-depth case study of India's diversity in friendships in Chapter 4 on the Russia-India 'special and privileged strategic partnership'.

Keeping one's doors open to multiple sides in an uncertain and transitioning world order is strategic common sense.

---

[103]Mishra, Rahul, 'From Non-Alignment to Multi-Alignment: Assessing India's Foreign Policy Shift', *The Round Table*, Vol. 112, No. 1, 2023, pp. 53–54.
[104]Jaishankar, Subrahmanyam, *The India Way: Strategies for an Uncertain World*, HarperCollins, New Delhi, p. 10.

But there are limits to multifariousness in India's strategic partnerships. The ideal of being 'a friend to all and enemy to none' is a luxury that a rising power cannot enjoy in a world which has forces aiming to prevent or suppress its upward ascent. The ancient Greek philosopher Aristotle's quip that 'a friend to all is a friend to none'[105] is apt for India as it has been choosy about its strategic partners on the basis of geopolitical criteria, and invested diplomatic capital in select special friends in a deep and trustful manner. The 'strategic' content in India's best strategic partnerships refers to some kind of counterbalancing or mobilizing against a shared adversary, or at least a shared problem. If India and another country do not see eye to eye on at least one specific threat or phenomenon of concern, and do not have any shared problem, then a real strategic partnership cannot be formed between them. By picking only seven of India's thirty-six or so formal strategic partnerships for detailed analysis, the larger point being made in this book is that friends in international relations have to coalesce against enemies, particularly in an era of global power transition and intense geopolitical tussles.

Jaishankar's assertion in 2023 that India is doing 'optimal positioning vis-à-vis the major power centres, less by hedging and more through active pursuit of interests and values,'[106] is the clearest indicator that strategic partnerships have a sharper and more security-oriented meaning for India today than in the early years of the post-Cold War era, when it signed partnerships with a disparate set of countries, with no quintessential thread holding them together. 'Hedging' or

---

[105]Thompson, Mark, 'Why Aristotle's Quote is More Relevant than Ever in Today's Society', *Medium*, 27 March 2023, https://tinyurl.com/ycxh7p4k. Accessed on 5 June 2024.
[106]Jaishankar, Subrahmanyam, '9 Years, 1 Big Footprint', *The Times of India*, 30 May 2023, https://tinyurl.com/4h7bmskj. Accessed on 5 June 2024.

'congaging' (strategy of simultaneously cooperating as well as countering) works when there is haziness or ambiguity in judging a country's conduct or intent. For a long time, like the USA, India was confused as to whether to engage or counterbalance China because Beijing acted subtly and nimbly in the pre-Xi Jinping period. In the Xi era, with China baring its claws and pushing India to the wall, India has no choice but to fight back through the classic combination of internal balancing (beefing up its own military capabilities) and external balancing (strengthening its network of meaningful friendships).

The Korean scholar Yong Soo Park has traced India's shift from hedging to balancing China to the period after 2010 amid a 'changed security environment' caused by China's 'aggressive expansionist activity'. Faced with an adverse national security scenario, India 'is improving its own military capabilities to counter China's threat, while at the same time, actively aligning with other countries such as the United States, Japan, and Australia that share a negative view of China's rise.' Park adds that this presents a marked change from the past, when 'India was passive in military cooperation with the United States to contain China due to its neutral foreign policy of non-alignment.'[107] India's discarding of non-alignment and adoption of alignment with a select group of friends based on strategic criteria, is a monumental alteration in behaviour, which is part and parcel of a newfound assertive strategic culture—a phenomenon I have analysed in my previous book.[108] A country that undergoes a fundamental remaking of its strategic culture will naturally reassess and recalibrate

---

[107]Park, Yong Soo, 'An Appraisal of Power Balancing Between India and China', *International Journal of Social Science Studies*, Vol. 11, No. 1, 2023, pp. 44, 46.
[108]Chaulia, Sreeram, *Crunch Time: Narendra Modi's National Security Crises*, 2022, Rupa Publications, New Delhi.

its friendships, and rethink the very purpose of its strategic partnerships. A partnership that India may have signed when it was in the 'congagement' and hedging mode will have to be updated to the balancing mode for that friendship to have relevance in the third decade of the 21st century.

In this context, India's most relevant strategic partnerships today have to be those which either explicitly or implicitly help its pushback against China, and to a lesser extent, China's proxy Pakistan. T.V. Paul considers strategic partnership as 'a soft-balancing tool only if it has a security component and is explicitly aimed at balancing the power or threatening behaviour of another state, but is below the level of a formal alliance.' He adds that if the bilateral relationship 'develops into anything more significant, such as allowing the use of [military] base facilities, then such an alignment counts as limited hard balancing.'[109] Assessing India's ways of tackling China in the Modi era, Paul refers to the former enhancing military cooperation with the USA, Australia and Japan, and argues that these three strategic partnerships 'display many elements of a soft balancing/limited hard-balancing coalition.'[110] In fact, all seven pivotal strategic partners of India covered in this book meet the standards of balancing.

The seven friends which appear in the subsequent chapters are vital enablers of India's balancing strategies (external, internal or both) against China and its 'all-weather strategic partner' Pakistan, which collude to hem India in and stymie its rise. Put differently, friends and enemies are two sides of the same coin in a geopolitically conflicted world. A friend who is not beneficial to deal with an enemy or an inimical phenomenon is of little value.

---

[109]Paul, T.V., *Restraining the Great Powers: Soft Balancing from Empires to the Global Era*, 2018, Yale University Press, New Haven, p. 26.
[110]Ibid., p. 138.

The seven countries selected for this book as India's closest friends stand out among its three dozen or so strategic partnerships (*see* Annexure, Table III) by virtue of their vital contributions in three domains—security, economy and geopolitical influence. Depending on geographical location, threat perceptions, economic capabilities, domestic political makeup, and the historical evolution of bilateral ties, each of these seven friends enables India with different weightages in these three domains. But viewed from a collective perspective, the sum total of these seven friendships adds up to a big fillip to India's rise as a leading power. By choosing Japan, Australia, the USA, Russia, France, Israel and the UAE as India's closest friends, we are in no way demeaning the value additions that accrue from other strategic partners. Friends like Argentina, Brazil, Greece, Mongolia and South Africa do not make the cut in this book, but there is no gainsaying their significance to India's 'Voice of the Global South' mission, and to the potential of vast untapped economic opportunities for India in emerging markets of Africa, Asia, Europe and Latin America. Yet, since these countries are neither players in the Indo-Pacific, nor active in the struggle against jihadist terrorism, and not closely knit in the field of security cooperation with India, they are not at the same level as the seven friends which are the main characters of this book.

In 2011, when India was still hedging vis-à-vis China and the world looked like a more benign place, a group of Indian scholars and former officials did a comparative study of six strategic partners of India— the USA, Russia, France, the UK, Germany and Japan—which were selected on the grounds that they happened to be the 'most active in the fields of defence cooperation, economic cooperation and political-diplomatic cooperation.'[111] On the yardsticks of India's nuclear strategy, its quest for a permanent seat in the UN Security Council, its stances on Pakistan, Afghanistan, Kashmir, and terrorism, the authors of the study ranked and evaluated which among these six friends mattered more to New Delhi. In their estimation, the USA got a cumulative numerical score of 18 out of 30, losing points due to its habit of hobnobbing with Pakistan during the GWOT. Russia scored higher than the USA, with a total of 23 out of 30, earning points over its consistent backing of India against Pakistan-sponsored terrorism. France secured 20, the UK got 15, Japan was awarded 14 and Germany came last, with 12. In the sphere of defence cooperation with India, the experts gave a score of 24 to Russia, 18 to the USA, 17 to France, 10 to the UK, 8 to Germany and 2 to Japan. On the criterion of economic cooperation with India, the ranking in descending order was USA (22), Japan (18), Germany (12), the UK (11), Russia (11) and France (10). Pooling together all dimensions, the report concluded that Russia was the most important strategic partner of India, while the USA came second, France stood third, and the UK, Germany and Japan followed lower down the order.[112]

If we fast-forward to the present era and look back at this list, the most striking aspect is that tackling China was not considered a principal foreign policy objective of India. The phrase 'Indo-Pacific' was hardly in vogue at that time, and did not find mention in that publication. To boot, another study in 2011 by an Indian think tank on a similar mission of comparatively evaluating India's strategic partnerships actually included China as one of its best friends, and found that on

---

[111]Kumar, Satish, S.D. Pradhan, Kanwal Sibal, Rahul Bedi and Bidisha Ganguly, 'India's Strategic Partners: A Comparative Assessment', Foundation for National Security Research, New Delhi, 2011, p. 1, https://tinyurl.com/4e3z9r34. Accessed on 5 June 2024.
[112]Ibid., pp. 13–14.

the basis of a composite score of 'economics, politics, defence, technology and people-to-people factors', China ranked third out of five countries in terms of value for India, ahead of Japan and the UK, but below the USA and Russia.[113]

In keeping with geopolitical realities of the third decade of the 21st century, particularly the Xi Jinping effect of radicalizing Chinese foreign policy to establish China's regional hegemony in Asia, this book places the China challenge right up front in India's priorities, even as Pakistan and jihadist extremism matter to a lesser extent. The premise guiding the chapters that follow rests on what General Bipin Rawat, the then Chief of Defence Staff of India, publicly acknowledged in 2021. He bluntly stated that there was 'no doubt' about China being India's 'enemy number one'.[114] As enemy number one's area of attention for establishing hegemony is the Indo-Pacific, it is this theatre which will make or mar India's rise as a leading power.

It is precisely due to the centrality of the Indo-Pacific in today's Indian strategic horizon, that Japan and Australia have been elevated to the top tier of New Delhi's friendships. The authors of the 2011 studies would rank these two friends more generously today. Also missing in the 2011 reports are Israel and the UAE. The reader will see in Chapter 6 how Israel muscled into India's strategic space, particularly in defence and counterterrorism, in the Modi era. The UAE has also stormed into India's top bracket of friendships in recent years by maximizing extraordinary economic and geoeconomic

---

[113]Gupta, Arvind, and Sarita Azad, 'Evaluating India's Strategic Partnerships using Analytic Hierarchy Process', Manohar Parrikar Institute for Defence Studies and Analyses, 17 September 2011, https://tinyurl.com/52khbt6t. Accessed on 5 June 2024.

[114]TNN, 'China Biggest Security Threat, Says General Bipin Rawat', *The Times of India*, 13 November 2021, https://tinyurl.com/wtw3vejj. Accessed on 5 June 2024.

coordination with India, as well as by aiding India's efforts to marginalize radical Islamist threats emanating from Pakistan. So, if one were to match the list of the 2011 studies with what we have presented in this book, the constants are France, Japan, Russia and the USA, but the new entrants—Australia, Israel and the UAE—tell their own remarkable stories. In my estimate, the latter three are relatively more strategic to India today, and will be so in the future, than Germany and the UK. If one visualizes the seven strategic partners in this book on a world map, it looks like an elongated arc starting with Russia's Far East and Japan in Northeast Asia, dipping down to Australia in Oceania, then turning west to Israel and the UAE, and then further afield to France and the USA. It is India's own arc of friendship that can be perceived as a global string that joins the key dots from multiple outward-spanning concentric circles or *mandala*s envisaged by Kautilya two-and-half millennia ago, when the geographical extent of the known world was much smaller.

BEST FRIENDS FOREVER?

Friendship and enmity are age-old concepts that figure prominently in India's ancient statecraft. Kautilya, who advised the Mauryan emperor Chandragupta (350–295 BCE), wrote extensively about the nature and typology of friends and foes, and constructed a whole system of international relations based on the complex interplay among them. In past decades, it was fashionable to assert that due to the effects of economic globalization, interdependence and thick institutionalization of issues in multilateral forums, modern-day foreign relations had grown complex and protean, and no dyad of countries could be classified straightforwardly as friendly or inimical. Competition-cum-cooperation, we were told, was the new normal as countries which worked together on one issue might square off against each other on another issue. This mixed-up, ambiguous reading of world politics was reflected in how strategic partnerships have been seen as 'primarily "goal-driven" rather than "threat-driven" arrangements' in which 'no state is identified by the partnership as a "threat", though the partnership may be concerned with joint security "issue-areas"—such as terrorism, separatism, religious fundamentalism.'[115]

But can strategic partnerships forever remain apolitical so as to avoid targeting a shared threat in the form of a rival nation-state? This book posits that, in the current era of global power transition, emerging multipolarity and fierce geopolitical rivalries, strategic partnerships involve balancing of adversaries as their prime function. It is true that most strategic partnerships have not morphed into full-fledged alliances, but worsening enmities and conflicts do hold out a possibility that some of them might be compelled to turn back the clock and revert to alliances or adopt alliance-like features while remaining on the borderline of partnership and alliance. The comparative survey of the strategic partnerships of the USA, China and India in the present Introduction suggests that all three intend to harness their friendships to counter their opponents through a mix of hard balancing and soft balancing.

As the China-USA 'new Cold War' hots up, and as the China-India contest deepens in the Indo-Pacific, all three countries are seeing strategic partnerships as devices to push back against their adversaries in economic, military and geopolitical realms. The same can be said for the remaining six friends of India which are covered in this book. All of them are eyeing the region and the world around them with

---

[115]Wilkins, Thomas, op. cit., p. 68.

trepidation and seeking security in tighter and substantively more 'strategic' partnerships.

In many of the case studies of India's friendships in this book, the dilemma of whether a strategic partnership is sufficient, or will it be forced by circumstances to evolve into a hard military alliance, is a real and haunting one. If deterrence of China based on strategic partnerships fails in the Indo-Pacific, then is not alliance the last refuge and the ultimate protection? Eruption of major wars in Eastern Europe and West Asia/the Middle East have ruffled feathers in India and elsewhere as to where the world order is going, and whether the assumptions of the past two decades will just be blown away. If China invades and occupies Taiwan or launches a limited war against India along the disputed Himalayan borders, will strategic partnerships be enough to hold the fort? If the already severe security climate in the Indo-Pacific reaches a moment of reckoning as Chinese aggression peaks, something akin to the critical inflexion point of 1971 will crop up again in India. In that fateful year, as Bangladesh was struggling for liberation from Pakistan, India discarded its cherished non-alignment policy in all but name, and signed a Treaty of Peace, Friendship and Cooperation with the Soviet Union to ward off the imminent threat posed by the 'Beijing-Washington-Islamabad axis'[116].

The future direction and content of India's strategic partnerships depend greatly on China's behaviour. If Beijing decides to move past its 'salami slicing' and 'grey zone warfare' tactics of gradually and slowly altering the territorial status quo in the Indo-Pacific through small cuts and nibbles, and initiates large military invasions and occupations, then India as well as its seven strategic partners covered in this book

---

[116]Chaudhuri, Sailen, *Beijing-Washington-Islamabad Entente: Genesis and Development*, 1982, Sterling, New Delhi.

will need to re-evaluate and reinvent their friendships. The journey from non-alignment to multi-alignment to alliance is not a theoretically remote proposition for India and its friends in light of the revisionist ambitions and actions of China. The analogy from human interpersonal relationships is informative here. It is not uncommon for friends to become lovers and then spouses. The degree of security may be maximum in marriage, but it also limits autonomy and flexibility in life choices.

For the moment, all we can conclude is that only strategic partners can be converted into allies. A brand-new alliance with a country that is not already a strategic partner with a history of close bilateral cooperation is unthinkable. So, for the present and the future, India will prize and cling to its strategic partners, even if some of them like Russia have moved uncomfortably closer to India's main adversary China, and some more might gravitate in directions that cannot be foreseen at present.

Thousands of years ago, Kautilya wrote about a category of friends who may have intimate ties with one's enemies:

> Whoever is of an amicable nature is a true friend; whoever sides also with the enemy is a mutable friend and who is indifferent to neither (the conqueror and his enemy) is a friend to both.[117]

The notion of a 'mutable friend', i.e. one who is likely to change, need not be seen in a negative vein as someone who could abandon or betray you. In the chapters that follow, the reader will encounter friends of India who conversely worry that India is mutable and not very firmly and conclusively on their side. The inbuilt uncertainty of the global power transition contains room for strategic shifts and adjustments

---

[117]Shamasastry, Rudrapatna, op. cit., p. 404.

by every country. India's major task in years and decades to come will be to update the content and parameters of its friendships in ways that keep up with the challenging times that lie ahead.

1

FEEDING THE KOI FISH: JAPAN AND INDIA IN BROADER ASIA

*Japan has undergone "The Discovery of India",
by which I mean we have rediscovered India as a
partner that shares the same values and interests,
and also as a friend that will work alongside us
to enrich the seas of freedom and prosperity, which
will be open and transparent to all.*[118]

—Shinzo Abe, Prime Minister of Japan, 2007

In the fall of 2014, just before Japan and India elevated
their bilateral ties from 'strategic and global partnership'
to 'special strategic and global partnership' (*see* Annexure,
Table III), two men clad in black outfits walked out to an
open area in a Kyoto guest house. In the dark, under the
glare of flashing bulbs and news media, they scooped out
feed from identical containers, and began sprinkling it into
a pond of colourful koi fish (carp). As the fish leapt to the
surface to gobble up the feed, the two benefactors looked at

---

[118]MOFA, '"Confluence of the Two Seas", Speech by H.E., M. Shinzo
Abe, Prime Minister of Japanat the Parliament of the Republic of India',
Ministry of Foreign Affairs of Japan, 22 August 2007,
https://tinyurl.com/mps3kjpb. Accessed on 5 June 2024.

each other with visible fondness, chatted with the aides, and posed for the shutterbugs. Despite a hectic summit diplomacy schedule, Prime Ministers Narendra Modi and Shinzo Abe made sure they performed the traditional Japanese ceremony of feeding the koi, which 'represents perseverance in adversity and the strength of purpose, aspirations and advancement', and is believed to 'bring good fortune or luck'.[119]

A year later, in the winter of 2015, Abe returned the gesture when he came to India to unveil a 'Japan and India Vision 2025 Special Strategic and Global Partnership Working Together for Peace and Prosperity of the Indo-Pacific Region and the World'. Dressed in traditional North Indian attire, he stood beside Prime Minister Modi on the lamp-lit banks of the holy Ganges in Varanasi and diligently performed *aarti* (in this context, venerating the river) amid group-chanting of Sanskrit verses by priests. It was an experience that mesmerized Japan's most charismatic and, eventually, the longest-serving, post-World War II leader. The symbolic event left no doubt that Japan and India were bound by not just contemporary materialistic interests, but by also a far deeper civilizational camaraderie that went back millennia between Hinduism and Buddhism, the latter having spread to Japan from India through China and Korea.

Abe knew that Varanasi held 'a special place in the religious and cultural tradition of Japan, as the city is also home to Sarnath, a place about 12 km from the main city where Gautam Buddha had delivered his first sermon upon attaining Enlightenment.'[120] It was, therefore, befitting that Abe and

---

[119]NDTV, 'Also Part of PM Modi's Japan Visit, Feeding Fish and Special Gifts', *NDTV*, 30 August 2014, https://tinyurl.com/bddfkvxj. Accessed on 5 June 2024.

[120]Dixit, Pawan, and Sudhir Kumar, 'Ganga Aarti at Varanasi Ghat Leaves Japan PM Mesmerized', *Hindustan Times*, 13 December 2015, https://tinyurl.com/2349b4bt. Accessed on 5 June 2024.

Modi paired up Varanasi and Kyoto as sister cities, with an eye on sharing urban-planning techniques, while preserving ancient heritage.[121] Apart from contributing to several water purification and sanitation projects across major Indian cities, Japan played a vital role in the cleaning up of the holy river in Varanasi through financial and technical assistance for India's National Mission for Clean Ganga.[122]

The 21st-century bond of geopolitics and economics—which Abe and Modi diligently shepherded until the former stepped down from office due to health reasons, and was later tragically assassinated—is set against the backdrop of deep-layered bilateral cultural respect and empathy over millennia. Unlike other strategic partnerships of India, the significance of a cosmological regard for India, which was known as *Tenjiku* or Centre of Heaven/Human World in the Japanese Buddhist worldview[123], is a unique bilateral cement.

In recent centuries, the mutual civilizational veneration was furthered by profound appreciation for each country's stances during the trying period of European colonial domination over Asia. Japan's rise as Asia's first industrial and military power, and its victory over Russia in 1905, had charged up Indian nationalists, who began to believe that if 'Japan, an Asiatic country' could trounce 'a great European power', then 'Asia could still defeat Europe as it had done so often in the past.'[124] The feeling was reinforced during World

[121]Ramachandran, Smriti Kak, '5 Areas Identified for Varanasi-Kyoto Deal', *The Hindu*, 13 January 2015, https://tinyurl.com/9rnyx44w. Accessed on 5 June 2024.

[122]JICA, 'Projects in India', Japan International Cooperation Agency, June 2022, https://tinyurl.com/4cdz7yuv. Accessed on 5 June 2024.

[123]Lentin, Sifra, 'India-Japan: Bound by the Ancient Tenjiku', *Gateway House*, 21 March 2023, https://tinyurl.com/5d5s4cjr. Accessed on 5 June 2024.

[124]Nehru, Jawaharlal, *Glimpses of World History*, 1934, Asia Publishing House, New York, p. 479.

War II, when India's revolutionary hero Subhas Chandra Bose allied with militarist Japan against British colonialism, and sowed mutual sentimental attachment among ordinary Indians and Japanese. The dissenting judgement given by India's Radhabinod Pal in the Tokyo War Crimes Tribunal, absolving Japanese leaders from charges of war crimes and crimes against humanity, also provided a defeated nation solace—that at least one country stood by it at a moment of deep humiliation and suffering.[125]

Notwithstanding the freeze in relations caused by the Cold War divide, when Japan stayed loyally within the Western bloc under the USA's umbrella, and India shuffled between non-alignment and de facto alliance with Soviet Russia, the afterglow of a sibling-like feeling remained in the historical memory and popular consciousness of Japanese and Indians alike. Compared to the other six friends of India, covered in the later chapters of this book, the lingering fraternal affection for Japan is a singular and extraordinary legacy, which helps explain why it was not so difficult to revive special bilateral relations to suit contemporary needs around the turn of the millennium.

Since its surrender to the USA and Allied Powers in 1945, Tokyo has remained a steadfast ally of Washington. However, India today has the privilege of a longer historical experience, and perceives Japan not as a feeble lackey of Western powers, but as a proud civilization and a pioneering modernizer, with tremendous latent energy that could be tapped to attain balance and stability in Asia.

---

[125]Deb, Sandipan, 'Radhabinod Pal: The Forgotten Indian and the Japanese Hero', *Mint Lounge*, 6 April 2018, https://tinyurl.com/4js9et44. Accessed on 5 June 2024.

A REDISCOVERY BETWEEN QUASI-FRIENDS

From India's standpoint today, Japan continuing to be an entrenched ally of the USA, while also attempting to chart out a course as a normal power, less fettered by restrictions imposed by the USA during its post-1945 occupation of the country, is not a contradiction. India's willingness to be open-minded and to enter into strategic partnerships with Western countries as part of its omni-directional, multi-alignment strategy around the turn of the millennium (*see* Annexure, Table III) meant that Tokyo's tag as Washington's long-standing top ally in East Asia made it doubly attractive to New Delhi. The synergies of the India-USA strategic partnership started to rub off positively on the India-Japan strategic partnership from the year 2000, reversing the Cold War era alienation, when India was wary of Japan for its pro-Western identity. Tokyo's decision to establish a 'global partnership' with New Delhi in 2000[126] was in step with Washington's push earlier that year to pursue a 'qualitatively new relationship' and 'stronger partnership' with New Delhi[127] (*see* Chapter 3). If Washington could quickly and pragmatically cast aside the economic sanctions, and stop cold-shouldering New Delhi after India's 1998 nuclear tests, Tokyo saw no reason for it to keep alienating New Delhi over concerns that it was a non-signatory to the Nuclear Non-Proliferation Treaty (NPT). Japan took the USA's cues in imposing sanctions on India in 1998, and again looked up to the precedent set by the USA while lifting restrictions in 2000. By 2015, Japan went so far as to sign a civilian nuclear agreement with India—the first and only such deal

---

[126]MEA, 'India-Japan Bilateral Relations', October 2023, Ministry of External Affairs, https://tinyurl.com/5ycnxnw2. Accessed on 31 August 2024.
[127]CWH, 'Joint Statement: US-India', Clinton White House, 15 September 2000, https://tinyurl.com/bdd85x92. Accessed on 9 June 2024.

inked by Tokyo with a non-NPT country, involving transfer of nuclear power technology and components.

When Japan took a strategic U-turn vis-à-vis India in 2000, the emerging triangular dynamic of Japan-USA-India relations was evident in the narrative of Hiroshi Hirabayashi, the then Ambassador of Japan to India. He recalled how impressed he was to witness American President Bill Clinton's landmark visit to India in March 2000, and immediately thereafter, he insisted to his headquarters in Tokyo that 'the Japanese prime minister should also visit India.' In August 2000, the landmark India visit of Yoshira Mori, the then Prime Minister of Japan, was truly 'epoch-making' as it set the ball rolling for a progressively unbreakable strategic partnership.[128] Subsequently, with Japan and India engaged in trilateral civilian coordination with the USA through dialogue mechanisms like JAI (Japan-America-India), and in trilateral joint military exercises like Malabar (2015–19), one could observe an undoubted external stimulus from Washington, which brought Tokyo and New Delhi closer. For a country like Japan that historically hewed to the USA's foreign policy preferences in judging whether a country is a friend or a foe, the USA's friendship with India was closely watched, and sought to be emulated or multiplied through its own friendship with India.

To better understand how the USA has encouraged, if not midwifed, the Japan-India strategic partnership in the Indo-Pacific, it is useful to compare it to the Japan-Australia quasi-alliance. A quasi-alliance refers to 'two states that remain non-allied but share a third power as a common ally.'[129] Both Japan and Australia are treaty allies of the USA and, thus,

---

[128]Hirabayashi, Hiroshi, *India: The Last Superpower*, 2021, Aleph, New Delhi, pp. 89–90.

[129]Cha, Victor, 'Abandonment, Entrapment, and Neoclassical Realism in Asia: The United States, Japan and Korea', *International Studies Quarterly*, Vol. 44, No. 2, 2000, p. 261.

are indirectly aligned to each other by virtue of belonging to the larger Washington-led alliance system in Asia. In the wake of growing fears of the challenge posed by Beijing's territorial expansionism, Tokyo and Canberra moved from indirect alignment to direct alignment by forming their special strategic partnership in 2014. Thomas Wilkins argued that this advanced bilateral partnership was the product of 'a policy blessed by Washington to "connect the spokes"' in its hub-and-spokes alliance architecture in the Indo-Pacific, and to give its allies 'more individual (and collective) responsibility for their own defence within the system.'[130]

Earlier in the present Introduction, we referred to the USA's reliance on an offshore balancing strategy in the Indo-Pacific, where its local allies and partners are motivated to be more active and better connected among themselves as a web or network to counter China's threat. If Australia and Japan can be aligned by virtue of being quasi-allies through the USA, then one can see India and Japan aligning by virtue of the former being a strategic partner of the USA, and the latter being an ally of the USA.

Compared to full-fledged alliances, strategic partnerships have their limitations, but one can postulate that Japan and India are quasi-friends, when seen through the prism of the USA's grand strategy in Asia. Washington's desire to put up a united front of its allies and partners to contain China's aggression is visible in its diplomacy to patch up historical animosities between Japan and South Korea (quasi-allies), speed up the special strategic partnership between Japan and Australia (quasi-allies), and endorse the special strategic and global partnership between Japan and India (quasi-friends).

---

[130]Wilkins, Thomas, 'From Strategic Partnership to Strategic Alliance? Australia-Japan Security Ties and the Asia-Pacific', *Asia Policy*, Vol. 20, 2015, p. 101.

While the USA's hand in the Japan-India friendship must be given its due, it would be incorrect to attribute the entire momentum gained between Tokyo and New Delhi merely to Washington's geostrategic game plans. Beijing's communist propaganda often paints bilateral and minilateral strategic partnerships among Asian countries as unwanted offspring of the USA's evil schemes and plots to suppress China, and to divide and rule over Asia. In 2023, when the air forces of Japan and India conducted their first joint fighter jet exercises off Japan's east coast, Chinese government mouthpieces claimed that they were held 'under the instigation of the US', and that 'both Japan and India are being lured by the US to join its Indo-Pacific strategy in containing China.'[131] Such sweeping Chinese denunciations are meant to portray Japan and India as mindless puppets being misled and exploited by the USA. On the contrary, Tokyo and New Delhi represent proud countries, with their respective national interests and visions for national rejuvenation. Today, Japan and India have agency of their own, and cannot be reduced to being pawns of the USA.

RISING SUN, LEAPING TIGER

'Quasi-friends' is just one angle in a multi-dimensional Japan-India strategic partnership, not the complete story. The maximum explanatory weightage for advances in Japan-India friendship lies in each side's aspirations to rise to a higher level in the regional and global orders. For Japan's restless nationalistic politicians and radical conservatives like Abe, friendship with India was an essential step towards the larger national renaissance project of drastically shaking up their

---

[131]Xuanzun, Liu, 'Japan, India Start Fighter Jet Drills, With Growing Military Ambitions Instigated by US Against China', *Global Times*, 16 January 2023, https://tinyurl.com/mw6jy96x. Accessed on 5 June 2024.

country, which had been mired in a long history of gradual evolution, dependence on the USA, and lost decades of slow economic growth and relative decline since the 1990s. During his brief first stint as Prime Minister in 2007, Abe delivered a landmark address in the Indian parliament, mooting a 'broader Asia that broke away geographical boundaries', and which involved a 'dynamic coupling' of the Pacific and Indian Oceans. He urged that 'it is incumbent upon us two democracies, Japan and India, to carry out the pursuit of freedom and prosperity' in this expanded region, which he termed the 'Arc of Freedom and Prosperity' along the 'outer rim of the Eurasian continent'. For this ambitious vision to connect and integrate this region, he insisted that 'the Strategic Global Partnership of Japan and India is pivotal.'[132]

By seeding the concept of the Indo-Pacific, with Japan and India as two pillars holding up its two corners, Abe revealed a profound Japanese strategic evolution. Instead of being complacent that the alliance with the USA was all Japan needed to be safe and secure in Northeast Asia, he institutionalized a revolutionarily proactive foreign policy to expand Japan's influence beyond just its backyard. In his own words, 'It is the responsibility of anyone involved in politics to always think of what Japan can do to contribute more to the peace and stability not just of Japan and the region, but of the entire world.'[133] According to Abe's foreign policy speech-writer and confidante, Tomohiko Taniguchi, as early as 2006, the Japanese leader had realized that 'the Asia-Pacific concept had become outdated,' and that 'there was a need for a larger concept that would balance China's intimidation, as well as a framework that would encompass

---

[132]MOFA, 'Confluence of the Two Seas', op. cit.
[133]Mirror Now, 'Shinzo Abe Passes Away: Most Memorable Quotes by Former Japan Prime Minister', *Times Now*, 9 July 2022, https://tinyurl.com/muwj22fy. Accessed on 5 June 2024.

and emphasize fast-growing India as one pole, both politically and economically.'[134] Takenori Horimoto, an India specialist in Japan, has echoed this interpretation and written that the Indo-Pacific was 'a strategic concept designed to encourage India to get involved in the Pacific maritime domain as a counter to China.' Horimoto says Abe thought 'the geographical concept of Asia-Pacific was insufficient to meet Chinese power by US forces alone,' and hence wanted to 'involve India in the Pacific sphere so that Japan can add its countervailing power vis-à-vis emerging China.'[135]

Like the proverbial canary in the mine, Abe brilliantly read China's strategic shift towards a menacing path very early. When Western allies of Japan still thought of China as a responsible stakeholder, which could be co-opted and moderated, Abe saw through the hidden intent of the dragon, and advocated a counterbalancing coalition under the rubrics of a 'confluence of the two seas' (Pacific and Indian Oceans) and 'democratic security diamond'.[136] Japan's willingness to come out of a shell and engage boldly with Taiwan (a self-governed island claimed by China), Pacific Island nations and Southeast Asian countries jostling with China over territorial disputes, and Tokyo's launch of a special strategic and global partnership with New Delhi, were fruits of Abe's drive to restore Japanese greatness through coalitions with like-minded countries.

Upon returning to the premiership in 2012, Abe and his radical conservative political allies in Japan were convinced that Japan can only lead the Indo-Pacific in collaboration with

[134]Taniguchi, Tomohiko, 'Shinzo Abe's Japan and a New Asia' in Baru, Sanjaya, ed., *The Importance of Shinzo Abe: India, Japan and the Indo-Pacific*, 2023, HarperCollins, Gurugram, p. 10.
[135]Horimoto, Takenori, 'Japan-India Relations: Mapping Abe's Diplomacy,' in Baru, Sanjaya, ed., op. cit., p. 103.
[136]Abe, Shinzo, 'Asia's Democratic Security Diamond', *Project Syndicate*, 27 December 2012, https://tinyurl.com/yc668485. Accessed on 12 August 2024.

countries like India. As a middle power with self-imposed shackles on its military since World War II, Japan could not realistically reshape the regional order unilaterally or in alliance just with the USA. It needed strong friends to project power and found one in India, whose mantra of a 'leading power' was a match made in heaven. Abe's 2013 speech in Washington, where he assured an elite American audience that 'Japan is not, and will never be, a tier-two country,' is notable for his emphasis on a USA-plus strategy. The task for Japan's foreign policy, he declared, was to 'work even more closely with the U.S., Korea, Australia and other like-minded democracies throughout the region,' and to emerge as 'a rules-promoter, a commons' guardian, and an effective ally and partner to the U.S. and other democracies.'[137] The stress on *other* was significant here, as Japan was convinced that it could not rise alone simply by remaining a docile hub in the USA's hub-and-spokes system.

One propelling factor behind Japan turning to India has been nagging doubts about the USA's iron-clad commitment to defending its allies in Asia in the event of a frontal attack by China. As the USA has often been militarily preoccupied in multiple conflict zones globally, including West Asia/the Middle East and Europe, questions have been raised on how focused it will be on power projection and deterrence in the Indo-Pacific. The Indian academic Shamshad Khan wrote in 2017 that 'in Japanese strategic thinking, India figures as an important partner as it realizes that its security ally—the US is overstretched with military missions in Iraq, Syria and Afghanistan, and thus it is not focusing much on East Asian regional security. Japanese defence planners have also noted

[137]Kantei, '"Japan is Back", Policy Speech by Prime Minister Shinzo Abe at the Center for Strategic and International Studies (CSIS)', 22 February 2013, Prime Minister of Japan and his Cabinet, https://tinyurl.com/4ms8ju5c. Accessed on 5 June 2024.

that with the rise of China, there has been a relative decline of US power in the region. Thus, they need someone to fill the void. India certainly fits in that calculation.'[138]

During Donald Trump's presidency (2017–2020), even though the USA publicly asserted that it aimed to pull out of other conflict zones and redirect its full strategic attention to the Indo-Pacific, the isolationist abandonment winds in USA's foreign policy left Japanese leaders nervy and 'sleepless'.[139] Investing in closer partnerships with rising power India, and middle powers like Australia, Indonesia and Vietnam, makes sense as a strategy for an anxiety-ridden Japan.

Single-handedly, India cannot obviously be a substitute for the USA. But as a member of a network of special friends of Japan, where each has a designated role to perform, India has the means to block China's expansion in the Indian Ocean Region (IOR), and relieve Tokyo of Chinese strategic pressure in the East and South China Seas. In 2023, Sibi George, the Ambassador of India to Japan, described how the regional division of labour is central to the Japan-India friendship: 'I consider Japan the most important partner for us. Any development in this part of the region has an impact on India and that region. Similarly, any development in the Indian Ocean, which is a key sea lane to Japan's energy security, is very important. Any development in that region will have a direct impact on this region. We are partners in peace for the mutual benefit of our two countries.'[140]

[138]Khan, Shamshad, *Changing Dynamics of India-Japan Relations: Buddhism to Special Strategic Partnership*, 2017, Pentagon Press, New Delhi, p. 69.

[139]Mead, Walter Russell, 'China and Trump are Making Japan Nervous', *The Wall Street Journal*, 16 September 2019, https://tinyurl.com/3sbw7wac. Accessed on 5 June 2024.

[140]YS, 'Strong Japan-India Relationship Good for Indo-Pacific Security, Speakers at Yomiuri International Forum Say', *Yomiuri Shimbun*, 3 October 2023, https://tinyurl.com/yc6xd8rr. Accessed on 5 June 2024.

Frequent critical references to China's unilateral and coercive behaviour in the East and South China Seas, and in the IOR in Japan-India communiqués and official statements[141], joint Japan-India and minilateral naval exercises in these sub-regions, and joint Japan-India initiatives to offer alternatives to Chinese loans and investments in those areas, emanate from the mutually shared assessment in Tokyo and New Delhi that the fates of the two oceans are inextricably linked by China's rise and its hegemonic 'two-ocean strategy'.[142]

For decades, Japanese strategists have viewed China's territorial expansionism and appetite for maximizing economic influence with increasing unease. Two scary prospects have them worried. The first is Abe's likening of China's ever-expanding strategic frontier to Nazi Germany's Lebensraum (living space). He warned: 'This very dangerous idea posits that borders and exclusive economic zones are determined by national power, and that as long as China's economy continues to grow, its sphere of influence will continue to expand.'[143] The second nightmare is of China implementing its 'three-stage scenario' for naval expansion by dominating the 'first island chain' (including Japan's Senkaku Islands and the South China Sea), the 'second island chain' (including Japan's Ogasawara Island and Indonesia), and the 'third island chain' (terminating the USA's military dominance and pushing

[141]MEA, 'India-Japan Summit Joint Statement Partnership for a Peaceful, Stable and Prosperous Post-COVID World', 19 March 2022, Ministry of External Affairs, Government of India, https://tinyurl.com/yuj2s999. Accessed on 5 June 2024; PMO of Japan, 'Policy Speech by Prime Minister Kishida Fumio at the Indian Council of World Affairs (ICWA)', 20 March 2023, https://tinyurl.com/4v36hfhr. Accessed on 5 June 2024.
[142]Mohan, C. Raja, 'China's Two-Ocean Strategy Puts India in a Pincer', *Foreign Policy*, 4 January 2022, https://tinyurl.com/34jhcsrz. Accessed on 21 February 2024.
[143]IE, 'Ex-Japan PM Says China Eyeing Nazi-Type "Lebensraum"', *The Indian Express*, 19 October 2010, https://tinyurl.com/4a843w3j. Accessed on 5 June 2024.

it out of the Pacific and Indian Oceans).[144] In its mission to forestall such disastrous outcomes for Japan's national security, Japan has found India to be indispensable. The 2022 National Security Strategy of Japan unhesitatingly labelled China as its 'unprecedented and greatest strategic challenge', and vowed to 'build a multi-layered network among its ally and like-minded countries [...] Australia, India, the ROK [South Korea], European countries, ASEAN countries, Canada, NATO, EU, and others.'[145]

Among all these players, as India is the rising power with the greatest potential to one day equal China and the USA, Japan views it as key both for its soft and hard balancing strategies. For instance, it has emphasized the value of joint trainings of its maritime self-defence forces with the Indian Navy. Due to the constraints of the USA-drafted post-war Constitution, for a long time Japan did not build a strong navy to project power away from its shores. Only after Abe's creative and determined efforts to reinterpret the Constitution, legislate new operational parameters, and increase defence spending did Japan begin coming out of its cocoon. This evolution was reflected in policies followed by his successors like Prime Minister Fumio Kishida, who noted that 'joint training with India and the U.S.', Australia and the UK will make Japan's fledgling navy a 'Force for Peace'[146]. Such views demonstrated how the more experienced and battle-ready

[144]Narushighe, Michishita, 'The Future of Sino-Japanese Competition at Sea', *Nippon*, 23 March 2012, https://tinyurl.com/2wxfvt57. Accessed on 5 June 2024.

[145]CAS, 'National Security Strategy of Japan', December 2022, Cabinet Secretariat, pp. 9, 13, https://tinyurl.com/23863v89. Accessed on 5 June 2024.

[146]MOFA, 'Japan's New Plan for a "Free and Open Indo-Pacific–Together with India, as an Indispensable Partner"', 20 March 2023, Ministry of Foreign Affairs of Japan, https://tinyurl.com/3utces3d. Accessed on 5 June 2024.

Indian military was seen as beneficial for uplifting neophyte Japan's fighting capabilities.

The signing of the Japan-India Acquisition and Cross-Servicing Agreement (ACSA) in 2020 was a milestone in this direction. It granted the two countries' armed forces access to each other's logistical supplies like fuel, oils, lubricants, spare parts and maintenance during trainings and bilateral exercises, enhanced interoperability, and created openings for the Indian Navy to be able to utilize Japan's first long-term overseas military base in Djibouti at the western end of the IOR, while Japan's maritime forces would reciprocally be able to harness India's geopolitically crucial Andaman and Nicobar Islands that straddle the chokepoint of the Strait of Malacca and rein in China's expansionism.[147] The need for Japanese forces to physically fight to defend India if it is under attack from China along the Line of Actual Control (LAC) or in the Indian Ocean, and vice versa, may not arise. Unlike the security obligation Japan owes to its ally, the USA, which was upgraded in 2015 to enable Japan's military to participate in foreign conflicts for 'collective self-defence' in support of its ally[148], the strategic partnership with India contains no such obligation. Yet, the Japan-India double act of applying simultaneous pressure on China on different fronts is of strategic import.

India's Act East policy of increasing its economic and military foothold and activity in Southeast Asia, Northeast Asia and the Pacific Islands, and Japan's Free and Open Indo-

---

[147]Chaudhury, Dipanjan, 'Indo-Japan Mutual Logistics Pact Can Enable Navies Access to Djibouti & Andamans', *The Economic Times*, 27 August 2020, https://tinyurl.com/553dv6eb. Accessed on 5 June 2024.

[148]MOFA, 'Japan's Legislation for Peace and Security: Seamless Responses for Peace and Security of Japan and the International Community', Ministry of Foreign Affairs of Japan, March 2016, https://tinyurl.com/4ax8pxj8. Accessed on 5 June 2024.

Pacific (FOIP) strategy intersect and complement each other. Japan's construct of the Indo-Pacific provides India entry and acknowledgement as a major power and stakeholder in determining the regional security and prosperity of East Asia. There was a time when Asia meant only China, Japan and the Koreas in the eyes of prominent world capitals. By popularizing and institutionalizing the Indo-Pacific and broader Asia, Japan carved out space for India to move on its eastern flank and demonstrate its might as a rising power. On the other hand, India courted and seconded Japan's involvement in security and economic development of neighbours such as Bangladesh, Myanmar, Sri Lanka and the Maldives, as an alternative to China[149], thereby creating chances for Japan to assume a role far beyond East Asia, and expand the ambit of its influence.

Japan's 'normalization' and transition from a pacifist power to a military power through a steady and sustained arms build-up under Abe and his successors have also been widely welcomed in India. Unlike East Asian countries, which carry scars from the traumatic historical memories of Japanese imperialism before and during World War II, and express rhetorical concerns about its recrudescence, India has no emotional hangover to be worried about a rearmed Japan that is acquiring significant offensive counter-strike weapons capabilities.

In 2022, when then Prime Minister Kishida's government released a new National Security Strategy, and announced a record $320 billion plan to equip Japan with long-range missiles, fighter jets, submarines and warships, catapulting Japan to the ranks of the third largest defence spender after the

---

[149]Macan-Markar, Marwaan, 'Sri Lanka, Maldives See Japan Wade into Indian Ocean Contest', *Nikkei Asia*, 28 July 2023, https://tinyurl.com/3nbe9j8s. Accessed on 17 June 2024.

USA and China[150], Indian commentators gave it a unambiguous thumbs-up. For India, this portended a genuinely multipolar Asia where a 'bold Japan' would be 'determined not to allow unilateral change of status quo by force in the Indo-Pacific and do what it takes to defend the core tenets of a rules-based order.'[151] Japanese strategist Satoru Nagao underlined that 'if both India and Japan possess long-range strike capabilities, this combined capability makes China defend multiple fronts. Even if China resorts to adventurism along the India-China border, it will still need to expend a certain amount of its budget and military assets to defend itself against Japan.'[152] India has also appreciated Japan shedding old inhibitions about offering foreign aid to like-minded countries in the Indo-Pacific for the purpose of acquiring military hardware. The prospect of Japan's Official Security Assistance (OSA) to the Philippines, Malaysia, Bangladesh, Fiji et al., was applauded in India as 'another step in Japan's march towards a more robust and proactive defence posture'.[153]

Compared to India's friends like the USA, Russia and France, its direct bilateral defence cooperation with Japan has not been robust until now because of Japan's slow and gradual assumption of the status of a normal power with a willingness to acquire and wield military force as an instrument of statecraft. But the future promises to be

[150]Kelly, Tim, and Sakura Murakami, 'Pacifist Japan Unveils Biggest Military Build-Up Since World War Two', *Reuters*, 17 December 2022, https://tinyurl.com/4a7w7ufv. Accessed on 17 June 2024.
[151]Basu, Titli, 'Japan's National Security Strategy is Good News for Indo-Pacific', *Hindustan Times*, 9 January 2023, https://tinyurl.com/mwu4xhb9. Accessed on 17 June 2024.
[152]Nagao, Satoru, 'How Japan's New National Security Strategy Impacts Cooperation with India', *The Economic Times*, 26 December 2022, https://tinyurl.com/mr3yca4r. Accessed on 17 June 2024.
[153]PTI, 'Japan to Offer Military Aid to Like-Minded Countries in a Bid to Counter China', *The Economic Times*, 13 April 2023, https://tinyurl.com/2k8vsr5z. Accessed on 17 June 2024.

exciting. Although Japan's internal divisions and debates about normalization have been 'arduous' and 'exceedingly difficult', the Abe-initiated neo-conservative push has finally succeeded in operationalizing the demand that 'Japan has to change with the times, live up to its alliance responsibilities [vis-à-vis the USA], fulfil its obligations as a responsible global power and look after its own interests and security.'[154] As Japan has exorcized its doubts and stepped out more confidently to face what its leaders call 'the most severe and complex security environment since the end of World War Two'[155], its readiness to engage in defence diplomacy with strategic partners like India has naturally increased. The 2+2 ministerial dialogue, involving foreign and defence ministers of India and Japan, which commenced in 2019, indicated that, henceforth, the defence leg of the strategic partnership would not lag behind the economic leg. If these integrated consultations yield concrete deliverables through co-development and coproduction of sensitive military equipment like unmanned aerial vehicles (UAVs), anti-drone systems, robotics, underwater communication, lithium-ion battery technology and intelligence systems[156], then the Japan-India friendship could claim that it excels not only in external balancing, but also in internal balancing.

---

[154]Teo, Victor, *Japan's Arduous Rejuvenation as a Global Power: Democratic Resilience and the US-China Challenge*, 2019, Palgrave Macmillan, Singapore, pp. 195, 202.
[155] Tomisawa, Ayai, 'Japan's Premier Vows to Secure Funding to Boost Defence: NHK', *Bloomberg*, 11 November 2023, https://tinyurl.com/5257pbxb. Accessed on 24 June 2024.
[156]Singh, Dalip, 'India, Japan Identify Key Areas of Defence Cooperation Ahead of 2+2 Dialogue at Tokyo', *The Hindu Business Line*, 31 August 2022, https://tinyurl.com/mtku48ex. Accessed on 17 June 2024.

THE FIVE REVOLUTIONS

Economic and geoeconomic cooperation forms the bedrock of the Japan-India friendship. These elements predate the bilateral military and geopolitical coordination, and continue to produce visible and concrete yields for the people of both countries, and for residents of the wider Indo-Pacific. In 2023, India's External Affairs Minister Subrahmanyam Jaishankar recounted four revolutions of the Indian economy at historic junctures that have been spurred by collaboration with Japan:

> There is the Maruti revolution where it wasn't just the Suzuki car coming in, it wasn't only about a car coming in, it was a way actually for the entire lifestyle, it was a thinking, it was an industrial culture which got changed. The second revolution was the metro revolution. I think it's had a very profound impact on the urban infrastructure of India. The third revolution is in the making which is the high-speed rail [...] when we complete that project, people will see in India what an enormous ripple impact it has [...] And the fourth revolution which I see on the horizon which is emerging and critical technologies and semiconductor sphere [sic] where again I do believe that there is a huge potential for us to work on.[157]

The seminal contributions of Japan to India's economic fortunes cannot be overstated. India has been the largest recipient of Japanese Official Development Assistance (ODA), which began in 1958, and has covered wide-ranging sectors such as agricultural techniques, power generation, public transportation, forestry and biodiversity, healthcare, human resource development, disaster mitigation and water

---

[157]MEA, 'Remarks by EAM, Dr. S. Jaishankar at the 2nd India-Japan Forum 2023', 28 July 2023, Ministry of External Affairs, Government of India, https://tinyurl.com/3h3h3je5. Accessed on 17 June 2024.

management.[158] The evidence is unequivocal that Japanese aid has helped improve public policies and life chances at the grassroots level in almost all states of India. For a poor developing nation like post-independence India, which was non-aligned or leaned towards the Soviet Union, to get advanced know-how and best practices transferred from the main ally of the USA in Asia, meant much more than just material benefits. Japan's great reputation and goodwill among India's people stem not only from its association with high quality and finely finished products, but also from the legacy of being a generous developmental partner with no political conditionalities that gave loans and grants, based on priorities identified by India. Japan's soft power strategy of spreading its influence through ODA has no bigger poster child than India. To cite Sibi George, Ambassador of India to Japan in 2021, 'India's continued rise in the global stage is supported by Japan, and Japan's continued rise as a global leader is supported with its ODA initiatives in India.'[159]

A noticeable emphasis in Japan's ODA and foreign investment in India since the special strategic and global partnership came into being in 2014, has been on infrastructure, connectivity and industrialization to bolster Modi's 'Make in India' campaign of revving up domestic manufacturing for Indian and world markets. Having visited Japan and invited Japanese industrial and business houses to his native state Gujarat while he was Chief Minister (2001–14), 'Modi believed that Japan, endowed with superior technological skills and financial strength, could to a large extent fulfil

---

[158]MOFA, 'Overview of Japan's ODA to India', Ministry of Foreign Affairs of Japan, June 2011, https://tinyurl.com/mmdrn7p6. Accessed on 17 June 2024.

[159]PTI, 'India Top Recipient of Japanese Financial Aid Since 2003, Surpassing China', *The Economic Times*, 26 March 2021, https://tinyurl.com/mr2zez6k. Accessed on 17 June 2024.

many of India's development aspirations,' and looked to Japan as he embarked on an 'integrated infrastructure programme involving the construction of roads, railways, airports and waterways.'[160] As if ordained by Modi and Abe's close friendship, the Japanese leader had almost simultaneously initiated an 'infrastructure system export strategy' with 'the clear objective of capturing global markets' and making it 'the central aspect of [...] Japan's economic rejuvenation'. Apart from 'fulfilling the needs of developing countries like Indonesia, Vietnam, India and Thailand,' Abe wanted to put on the table a Japanese alternative for 'stemming the growing influence of China,' which had begun to overshadow Japan through its own mega infrastructure projects via the Belt and Road Initiative (BRI).[161] The iconic Delhi-Mumbai Industrial Corridor (DMIC), Chennai-Bengaluru Industrial Corridor (CBIC), and Japanese Industrial Townships (JITs) across Indian states, where more than one hundred Japanese companies like Daikin, Isuzu, Kobelco, Yamaha and Hitachi have set up manufacturing units, are all extraordinary, to say the least. The positive effects of such game-changing Japanese initiatives on the Indian economy are visible, and show how Japan quietly, but surely, can match or even outdo China in the field of foreign economic assistance.[162]

Despite its typically understated style, Japan is far ahead of China as an investor in the Indian economy. As the fifth largest investor in India, with a cumulative FDI inflows of $41 billion for the period April 2000 to March 2024, and

---

[160]Kesavan, K.V., 'Infrastructure Connectivity and Corridors in Prime Minister Modi's Japan Policy', in Panda, Jagannath, ed., *Scaling Japan-India Cooperation in Indo-Pacific and Beyond 2025: Corridors, Connectivity and Contours*, 2020, KW Publishers, New Delhi, p. 78.
[161]Ibid., p. 83.
[162]Mishra, Amit, 'Japan Industrial Townships in India: A Silent Triumph Celebrating Modi-Abe Duo's Legacy', *Swarajya*, 20 July 2023, https://tinyurl.com/mrxtjxpw. Accessed on 17 June 2024.

as many as 1,439 of its companies active in sectors ranging from automobiles and electronics to textiles and chemicals, Japan is nothing short of an economic colossus in the Indian context.[163] The dedicated Japan clearance windows and Japan-Plus desk arrangements of the Modi government have paved the way for a steady surge of Japanese FDI which, as of 2023, exceeded FDI from all other special friends of India, except the USA and the UAE.[164] The Government of India's 'Make in India' portal named Japan second in its list of 'countries that are making big in India', following the USA and preceding the UAE, Germany and France.[165] Prime Minister Modi is on record while speaking in Kobe, Japan, that 'FDI means First Develop India,' and 'these days India is receiving the maximum FDI in its history.'[166]

The vote of confidence that the Government of Japan and Japan's Keidanren (Japan Business Federation) have given to India during its take-off stage to a high economic growth trajectory speaks volumes about timing and strategic trust.[167] It is also an indicator that Japan is not investing or lending in India for charity, but as a win-win proposition that generates healthy revenues and profits for Japanese corporations. Japan's decision in 2022 to invest an additional $42 billion in India

[163]Invest India, 'Japanese Investments in India: Overview and Opportunities', National Investment Promotion & Facilitation Agency, https://tinyurl.com/3j5pmpz5. Accessed on 17 June 2024.
[164]PTI, 'UAE Emerges as Fourth Largest Investor in India in FY–23', *The Hindu*, 11 June 2023, https://tinyurl.com/maxkaxp6. Accessed on 17 June 2024.
[165]MIN, '5 Countries that are Making Big in India', Make in India, https://tinyurl.com/5eunmuj4. Accessed on 17 June 2024.
[166]PIB, 'English Rendering of PM's Address to the Indian Community in Kobe, Japan', Press Information Bureau, 12 November 2016, https://tinyurl.com/bdz7tksf. Accessed on 17 June 2024.
[167]Venkatesh, Mahua, 'Japanese Firms Rank India as Top Investment Destination', *India Narrative*, 27 December 2022, https://tinyurl.com/49fjz8x7. Accessed on 17 June 2024.

until 2027 will simultaneously aid India's modernization, and expand opportunities for Japan's private sector. There has been some hand-wringing in India about relatively low bilateral trade volumes between the two countries, which hovered around $21 billion as of 2023, owing to non-tariff barriers that limit Indian exports to Japan despite the existence of a bilateral Free Trade Agreement (FTA)—known as the Comprehensive Economic Partnership Agreement (CEPA)—since 2011.[168] In Japan, India's decision not to join the Regional Comprehensive Economic Partnership (RCEP) agreement that would integrate all major economies of Asia and Oceania, due to fear of its market being flooded by state-subsidized Chinese goods, generated noticeable disappointment.[169] But as fast friends that share common democratic political systems, New Delhi and Tokyo understand each other's domestic compulsions, and have not allowed these trade-related disagreements from derailing the more impactful ODA and FDI-based exchanges. Both Japan and India have far higher bilateral trade figures with China than with each other. However, this does not make China a strategic partner or friend of either Japan or India. Bilateral trade volumes do not always reflect national strategy or state preferences, but indicate an aggregation of decisions and choices by individual companies, consumers and sectors, based on micro-level calculations, besides the complementarity of the two economies in terms of the composition of goods and services being traded. One need not wait for a miraculous jump in Japan-India trade to

[168]Sen, Amiti, 'India Asks Japan to Reduce Regulatory Barriers to Trade at WTO Review', *The Hindu Business Line*, 17 May 2023, https://tinyurl.com/54mtdyuz. Accessed on 17 June 2024.
[169]Haidar, Suhasini, 'Japan Still Hopes India Will Rejoin RCEP: Japan Cabinet Official Noriyuki Shikata', *The Hindu*, 20 March 2022, https://tinyurl.com/5au7szzj. Accessed on 17 June 2024.

conclude that Japan and India have truly uplifted each other economically in myriad other ways.

The 2023 bilateral agreement to establish the Japan-India semiconductor supply chain partnership, and the intent of Japanese electronics giants to invest billions of dollars in India for setting up state-of-the-art semiconductor factories, reflect how elevating this strategic partnership can be. Japan's share of 32 per cent of semiconductor equipment and 56 per cent of semiconductor materials[170] in the global supply makes this particular area of collaboration with India a future game-changer.

Over and above the four economic revolutions that Jaishankar enumerated, the Japan-India strategic partnership has produced a fifth revolution in the geoeconomic sphere. The two friends have joined hands to boost infrastructure, connectivity, skill enhancement, commercial capacities and resilient supply chains in a strategic zone spanning Northeast India, and going on to Bangladesh, Myanmar, Thailand, Vietnam, Sri Lanka and the Maldives. Under the Act East Forum roadmap for Northeast India—a region bordering China, that was fragile because of its underdevelopment and isolation from India's heartland—Japan has undertaken a variety of projects in sectors like bridges, highways, waterways, irrigation, agro-industries, tourism, water supply, sewerage, healthcare, sustainable forestry and renewable energy. Japan has more than lived up to its assurance in 2015 that 'for the enhancement of connectivity between SAARC [South Asian Association for Regional Cooperation] and ASEAN [Association of Southeast Asian Nations], Japan will strengthen its assistance by supporting development initiatives

---

[170]CNA, 'Japan, Taiwan Perfect Match in Semiconductor Sector: Pegatron Boss', *Focus Taiwan*, 21 February 2024, https://tinyurl.com/4ekcnstz. Accessed on 17 June 2024.

in Northeast India, which will serve as a connective node between the two regions.'[171]

That Japan standing by India in the Northeast is a sensitive issue can be gauged from China's objections to the Japan-led Asian Development Bank (ADB)-funded projects, and to direct bilateral Japanese assistance to India in Arunachal Pradesh, which is claimed by China on the dubious grounds that it is 'South Tibet' and rightfully belongs to China.[172] For India to rope in no other friend except Japan to scale up infrastructure so close to its militarized disputed frontier with Chinese-occupied territories, speaks highly of the strategic coordination between New Delhi and Tokyo.

Japan and India have teamed up not only in Northeast India. During the prime ministership of Sheikh Hasina in Bangladesh, Japan moved in there as a major commercial and developmental partner, and helped ensure an inseparable troika-like formation with India in the Bay of Bengal region.[173] The Japanese-financed deep-sea Matarbari Port in southern Bangladesh took off in close consultations with India, which backed Japan's foreign policy activism along its eastern littoral region. Researchers have noted that a rival deep-sea port which Bangladesh had considered in Sonadia with Chinese funding had to be aborted 'because of India's opposition, which the [government] in Dhaka could not simply override due to its overreliance on Delhi.' Given that 'India lacks the resources to offer an alternative to China on its own,' it 'welcomes

---

[171]MOFA, 'Policy Speech by Foreign Minister Fumio Kishida "Special Partnership for the Era of the Indo-Pacific"', 18 January 2015, Ministry of Foreign Affairs of Japan, https://tinyurl.com/bdz3czjy. Accessed on 17 June 2024.

[172]Patranobis, Sutirtho, 'China Reacts to India-Japan Cooperation in Northeast, Says No Room for "Third Party"', *Hindustan Times*, 15 September 2017, https://tinyurl.com/bdppwkve. Accessed on 17 June 2024.

[173]Bhatia, Rajiv, 'A New Troika for India's Northeast Region', *The Hindu*, 24 April 2023, https://tinyurl.com/4d83p5es. Accessed on 17 June 2024.

Japan to build the Matarbari Port, which seems to serve India's interest no less than Bangladesh's.'[174]

Japan and India also jointly implemented projects for widening roads, refurbishing bridges, providing rolling stock and constructing railway infrastructure in Bangladesh as part of an India-plus strategy of strengthening relationships with 'certain geopolitically important countries in the region, in concert with India's "Neighbourhood First" policy.'[175] In the context of Bangladesh joining the BRI, but trying to avoid overdependence on China in the Sheikh Hasina era, the Japan-India tag team was a counterbalancing presence that ensured Bangladesh's sovereignty and freedom of options. Bangladesh's decision in 2023 to release an official Indo-Pacific Outlook won applause in Japan, India and the USA, and demonstrated its 'willingness to deepen existing cooperation' with the Quad countries, with the ultimate goal of maintaining Dhaka's 'strategic autonomy'.[176] Following the overthrow of Hasina's government by organised mobs of protesters in 2024, it became even more imperative that Japan and India coordinate their economic assistance strategies to prevent China from seizing the opportunity to dominate Bangladesh.

Japan and India have also sought to team up in Myanmar, with the goal of integrating this trouble-torn country into their shared visions of FOIP and Act East. Tokyo and New Delhi have implemented 'soft infrastructure' plans for schools

---

[174]Mahmud, Faisal, and Ryohtaroh Satoh, 'Bangladesh Deep-Sea Port Promises Strategic Anchor for Japan, India', *Nikkei Asia*, 12 April 2023, https://tinyurl.com/mtvn7mfw. Accessed on 17 June 2024.

[175]Kurita, Masahiro, 'Japan's "India-Plus" Strategic Engagement with South Asia', *South Asian Voices*, 14 May 2020, https://tinyurl.com/4a9r2pzp. Accessed on 17 June 2024.

[176]Saimum, Rubiat, 'Bangladesh's Strategic Pivot to the Indo-Pacific', *East Asia Forum*, 9 June 2023, https://tinyurl.com/5b2empkt. Accessed on 17 June 2024.

in conflict-affected parts of Myanmar, and have also been instrumental in countering Chinese mega projects through their own alternative initiatives. Capitalizing on Myanmarese regimes' fear of overdependence on China, Japan built the Dawei and Thilawa special economic zones (SEZs), railways and energy plants in Myanmar worth billions of dollars. India's budgetary outlays in Myanmar have been smaller, but its completion of the deep-water Sittwe Port (not far from the Japan-built deep-sea Matarbari Port up north in Bangladesh), which would activate the Kaladan Multi-Modal Transit Transport Project linking Northeast India with ASEAN, have clear complementarities with Japan's proposal to set up a pan-regional 'industrial value chain' that weans away the Bay of Bengal region from China's hegemonic clutches.[177]

Japan and India had also acted in concert for infrastructure contracts in Sri Lanka for building the East Container Terminal (ECT) project in Colombo, but this was cancelled by Sri Lanka's corrupt and China-beholden government of the Rajapaksa clan. When the fruits of over-reliance on China came home to roost, and the Rajapaksa regime collapsed in 2022, Sri Lanka had to introspect about how much better it would have been had it not put all its eggs in the China basket. That China's BRI had a destabilizing and enslaving character was plain for all to see in the way it had devastated and wrecked Sri Lanka's economy, and forced it to concede the strategically located Hambantota Port for 99 years to Beijing. Ideas for Japan and India to return together to Sri Lanka and jointly launch projects in renewable energy, grid connectivity, oil pipelines, tourism and education, were subsequently revived, although clearing the rubble of Sri Lanka's humungous

---

[177]Yamada, Fumiko, 'Why Japan is Edging Closer to Bangladesh and India in the Region', *South Asia Monitor*, 16 April 2023, https://tinyurl.com/mr973xab. Accessed on 17 June 2024.

debt and distressed public finances introduced an element of caution in Tokyo and New Delhi.[178]

With nearshoring assuming greater significance in the present era of geopolitical competition and mistrust, Japan and India can be two nodal partners in the Indo-Pacific to integrate countries on the principle of trust and geographical proximity.

To cater to the western end of the Indian Ocean Region (IOR), Japan and India launched the Asia-Africa Growth Corridor (AAGC) in 2016. It was an ambitious concept to link Japan with ASEAN, South Asia and the east coast of Africa through a maritime corridor centred on industrial networks and quality infrastructure—a not-so-subtle emphasis to differentiate its work from China's BRI, which had blanketed Africa with costly roads, highways, railroads and bridges through unsustainable loans. The AAGC's B2B (business-to-business) model was premised on private sector companies and investors in Japan and India, pairing up and raising money for works tying Africa to their economies. But this free market-oriented approach could not match the BRI which involved direct governmental financing and stakes from China. 'Limited interest among Japanese companies' as opposed to overwhelming keenness of their Indian counterparts followed, and did not allow the AAGC to be scaled up.[179] Nonetheless, enormous potential remains for Tokyo and New Delhi to implement triangular cooperation in Africa, where both the Asian partners foresee phenomenal increases in trade volumes. It is worth noting that the Japan-India friendship helped Tokyo push the strategic envelope and define Indo-Pacific as inclusive

---

[178]Haidar, Suhasini, 'India-Japan Look to Restart Trilateral Cooperation with Sri Lanka, but with Caution', *The Hindu*, 10 August 2023, https://tinyurl.com/4swvuak7. Accessed on 17 June 2024.

[179]Singh, Gurjit, 'Trilateral Cooperation in Africa Gets Moving', *The Economic Times*, 9 August 2022, https://tinyurl.com/2mkhwv5u. Accessed on 17 June 2024.

of eastern and southern Africa. 'Bringing Africa into the Indo-Pacific construct was a signal from Japan to India that its priorities will be taken on board as well.'[180] Japan's Partnership for Quality Infrastructure (PQI) and its push within the Quad and the G7 to make infrastructure a keystone of coordinated foreign assistance mean that Japan-India 'nested partnerships' (bilateral, trilateral and quadrilateral) will deliver in one form or the other.[181]

The big takeaway from all these geoeconomic moves by Japan and India in the Indo-Pacific is that they mitigate India's encirclement and bottling up by China's string of pearls strategy, and present concrete alternatives to poorer countries so that they do not end up as vassal states of China. It is not an exaggeration to say that Japan has assisted India in sustaining its regional predominance in South Asia, a prerequisite for a rising power to demonstrate its status as a would-be great power in world politics (*see* earlier in the Introduction of this book), and also in making deeper forays into East Asia. Japan is a buoy that keeps India's 'leading power' dream afloat and swimming across the maritime expanses of the Indo-Pacific.

A FIREFIGHTING TEAM?

The longer-term prognosis for the Japan-India friendship is rosy, and we will witness many more milestones in its future evolution. But one nagging question remains: Can the two Asian powerhouses handle a major security emergency that might arise if China attempts an all-out assault on Taiwan,

---

[180]Gurjar, Sankalp, 'Expanding the Strategic Envelope: Indo-Pacific, Africa and Shinzo Abe', Indian Council of World Affairs, 14 July 2022, https://tinyurl.com/4pwhd4s7. Accessed on 17 June 2024.

[181]Basrur, Rajesh, and Sumitha Narayanan Kutty, 'Modi's India and Japan: Nested Strategic Partnerships', *International Politics*, Vol. 59, 2022, pp. 67–89.

a forcible takeover of Japan's Senkaku Islands or a limited war with India along the disputed Himalayan borders? Ever since Russia invaded Ukraine in 2022, Japan has been spooked by the dreadful prospect of China doing a Ukraine in Asia by invading Taiwan, which is just 111 kilometres from Japan's Yonaguni Island. The failure of previously constructed deterrence structures in Europe has starkly reminded Japanese of Abe's famous dictum that 'a Taiwan contingency is a Japan contingency.'[182]

At another end, India cannot rule out a limited conflict with China, which has bared its claws under Xi Jinping, and sought to impose its will on smaller Asian neighbours. Hypothetical games that the Indian military has studied if China attacks Taiwan include options of India 'serving as a logistics hub' for allied (presumably American and Japanese) warships and aircraft that resist China, or even of getting 'directly involved along their northern border, opening a new theater of war with China'.[183]

Can India also contribute more directly to Japan's security in its backyard in the East and South China Seas? Certainly, the growing naval capabilities of India and Japan will extend their power projection and warfighting reach further in time to come. But as one Indian commentator has pointed out, 'The challenge here for both nations is to tide over the indifference that exists between them towards each other's immediate security environment.'[184]

---

[182]Mukai, Yuko, 'Eyeing China and Taiwan, Japan Must Learn from the War in Ukraine', *Yomiuri Shimbun*, 21 October 2023, https://tinyurl.com/ymj9d3c7. Accessed on 17 June 2024.

[183]TNN, 'India's Military Studying Options for any China War on Taiwan', *The Times of India*, 8 September 2023, https://tinyurl.com/3rumrvkd. Accessed on 17 June 2024.

[184]Prabhakar, H.S., 'India-Japan Relations: Managing Security and Economic Interdependence in Asia', in Sridharan, E., ed., *Eastward Ho? India's Relations with the Indo-Pacific*, 2021, Orient Blackswan, Hyderabad, p. 96.

The question of what Japan can do for India if China launches an offensive across the LAC has not been mooted publicly. India is sufficiently equipped and armed to beat back a large-scale Chinese incursion in the Himalayas, but what are friends for if they do not come to each other's rescue in a grave crisis? Japan's quest for a special strategic and global partnership with India is indeed 'part of a wider adjustment' to 'systemic pressures' triggered by China's rise and apprehensions about the USA's security commitments.[185] But what if the system comes apart at the seams, and China goes for maximizing its strategic frontier at the cost of its neighbours? The answers to these riddles lie in Indo-Pacific minilateral coalitions, involving additional friends (*see* Chapters 2, 3 and 5) rather than purely Japan-India bilateral cooperation.

One last thought merits attention. Japan and India often hail their values-based partnership, and present their friendship as a bond between two democracies that share a common political culture. Is there potential for Tokyo and New Delhi to jointly undertake promotion of democracy in the Indo-Pacific? Neither country has had qualms in entering into strategic partnerships with authoritarian countries thus far, nor has either side tried to intervene in the internal affairs of Asian nations, with the goal of a regime change. But in cases like Myanmar, where democratic backsliding hands a clear advantage to dictatorial China to displace the influence of Japan and India, Tokyo and New Delhi have coordinated and demanded cessation of state-sponsored violence by the military junta, and a return to the path of democratic transition.[186]

---

[185]Envall, H.D.P., 'Japan's India Engagement: From Different Worlds to Strategic Partners', in Hall, Ian, ed., *The Engagement of India: Strategies and Responses*, 2014, Georgetown University Press, Washington, D.C., p. 40.
[186]ANI, 'India, Japan Urge Myanmar to End Violence, Return to Democracy', *NDTV*, 20 March 2022, https://tinyurl.com/45xun2p2. Accessed on 17 June 2024.

As a manifestation of a braver values-based foreign policy that Abe brought into effect, Japan has slammed human rights abuses in China and offered safe haven for activists agitating for freedom of persecuted minority communities like the Uyghurs and the Tibetans[187], and for democracy in Hong Kong[188]. Whenever democracy has been in peril due to the shenanigans of pro-China wannabe autocrats in neighbouring countries like Nepal, Maldives and Sri Lanka, India too has opposed such regimes.

Neither Japan nor India can strategically afford a universal Manichean division of the world into democracies versus dictatorships, especially not when Vietnam, a one-party state, is a close strategic partner to both Tokyo and New Delhi for counterbalancing Beijing. But to the extent possible, in countries where there exists a concurrence between realpolitik and idealism, it would make sense for Japan and India to live up to their reputations as democratic heavyweights in Asia. Creative Japan-India civil society development-focused joint programmes alongside traditional economic development-centric ones in select countries of the Indo-Pacific at risk of Chinese takeover could be incrementally implemented. Such projects will be less controversial and more impactful than if the USA or European countries went about preaching to developing countries in their loud Western liberal tone. Japan's promise that it will 'adopt an approach focusing on people' in its FOIP policies, and look to protect the 'dignity of individual people' in vulnerable countries across the region,

---

[187]ANI, 'Japan: International Conference Raises Human Rights Violations by China against Uyghurs', *The Times of India*, 31 October 2023, https://tinyurl.com/2nbvfadk. Accessed on 17 June 2024.

[188]Iwata, Emi, 'Protesters March in Shibuya to Call for Democracy in Hong Kong', *Asahi Shimbun*, 12 June 2023, https://tinyurl.com/yeyu7wp6. Accessed on 17 June 2024.

is a promising avenue for future Japan-India coordination.[189] Ironically, people-to-people linkages between Japan and India itself are modest, and hopes of India's surplus labour immigrating in large numbers to fill acute labour shortages in Japan as it grapples with critical demographic decline have not panned out.[190] Be that as it may, jointly addressing the rights and interests of ordinary people in third countries of the Indo-Pacific can add a powerful moral dimension to the Japan-India strategic partnership as a sustainable endogenous Asian alternative to the Beijing consensus.

---

[189]PMO of Japan, 'Policy Speech by Prime Minister Kishida at the Indian Council of World Affairs (ICWA)', op. cit.

[190]Seno, Shigeru, 'India Unlikely to Solve Japan's Labor Shortage', *Nikkei Asia*, 26 September 2023, https://tinyurl.com/uj5pwntp. Accessed on 17 June 2024.

2

REACHING THE TOP TIER: AUSTRALIA AND INDIA IN A NEW ERA

There was a time when it was said that 3C defines the relationship between India and Australia [...] These are—Commonwealth, Cricket and Curry. Later on, it was said that India and Australia relations are based on 3D, i.e. Democracy, Diaspora and Dosti [friendship]. Some people even said that India-Australia relations are based on 3E or Energy, Economy and Education [...] This probably has been true in different periods [...] Do you know what the greatest foundation of all these relations is? [...] Mutual Trust and Mutual Respect.[191]

—Narendra Modi, Prime Minister of India, 2023

In the early summer of 2023, a highly symbolic event took place off the western coast of India's commercial metropolis, Mumbai. As the sun shone bright, and media persons waited in anticipation for the perfect photo op and

---

[191]NM, 'PM Modi Addresses Community Programme in Sydney, Australia', Narendra Modi, 23 May 2023, https://tinyurl.com/ywxcmjz3. Accessed on 18 June 2024.

video frame, a foreigner dressed in a dark suit and red tie dramatically came into view atop a rising mobile platform, with the waters of the Arabian Sea gleaming in the background. He was flanked by Radhakrishnan Hari Kumar, the then Chief of the Naval Staff of India, and several white-clad Indian officers and sailors, all beaming with a sense of pride and camaraderie. The guest was Anthony Albanese, Prime Minister of Australia, who made history by becoming the first-ever foreign leader to be hosted and accorded a ceremonial guard of honour on India's indigenously manufactured aircraft carrier and largest warship INS *Vikrant*. A visual highlight was Albanese walking up to a point on the deck of the megaship, climbing atop India's indigenous light combat aircraft (LCA), sitting in the cockpit, nodding as an Indian fighter pilot explained how the mean machine worked, and then beaming with a thumbs-up signal towards the cameras. In his speech on board that day, Albanese declared that 'for Australia, India is a top-tier security partner' in the context of the Indian Ocean, which 'is central to both countries' security and prosperity', and emphasized that 'there has never been a point in our country's history where we've had such a strong strategic alignment.'[192]

Having witnessed that event, and juxtaposing it with the past, for an Australian leader to thus endorse and celebrate the growing might of the Indian Navy was an extraordinary 180-degree turnaround from an earlier era when Canberra had thought of the Indian military as a competitor, or a problem for Australian interests in the Indian Ocean. There was a period during the fading years of the Cold War when Australia announced a major shift in its military posture by redeploying naval assets to its western coast near Perth in

---

[192]ET, 'Australian Prime Minister Anthony Albanese Visits India's Homemade Aircraft Carrier INS *Vikrant*', *The Economic Times*, 9 March 2023, https://tinyurl.com/ycym3n6h. Accessed on 17 June 2024.

order to defend its economic interests in the Indian Ocean. Dubbed as the 'two-ocean strategy', it was meant to be a corrective to Australia's historic inclination to view itself as 'a Pacific Ocean state' whose strategic orientation was to the east around Sydney.[193] Canberra's two-ocean strategy clashed with New Delhi's decision around the same time to modernize and expand its naval fleet to perform 'out-of-area intervention capabilities'[194].

Although the two countries had remained core members of the British Commonwealth, they were estranged throughout the era of the East-West bloc confrontation, with Australia firmly ensconced in the Western camp as a treaty ally of the USA, and India gravitating between non-alignment and de facto alliance with the Soviet Union. Bilateral trust was low. Australian governmental and political circles in the late 1980s therefore expressed 'concern about India's views of its role as a regional policeman and the degree to which coercion enters into its calculations of enforcement,' and complained about India's nuclear weapons ambitions.[195] India's reliance on communist Russia for its naval build-up and its canvassing for an 'Indian Ocean zone of peace', free of nuclear weapons and American presence, grated with Australia, whose self-defined role after World War II was summed up by the notion of transferring loyalties from being a 'British colony' to becoming an 'American satellite'.[196] The mutual indifference

[193]DeSilva-Ranasinghe, Serge, 'The Politics of the Two-Ocean Navy', Australian Naval Institute, 15 June 2016, https://tinyurl.com/wdstpduj. Accessed on 17 June 2024.

[194]Hoyt, Timothy, 'Modernizing the Indian Armed Forces', *Joint Force Quarterly*, Summer 2000, p. 18.

[195]SSC, *Australia-India Relations*, 1990, Senate Standing Committee on Foreign Affairs, Defence and Trade, p. 71.

[196]McLean, David, 'From British Colony to American Colony? Australia and the USA During the Cold War', *Australian Journal of Politics and History*, Vol. 52, No. 1, 2006, pp. 64–79.

and prickliness at that stage involved India treating Australia as a 'US stooge' and Australia considering India an 'undesirable strategic ally'.[197]

TRANSCENDING THE CLICHÉS

The transformation in bilateral relations from that low point to the present high point takes us through a very instructive journey of deep re-evaluation and rethinking on both sides, spurred by big shifts in world politics. We can draw parallels between the onset of the Australia-India strategic partnership and the Japan-India strategic partnership. Like its quasi-ally Japan (*see* Chapter 1), Australia also first denounced India's 1998 nuclear weapons tests and downgraded relations, taking the cue from the USA. And just as Tokyo resumed high-level engagements with New Delhi from the year 2000, in line with Washington's decision to forget nuclear non-proliferation dogmas and move on, Canberra also readjusted its lens to repair and improve ties with New Delhi.

Within the next few years, the basis for a strong and reliable bilateral friendship was laid. The first step towards building a closer understanding was catalysed by two jarring events—terrorist attacks on the USA on 11 September 2001 (9/11), and the October 2002 bomb blasts which killed dozens of Australian citizens in Bali, Indonesia. They made Australia realize the urgent need for regional partners to counter the threat of jihadist extremism. India, which had been grappling with Pakistan-sponsored violent jihadists for decades, and whose military boasted of significant counterterrorism experience, became a natural go-to partner for Australia.

---

[197]Snedden, Christopher, 'Australia-India Relations: Strategic Dissonance', in Stoddart, Brian, and Auriol Weigold, eds., *India & Australia: Bridging Different Worlds*, 2011, Readworthy, New Delhi, p. 73

While Australian troops were fighting alongside American counterparts in the GWOT against Pakistan-supported hardline Islamists of the Taliban in Afghanistan, India too was backing the anti-Taliban forces there. So, Canberra and New Delhi found in counterterrorism the first concrete basis for strategic alignment. They began sharing intelligence and tactics in dealing with Islamist extremism, given the global nature of the threat posed by Al Qaeda and affiliated outfits.

The two diplomatic milestones in the lead-up to the declaration of the bilateral strategic partnership—the Australia-India Memorandum of Understanding (MoU) on Combating International Terrorism in 2003, and the MoU on Defence Cooperation in 2006—highlighted the 'fight against terrorism', and 'maritime cooperation to check [the] terrorist threat in Malacca Straits.'[198] Writing in 2007, the Australian diplomat Rory Medcalf mentioned 'recognition of common cause against Islamist terrorism' as an important facilitator for improved bilateral ties.[199]

The second boost to bilateral relations came in 2008. The year, as it is famously remembered, saw the world plunge into a once-in-many-generations financial crisis, bringing the global economy and national systems to their knees. With Western economies and polities under severe duress, the dragon roared. Beijing showed its first signs of military and diplomatic muscle-flexing at that time, owing to its belief that the Western model of capitalism was collapsing, and that China would not face strong resistance to its military expansionism and regional bullying of smaller neighbours from a USA which was fighting for the very survival of its economy.

China's so-called first assertive foreign policy before the

[198]PTI, 'India, Australia Sign MoU on Defence Cooperation', *Rediff*, 6 March 2006, https://tinyurl.com/5aewsbcb. Accessed on 17 June 2024.
[199]Medcalf, Rory, 'Uranium Thorn', *The Times of India*, 20 April 2007, https://tinyurl.com/3hzym36v. Accessed on 17 June 2024.

advent of President Xi Jinping caught the attention of both Australia and India. But at that time, the threat perception was not so acute. Take, for instance, the 2007 Malabar joint naval exercises, wherein the co-hosts India and the USA invited militaries of Australia, Japan and Singapore to conduct multilateral war games in the Bay of Bengal. Spurred by Prime Minister Shinzo Abe's fervent efforts to form a quadrilateral coalition that checks Chinese expansion (*see* Chapter 1), these unprecedented exercises were met by a fierce pushback and warnings from Beijing that attempts to strategically encircle it would backfire.

Australia, whose economy was already deeply intertwined with that of China, developed cold feet under the China-friendly government of Kevin Rudd, the then Prime Minister of Australia. Stephen Smith, the Australian Foreign Minister at that time, went to Beijing and, as his Chinese counterpart looked on approvingly, announced that 'so-called quadrilateral dialogue with India is not something that we are pursuing.' He also informed Indian leaders that Australia 'doesn't want to do anything unnecessarily that upsets any other country.'[200]

Manmohan Singh, the then Prime Minister of India, was himself worried about incurring China's wrath and losing the political support of China-friendly Indian communist political parties which could pull the rug from under the feet of his weak coalition government. He too backed out. Even the USA, which was preoccupied by the GWOT, and hoped to co-opt China to manage the nuclear challenges posed by Iran and North Korea, conveyed a signal that 'it wanted to go slow' on the Quad.[201] To China's great relief, the 2008

---

[200]Madan, Tanvi, 'The Rise, Fall, and Rebirth of the "Quad"', *War on the Rocks*, 16 November 2017, https://tinyurl.com/4exmnr2f. Accessed on 17 June 2024.
[201]Flitton, Daniel, 'Who Really Killed the Quad 1.0?', *The Interpreter*, 2 June 2020, https://tinyurl.com/y28n4bwr. Accessed on 17 June 2024.

Malabar exercises reverted to the bilateral India-USA format, and remained so until 2014, when Japan rejoined them. It was not until 2020 that the Royal Australian Navy (RAN) made a comeback to these strategic maritime games.

This is not to say that Australian politicians and decision makers were absolutely naïve or Pollyannaish about China during the noughties. The timing of the Australia-India strategic partnership's onset in 2009 (*see* Annexure, Table III) was linked to mounting anxieties on both sides about the need to close ranks against challenges posed by China's growing pushiness.

The Australian academic Ian Hall wrote that 'Beijing's new assertiveness after the Global Financial Crisis (GFC) of 2008–2009 unsettled both Canberra and New Delhi, stimulating another push for closer security ties and for more coordinated action.'[202] Even before the advent of President Xi Jinping, the Chinese dragon had begun revealing its fiercer side to smaller Asian neighbours, owing to a perception that the USA was weakening, and that the global configuration of forces would, henceforth, favour communist China rather than the decadent capitalist USA.

Fears that the USA, Australia's main security ally, might decline and give way to a Chinese-dominated order across the oceanic spaces that mattered to Canberra, had begun circulating even before the construct of the Indo-Pacific was mainstreamed. This was compounded by economically stagnant Japan, which was Australia's quasi-ally and its number one strategic partner in Asia. Having vowed that 'Australia has no greater friend in Asia than Japan,'[203] Canberra was dismayed by what seemed like a simultaneous descent of

---

[202]Hall, Ian, 'Australia and India in the Modi Era: An Unequal Strategic Partnership?' *International Politics*, Vol. 59, No. 1, 2022, p. 116.
[203]JT, 'Australia's Leader "Discovers' Asia"', *The Japan Times*, 7 April 2005, https://tinyurl.com/y3kajaz7. Accessed on 17 June 2024.

both the USA and Japan. Indian scholars contextualized the signing of the Australia-India strategic partnership in this shifting power equilibrium by writing that the 'US' relative decline in terms of global influence is accompanied by China's relative rise globally both in economic and political realms. At the same time, Japan's relative decline coincides with [sic] somewhat relative rise of India, again both economically and politically.'[204]

The 2009 Australia-India Joint Declaration on Security Cooperation talked of a 'common commitment to democracy, freedom, human rights and the rule of law' and professed 'deep respect for each other's contribution to promoting peace, stability and development in Asia.'[205] It was anodyne language compared to what Canberra and New Delhi publicly utter nowadays, but a step, nonetheless, in the right direction, by hinting that the China factor had begun to lurk in the background of their friendship.

The debate in Australia about how to adjust to a new regional order where China might be numero uno, was lively. In 2010, Australian pundit Hugh White laid out a set of choices for his country, while assuming that the USA would still manage to stay ahead of China in the regional power stakes. 'We can remain allied to America, seek another great and powerful friend, opt for armed neutrality, build a regional alliance with our Southeast Asian neighbours, or do nothing and hope for the best.'[206] After Xi took charge in Beijing and adopted a strident and hyper-nationalistic foreign

[204]Panda, Rajaram, and Pranamita Baruah, 'India-Australia Strategic Partnership: A Case for Holistic Approach', *India Quarterly*, Vol. 66, No. 2, 2010, p. 210.

[205]AHC, 'India-Australia Joint Declaration on Security Cooperation', Australian High Commission, 12 November 2009, https://tinyurl.com/zzdr5d7m. Accessed on 17 June 2024.

[206]White, Hugh, 'Power Shift: Australia's Future Between Washington and Beijing', *Quarterly Essay*, No. 39, 2010, p. 60.

policy, while Washington's relative decline was compounded by foreign policy isolationism under President Donald Trump, Australian anxieties deepened.

In 2017, White argued that America was fading and China would overtake it to be the dominant power in the Indo-Pacific, and called on Australians 'to start thinking for ourselves about how to make our way and hold our corner in an Asia dominated by China.'[207] One of the solutions he presented was for Australia to invest more in relationships with others, singling out India as 'the most important to us, because it will want to limit China's influence in the Indian Ocean Region, which should mean it has a long-term interest in limiting China's sway over Australia.'[208]

Gareth Evans, the former Australian Foreign Minister, also chimed in that 'neither we nor anyone else in the region should be under any illusion that the US will be there for us militarily in any circumstance where it does not also see its own immediate interests being under some threat.' His solutions to 'the big regional challenges we are all facing' were: 'Less United States. More self-reliance. More Asia,' i.e. shedding supine dependence on the USA, ramping up Australia's own military strength, and significantly upgrading 'partnerships with key regional neighbours like India, Indonesia, Japan and the ROK [South Korea].' Elaborating on the 'More Asia' prescription, Evans posited that 'a united front of middle powers' might be more effective in resisting China's aggressive behaviour 'than relying on the United States'.[209]

The same combination of internal balancing and external balancing which Japan embarked upon in response to the

---

[207]White, Hugh, 'Without America: Australia in the New Asia', *Quarterly Essay*, No. 68, 2017, p. 4.
[208]Ibid., pp. 62–63.
[209]Evans, Gareth, 'Asian Geopolitics in Transition', Asia Society, 29 November 2017, https://tinyurl.com/442h7dj7. Accessed on 17 June 2024.

China threat (*see* Chapter 1) drove Australia to announce a huge hike in defence spending of over $186 billion to acquire 'longer-range strike capabilities across air, sea and land'[210], and to expand the scope and intent of its strategic partnerships. The upgrade of the Australia-India friendship to a 'comprehensive strategic partnership' happened in parallel to the Australian military build-up plan in 2020, and was a clear response to hostile Chinese behaviour. The 'intensification of China's assertiveness across the Indo-Pacific' and 'mounting evidence of widespread attempts by Chinese interests to influence and interfere in Australian politics' convinced Canberra and New Delhi that a 'renewed effort had to be made in strengthening their strategic partnership as insurance against an erratic regime in Washington and an assertive one in Beijing.'[211]

It is noteworthy that the Australia-India strategic partnership was elevated to the next level not as a singular event, but as part of a series of moves Canberra made with Asian countries. Australia entered into a 'special strategic partnership' with Japan in 2014, a 'comprehensive strategic partnership' with Indonesia in 2018, with ASEAN in 2021, and with Vietnam in 2024, and a 'strategic partnership' with Thailand in 2020, and with the Philippines in 2023. Australia's defence coordination and military interoperability pacts with a range of like-minded countries, including India, mushroomed in the third decade of the 21st century, as if to keep pace with the alarm bells about China that were ringing louder. While none of the countries with which Australia pursued bilateral and minilateral partnerships was anti-American, the trend illustrated how Canberra set about forming a second line of defence with a wider set of friends

[210]Packham, Colin, 'Australia to Sharply Increase Defence Spending with Focus on the Indo-Pacific', https://tinyurl.com/3jhvwc8k. Accessed on 17 June 2024.
[211]Hall, Ian, 'Australia and India in the Modi Era', op. cit., p. 121.

as an insurance policy in case the USA backtracked from its traditional role as a security guarantor in the Pacific.

It was only after the Biden administration resumed normal service in the USA's foreign policy from 2021, and re-engaged in coalition confidence-building across Asia and Oceania, that Australia's fears of strategic abandonment by the USA reduced a bit. But given the vagaries and volatility in the USA's foreign policy due to changes in presidential administrations and domestic political polarization, Australia's determination to be strategically self-reliant and to stand up to China through means other than just the USA continued unabated. Historically sheltered as a 'lucky country' whose vast continental size, abundant natural resources, impregnable geographical location and steady economic growth were supposed to have been buttressed by a 'secure strategic situation from the beginning of the Cold War to the end of the unipolar moment,'[212] Australia has entered a new era where it has to reckon with hard realities.

The oft-cited Australian balancing act of avoiding 'a potential clash between its economic interests with China and its security ties with the United States'[213] remains a core dilemma for Canberra, but one of the ways to navigate the tricky conundrum is to look at options beyond the two great powers, diversify relationships, and build webs of friendships with middle and rising powers so that the concept of the Indo-Pacific and the principle of a 'rules-based order' become regional realities, and shield Australian interests.

---

[212]Dunley, Richard, 'The End of the "Lucky Country"? Understanding the Failure of the AUKUS Policy Debate', *Australian Journal of International Affairs*, Vol. 77, No. 3, 2023, p. 322.
[213]Blaxland, John, 'Strategic Balancing Act: Australia's Approach to Managing China, the USA and Regional Security Priorities', *Security Challenges*, Vol. 13, No. 1, 2017, p. 20.

INDO-PACIFIC COUSINS

Thus far, we have analysed the evolution of the Australia-India strategic partnership through a bilateral prism derived from fundamental national needs of the two friends, while placing the competition between China and the USA in the backdrop. But there would be no 'comprehensive strategic partnership' between Australia and India today had the idea of the Indo-Pacific not taken root and bloomed.

Though Japan's Shinzo Abe was undoubtedly the progenitor and proselytizer-in-chief of the Indo-Pacific (*see* Chapter 1), Australian officials were its ardent adherents. Medcalf recalled that the conversion to Indo-Pacific from the old Asia-Pacific, a concept that Australia had conceived and championed through the creation of the Asia-Pacific Economic Cooperation (APEC), was propelled by 'the logic that Australia's region was changing to a two-ocean system, with China turning south and west and India turning east,' and egged on by politicians from Western Australia who stressed the centrality of the Indian Ocean to their part of the country, and to the overall national interests.[214] Prime Minister Julia Gillard's clarion call in a 2012 White Paper for Australia to become 'a more Asia-literate and Asia-capable nation,' and its acknowledgement that the term Indo-Pacific implied 'the western Pacific Ocean and the Indian Ocean would come to be considered as one strategic arc,' confirmed Australia's 'Asianist' identity was ripening.[215] While labelling China and India as equally important partners to engage with, Gillard's government predicted that 'India's growing economic

[214]Medcalf, Rory, *Indo-Pacific Empire: China, America and the Contest for the World's Pivotal Region*, 2020, Manchester University Press, Manchester, p. 106.
[215]AG, 'Australia in the Asian Century', Australian Government, White Paper, October 2012, pp. iii, 74, https://tinyurl.com/58kw9ny6. Accessed on 13 March 2024.

and strategic weight will increasingly influence the balance of power within Asia, and amplify India's global influence,' and that 'the wider regional construct of the Indo-Pacific, linking the Indian and Pacific Oceans as one strategic arc that includes Southeast Asia, illustrates this influence.'[216] As the Indo-Pacific idea advanced, Australia's ambivalence about China and its habit of coupling China with India as two equally trustworthy friends in Asia receded.

The Malcolm Turnbull government's White Paper in 2017 declared that 'Indo-Pacific democracies of Japan, Indonesia, India and the Republic of Korea are of first order importance to Australia,' and singled out India as the country which 'now sits in the front rank of Australia's international partnerships,' and with whom 'we have common interests in upholding international law, especially in relation to freedom of navigation and maritime security.'[217] The 2020 upgrade of the Australia-India friendship to a 'comprehensive strategic partnership'—which happened amidst a sharp deterioration in Australia-China relations due to Chinese threats and coercive economic actions following the Scott Morrison government's demand for an international probe into the origins of the Coronavirus pandemic in China—was anchored in a common understanding of the Indo-Pacific between Canberra and New Delhi. The two friends labelled their advanced partnership to be 'in line with India's increasing engagement in the Indo-Pacific region through her Indo-Pacific vision and Australia's Indo-Pacific approach and its Pacific Step-Up for the South Pacific.'[218] Step-Up was a

---

[216]Ibid., p. 232.

[217]DFAT, 'Opportunity, Security, Strength', Department of Foreign Affairs and Trade, White Paper, 2017, pp. 40, 42, https://tinyurl.com/bdd7u2sz. Accessed on 17 June 2024.

[218]DFAT, 'Joint Statement on a Comprehensive Strategic Partnership between Republic of India and Australia', 4 June 2020, Department of Foreign Affairs and Trade, https://tinyurl.com/49khyfyz. Accessed on 17 June 2024.

concerted strategy by Canberra to ward off Beijing's challenge in its zone of influence. In other words, Australia saw that India was upping its game across the region and vice-versa, and hence, each rose in the other's esteem.

As a middle power whose 'interests are simply too extensive for it to protect and advance on its own,'[219] Australia increasingly looks up to India and other Indo-Pacific friends to sustain the security of sea lanes and freedom of navigation for its economic needs. In the western part of the Indo-Pacific, since India has the 'largest navy and coastguard of any littoral state' between the straits of Hormuz and Malacca, it 'is an appealing strategic partner for Australia, the world's largest island-state' whose commercial trade with Western countries depends on friendly powers staying in control of the Indian Ocean.[220] In 2019, Marise Payne, the then Foreign Minister of Australia, was not exaggerating when she said in New Delhi that 'our respective futures are intertwined and heavily dependent on how well we cooperate on the challenges and opportunities in the Indian Ocean in the decades ahead.'[221]

Australian and Indian security establishments have consulted and coordinated closely in three sub-regional institutions in particular—the Indian Ocean Naval Symposium (IONS), the Indian Ocean Rim Association (IORA) and the Information Fusion Centre—Indian Ocean Region (IFC—IOR). The bilateral 2+2 ministerial dialogues, involving foreign and defence ministers, have been instrumental in mooting and implementing joint initiatives for closer interoperability of the

---

[219]Medcalf, Rory, *Indo-Pacific Empire*, op. cit., p. 156.

[220]Gopal, Darvesh, and Dalbir Ahlawat, 'Australia-India Strategic Relations: From Estrangement to Engagement', *India Quarterly*, Vol. 71, No. 3, 2015, p. 212.

[221]MFA, 'Address to the Raisina Dialogue', Minister for Foreign Affairs, Australia, 9 January 2019, https://tinyurl.com/ua3k9u66. Accessed on 17 June 2024.

two militaries in the IOR. It was not a coincidence that India began the practice of a 2+2 with Australia in 2021, following similar institutionalized formats to facilitate defence diplomacy with the USA in 2018 and Japan in 2019, while preceding likewise arrangements with Russia in 2021 and the UK in 2023. Even at the summit level of bilateral diplomacy, Australia and India have focused on the IOR as a vital subset of the broader Indo-Pacific cooperation. In the first annualized summit meeting between Prime Ministers Albanese and Modi in 2023, for example, the leaders appreciated 'the increasing interoperability between the respective forces through implementation of the India-Australia Mutual Logistics Support Arrangement [MLSA]' and 'welcomed the arrangements between the two countries for enhancing Maritime Domain Awareness in the Indian Ocean Region, increased defence information sharing and consolidation of mutual access that continue to deepen operational defence cooperation.'[222]

Australia's nightmare of not having a friendly democratic power to keep the IOR free and open for its mercantile commerce has, to an extent, been mitigated by India's proactive naval diplomacy in the Modi era. More can be done. The presence of Indian forces in the Cocos (Keeling Island) and Christmas Island, which are Australian territories in the IOR, carry potential for 'expanding the strategic reach of the Indian military' as these outposts lie east of the Andamans and next to the maritime choke points of the straits of Malacca, Sunda and Lombok.[223] In 2024, Philip Green, the Australian High Commissioner to India, cited the 'landings of Australian P8

---

[222]HCI, '1st India-Australia Annual Summit: Joint Statement (March 10, 2023)', 21 May 2023, High Commission of India, https://tinyurl.com/2s477ety. Accessed on 17 June 2024.

[223]Peri, Dinakar, 'Two Indian Military Aircraft Visit Australia's Strategic Cocos Islands', The Hindu, 30 July 2023, https://tinyurl.com/5n6j96w7. Accessed on 17 June 2024.

aircraft on the Andaman and Nicobar Islands and the landings of [Indian] Dornier aircraft on our Cocos (Keeling) Islands' as 'a pointer to the future of how we might be able to use each other's geography to greater benefit.' He mooted the ambition of moving from interoperability to 'interchangeability', wherein 'we will be able to put elements of the Australian defence forces into elements of Indian defence forces, and for them to be operating together seamlessly.'[224]

The geopolitical analyst Dhruva Jaishankar has suggested that there is also room for India to capitalize on the Five Power Defence Arrangements (FPDA) among Australia, Malaysia, New Zealand, Singapore and the UK, which 'give Australia a firm security toehold in Southeast Asia, where India's activity and interests have increased.'[225] Australian scholars Simon Bateman and David Brewster envisage 'a broad arrangement in maritime surveillance' of the IOR through 'a network of facilities potentially available to Australia, India and other partners' which 'could include Diego Garcia, Djibouti, French Reunion and the new Indian-built facility on Mauritius' Agaléga Island.'[226] In the eventuality of war with China, or just to sustain fiercer geostrategic competition with it, India will benefit from dense networks of interoperability and intermingling that its forces and Australian counterparts enter into in pivotal locations. The 2024 Australian National Defence Strategy's commitment to increase 'the depth and

[224]Mattoo, Shashank, 'Australian Envoy Says Ties with India at Historic High', *Mint*, 16 February 2024, https://tinyurl.com/yc83nj96. Accessed on 17 June 2024.

[225]Jaishankar, Dhruva 'The Australia-India Strategic Partnership: Accelerating Security Cooperation in the Indo-Pacific', Lowy Institute, September 2020, https://tinyurl.com/yvpjk7np. Accessed on 17 June 2024.

[226]Bateman, Simon, and David Brewster, 'Australia and India: Working Together and with Others in Maritime Security', in Bradford, John F., et al, eds., *Maritime Cooperation and Security in the Indo-Pacific Region*, 2022, Brill, pp. 283–284.

complexity' of security cooperation with India, and 'seek opportunities with India to drive practical bilateral and multilateral cooperation, defence industry cooperation and information sharing,'[227] holds great promise.

To consolidate and expand the impact of Australia-India strategic ties across the Indo-Pacific, drawing in third countries, and triangulating with them, has emerged as a favoured approach in Canberra and New Delhi. The launch of the Australia-India-Indonesia trilateral in 2022 was a regional milestone. As the leader and biggest military power of ASEAN, Indonesia is vital for realizing the vision of FOIP. Yet, it has been hesitant to associate with the Quad, or any other counterbalancing coalitions out of fear of the fallout on its economy, which is intertwined with China through trade and BRI infrastructure loans, and concerns that Beijing will retaliate through pressure on Jakarta over their territorial dispute in the Natuna Islands.

Persuading the Indonesians to form the trilateral with Australia and India was an achievement in itself. To achieve this outcome, the pre-existing strategic partnerships that Australia and India already had with Indonesia came in handy. Canberra and New Delhi's shared motto of 'ASEAN centrality' in the Indo-Pacific was also relevant, since bolstering the regional institution of Southeast Asian countries is a core foreign policy goal for Jakarta. Though the trilateral kicked off with an agenda of safe subjects for Indonesia like cooperation in IORA, G20, maritime governance and blue economy[228], it was instructive that the three sides gained enough momentum to launch their maiden trilateral joint naval exercises in

---

[227]AG, 'National Defence Strategy', Australian Government, April 2024, p. 49, https://tinyurl.com/23393z7e. Accessed on 17 June 2024.
[228]Saha, Premesha, 'The Australia-India-Indonesia Trilateral Finally Takes Off', Observer Research Foundation, 4 October 2022, https://tinyurl.com/3yhy4ptr. Accessed on 30 March 2024.

2023 to 'improve their collective capability to support a stable, peaceful and secure Indo-Pacific region.'[229] As China's harassment of Indonesia over the Natunas mounts, one can expect this trilateral to gain more strategic content. Such is the deteriorating geopolitical environment in the Indo-Pacific that even if a country wants to veer away from hard security and balance-of-power issues in its diplomacy, they cannot be kept off the table for long.

Another notable Indo-Pacific trilateral ministerial dialogue forum involving Australia and India has been with France. Dubbed IFA (India-France-Australia), it began in 2021 with a pledge to 'work together with a range of partners to promote the rules-based maritime order based on respect for sovereignty and international law.'[230] Since France has territories in the IOR, and has sought to defend them from Chinese hegemony, it was not reluctant to join the trilateral. Yet, an unfortunate sequence of events involving Australia's cancellation of a submarine purchase deal with France and instead opting for the USA's alternative offer under the umbrella of a new alliance called AUKUS (Australia, UK and USA), almost destroyed the India-France-Australia trilateral. Canberra and Paris assiduously worked to repair lost trust and could revive the trilateral with New Delhi by 2023, thanks to the unmissable realization that internal squabbles among Indo-Pacific powers would only hand over the region on a platter to expansionist China.[231]

---

[229]TNIE, 'First Maritime Exercise Held Between India, Australia and Indonesia', *The New Indian Express*, 22 September 2023, https://tinyurl.com/33fsv9ws. Accessed on 17 June 2024.

[230]MEA, 'India-France-Australia Joint Statement on the Occasion of the Trilateral Ministerial Dialogue (May 04, 2021)', Ministry of External Affairs, Government of India, 5 May 2021, https://tinyurl.com/ntu757j6. Accessed on 17 June 2024.

[231]Bhaumik, Anirban, 'France, Australia to Restart Trilateral Initiative with India to Counter China', *Deccan Herald*, 15 September 2022, https://tinyurl.com/yc5kpnu6. Accessed on 17 June 2024.

A fuller account of France's role in the Indo-Pacific and its strategic partnership with India can be found in Chapter 5. Here, it suffices to note that the Indo-Pacific dynamics have created space for more trilaterals involving Australia and India. While the Australia-Japan-India (AJI) trilateral has existed since 2015, and so has the Japan-America-India (JAI) trilateral since 2018, the more interesting combinations will be outside the Quad parameters. A new trilateral or quadrilateral where India pairs up with Australia and Japan and brings in Vietnam and/or the Philippines cannot be ruled out. Defence minister-level dialogues among Australia, Japan, the Philippines and the USA have seeded talk of a 'new Quad' without India,[232] but New Delhi will not want to be left out in this proliferating alphabet soup of minilaterals in the Indo-Pacific.

One promising arena for harnessing jointness between Australia and India is in the Pacific Island nations, which fall within Canberra's traditional sphere of influence, but where China has intruded with economic and security assistance packages. Just as India is apprehensive of China's encroachments in South Asia, Australia has watched with unease as China forced its way into its backyard, using BRI loans and non-transparent security deals with local elites in the tiny Pacific Island countries. Given that both New Delhi and Canberra feel they have to defend turf against the Chinese juggernaut, they are consulting closely with each other on how to put up a united resistance front. In 2023, after Prime Minister Modi visited Papua New Guinea for the third Forum for India-Pacific Islands Cooperation (FIPIC) before touching down in Australia, Vinay Mohan Kawatra, then India's Foreign Secretary, publicly mentioned that 'naturally, this is

---

[232]Nakamura, Ryo, 'Philippines to Step Up Ties with U.S.-Japan-Australia Coalition', *Nikkei Asia*, 3 June 2023, https://tinyurl.com/292x35p8. Accessed on 17 June 2024.

an area where Australia [...] has traditionally had strong presence. And naturally, our cooperation with Australia can be synergetic in a manner that is beneficial to the countries of the Pacific, which are, of course, countries of the Global South also.'[233]

Australia has been strategizing a pushback against China in the Pacific Islands in concert with the USA. Bringing India in will help its cause. The Australia-India Indo-Pacific Oceans Initiative Partnership (AIIPOIP)'s call for joint funding of projects for maritime ecology and security has a specific focus on the Pacific Islands Forum (PIF). India's Coalition for Disaster Resilient Infrastructure (CDRI), of which Australia is a member, has also targeted Small Island Developing States (SIDS) in the Pacific to assist them with projects that can withstand the adverse effects of climate change. The Supply Chain Resilience Initiative (SCRI), which Australia and India launched in 2021 together with Japan, to support 'enhanced utilization of digital technology' and 'trade and investment diversification' across the Indo-Pacific[234], can be another institutional means to wean away Pacific Islands and ASEAN countries from China's stranglehold.

Indo-Pacific complementarity between Australia and India also goes in the other direction, i.e. in India's surrounding sub-region. The New Zealand-based scholar Manjeet Pardesi has argued that just as India 'should approach the South Pacific by keeping Australia and New Zealand in the loop,' Australia must 'tailor its growing presence in the Indian Ocean by

---

[233]MEA, 'Transcript of Special Briefing by Foreign Secretary on Prime Minister's Visit to Australia (May 24, 2023)', Ministry of External Affairs, Government of India, 27 May 2023, https://tinyurl.com/4cjnfej6. Accessed on 17 June 2024.

[234]HBL, 'India, Japan and Australia Launch the Supply Chain Resilience Initiative', *The Hindu Business Line*, 6 December 2021, https://tinyurl.com/mryewaa9. Accessed on 17 June 2024.

keeping India in the loop' and 'approach regional partners such as Sri Lanka, Bangladesh, and the Indian Ocean island-states together with India in various trilateral fora.' This way, he contends, Australia and India can pool their limited resources in the region and 'also prevent any political misgivings in New Delhi as Canberra assumes a larger regional role.'[235]

Chapter 1 elaborated on how Japan and India collaborated in triangular mode in South and Southeast Asian countries like Sri Lanka, Bangladesh and Myanmar. Australia can replicate this model together with India in South Asian countries such as Bangladesh, with whom it already has a robust relationship, and Sri Lanka, where it has a sizeable diaspora connection. Shared membership of the IORA and of the British Commonwealth means that Bangladesh, the Maldives and Sri Lanka present the best opportunity for Australia-India joint public works and capacity-building programmes. All in all, Australia is eager to partner with India for 'the region's thickening architecture'[236], and their creative triangulation and minilateralism will be necessary to keep the Chinese at bay. If Japan and India are siblings in the Indo-Pacific (see Chapter 1), Australia and India are close cousins.

NOT THE 'NEW CHINA'

As explained in the Introduction of this book, strategic partnerships enable counterbalancing of adversaries through multiple means and domains. They are not limited to defence and geopolitics. As a commercial nation governed by capitalist values and business instincts, Australia had sought to unlock

---

the benefits of accessing India's vast and fast-growing market of consumers for decades, but was frustrated by New Delhi's trade protectionism and slow-dialling of bilateral trade negotiations. Even as other elements made progress after the bilateral strategic partnership was announced in 2009, India could not hold a candle to China as an economic proposition for Australian exporters. As of 2019, Australia-India annual trade stood at just $19 billion, while Australia-China trade exceeded $200 billion. But given the geopolitical fractures and trust deficits between China and the West, to which Australia will always belong in some measure, owing to its alliance with the USA and its political culture as a democracy, a question that nagged Australians was whether excessive economic exchange with China was healthy, or a trap limiting their autonomy and sovereignty.

This dilemma came to a head when the Coronavirus pandemic broke out in 2020, and exposed the dependency of the Australian economy on China. Sparring with Canberra over the controversial origins of the pandemic in Wuhan, Beijing angrily issued a public dossier listing 14 grievances and slapped 'trade strikes on up to a dozen [Australian] products including wine, beef, barley, timber, lobster and coal'.[237] Nasty tirades in Chinese government mouthpieces that challenging China would hurt Australia's economy fatally and warnings that 'it won't be so easy for Australia to find a comparably large export market, or a supply of high-quality and cheap imported goods, or a strong group of investors to replace China's,'[238] grated on Australian nerves. They steeled

[237]Kearsley, Jonathan, Eryk Bagshaw and Anthony Galloway, '"If You Make China the Enemy, China Will be the Enemy": Beijing's Fresh Threat to Australia', *The Sydney Morning Herald*, 18 November 2020, https://tinyurl.com/mupfz3jn. Accessed on 17 June 2024.
[238]Lei, Yu, 'Australia Risks Backsliding into a Poor Country in Asia Pacific', *Global Times*, 31 August 2020, https://tinyurl.com/33y354c4. Accessed on 17 June 2024.

Canberra to finally act on the long-postponed diversification of its economic partnerships. The path to escaping China's economic blackmail lay in making more friends and adding new layers to existing friendships.

With China-Australia relations sinking to a low, the statistical reality of booming trade with China and lacklustre trade with India was no longer a fact but an anomaly that had to be fixed. Australia began looking at India afresh from the lens of how to safeguard its economy against excessive reliance on China, and how to tap other markets. The China-Australia spat could not have been better timed because India had almost simultaneously embarked on a new export-oriented economic strategy, and begun warming up to FTAs with trusted friends after a decade of shying away from signing them. The negotiations for an Australia-India FTA, which had dragged on fruitlessly from 2011 to 2016, were relaunched in September 2021, and an interim 'early harvest' deal known as the Economic Cooperation and Trade Agreement (ECTA) was signed in April 2022.

The urgency and speed with which the ECTA was concluded, and the uninterrupted bipartisan support it received in Canberra even though Australia transitioned from the Liberal Party government of Scott Morrison to the Labour Party government of Anthony Albanese, spoke volumes. Also, Australia made more concessions to India than it got in return. Sensitive sectors for India like agriculture and dairy were not opened up for Australian exporters through the ECTA. Still, there was a euphoric feeling that the deal, which was predicted to double bilateral trade to over $50 billion, would lead to bigger wins. Canberra hailed it as marking 'the opening of one of the biggest economic doors there is to open in the world today.'[239] Piyush Goyal, India's Commerce Minister, called the agreement, which would grant Indian exporters lower import duties from Australia than competitors from China, Vietnam and Bangladesh, a 'labour of love' and a 'complete win-win'.[240]

The full FTA, when signed, was projected to 'take economic ties between the two countries to a strategic level as Australia is expected to offer assured supplies of critical minerals such as lithium and cobalt to India without any disruption.'[241] The phrase 'critical minerals' has become a buzzword in Australia-India friendship. Australia's extractive industries have 'reserves of at least 21 of the 49 critical minerals identified by the Indian Government,' including antimony, zircon, tantalum and rare-earth minerals. Through these raw materials, Canberra is poised to be a leading contributor for 'India's ambition to take a major role in global advanced manufacturing'.[242]

For India's energy security, Australia had high hopes of exporting large quantities of uranium to strengthen India's nuclear power generation, following the signing of a bilateral Civil Nuclear Deal in 2014. This agreement had immense symbolic value, as New Delhi resented the fact that Canberra had been selling uranium to an arch nuclear proliferator like China, but was withholding it from a responsible nuclear

---

[239]Tan, Su-Lin, 'Can India Fill the China-Shaped Hole in Australia's Economy?' *South China Morning Post*, 2 May 2022, https://tinyurl.com/wrc7f47x. Accessed on 17 June 2024.

[240]Agarwal, Ayushi, 'India-Australia Trade Agreement: Piyush Goyal says India Can Now Sell More Competitive Goods to Global Market', *CNBC*, 29 December 2022, https://tinyurl.com/43abhct2. Accessed on 17 June 2024.

[241]Jayaswal, Rajeev, 'After FTA, India and Australia to Boost Economic Ties', *Hindustan Times*, 21 November 2023, https://tinyurl.com/3j4xuz77. Accessed on 17 June 2024.

[242]DFAT, 'Australia-India ECTA Benefits for the Australian Critical Minerals and Resources Sectors', November 2022, Department of Foreign Affairs and Trade, https://tinyurl.com/4hpyhuef. Accessed on 17 June 2024.

power like India on grounds that the latter had not signed the NPT. But the deal's commercial dividends for Australia did not materialize as India's nuclear energy capacity remained small compared to its wind and solar electricity expansion.[243] Australia has grown in stature in India's fossil fuel market, accounting for a bigger share of its coal, gas and iron ore imports.

With clean energy posited to be the way of the future, Australia and India also intend to make coordinated investments and trade in green hydrogen and related cutting-edge fields so that India's 'decarbonization without deindustrialization' pathway to becoming a high-income country can be realized.[244] In Chapter 1, we saw how Japan adds to India's hard power through economic means. If Canberra and New Delhi learn from the past, adjust misplaced expectations and go after feasible and scalable goals, Australia will not be far behind as a top economic booster of India in time to come.

From the Australian perspective, India cannot by itself be the 'new China', i.e. a single giant vacuum cleaner that sucks up Australian industrial minerals with an assured and voracious demand. Even before the China-Australia row escalated in 2020, Peter Varghese, the former Australian High Commissioner to India, had clarified that India was a different economic entity compared to China, and must be 'understood on its own terms', as its main motor was growth in services. His observation in 2018 that 'a growing Indian economy will need more of the things Australia is well placed to provide from education services to resources and energy;

---

[243]Ramana, M.V., and Cassandra Jeffery, 'No Market for Australian Uranium in India', *East Asia Forum*, 23 June 2020, https://tinyurl.com/yszkwje7. Accessed on 17 June 2024.
[244]Turnbull, Malcolm, and Arunabha Ghosh, 'Energy-Hungry India has a Natural Green Ally in Australia', *The Australian Financial Review*, 24 May 2023, https://tinyurl.com/49bhtyt7. Accessed on 17 June 2024.

from food to health care; from tourist destinations to expertise in water and environmental management,'[245] is worth heeding for corporations and government planners on both sides.

Focusing on services and small and medium enterprises does not mean Australia's mining giants lack prospects in India. In 2023, when Australia tried a thaw with China, and Beijing lifted its ban on Australian mineral exports, a fascinating new reality emerged. There was a clear 'reluctance by Australian exporters to bet as big again on a country that is prepared to use economic coercion' and little enthusiasm for a 'pivot back to business as usual with Beijing'. Australian coal exporters had cultivated India, 'which needs coal to feed its burgeoning steel industry,' as a new market and stuck to it. The Carmichael coal mine in Australia's Queensland, for example, is owned by the Adani Group's Australian subsidiary, Bravus Mining & Resources, and ships millions of tonnes of coal to India for thermal power generation. India is only part of the solution for Australia's economic diversification strategy. In the aftermath of the trade war between China and Australia, the latter's cotton exporters shifted to Vietnam, barley exporters went to Saudi Arabia, and wine exporters redirected to Japan and ASEAN[246]. Australia has thus opted for a broad-based approach, and if India keeps growing economically, it will be there as one prominent flower in a bouquet of alternatives for Australia.

[245]Varghese, Peter, 'An India Economic Strategy to 2035: Navigating from Potential to Delivery', Department of Foreign Affairs and Trade, 2018, pp. 5–6, https://tinyurl.com/2s4h3twt. Accessed on 17 June 2024.
[246]Hoyle, Rhiannon, 'China Says Australia's Exporters Can Come Back. Some Say No Thanks', *The Wall Street Journal*, 4 November 2023, https://tinyurl.com/ekytw2vk. Accessed on 17 June 2024.

DIAL D FOR DIASPORA

The 2020 Joint Statement establishing a 'comprehensive strategic partnership' between Australia and India paid tribute to Indian Australians as the 'fastest-growing large diaspora', and credited them for 'enriching all aspects of bilateral ties'.[247] Numbering around one million (four per cent of Australia's total population) by 2024, people of Indian origin have poured into the land Down Under for economic opportunities, and become a powerful constituency that acts as a visible human bridge in the bilateral friendship. Like in the USA (*see* Chapter 3), the recently arrived waves of Indian immigrants are highly educated and skilled professionals, and managers whose net contributions to Australia's economy and society are unmatched by any other immigrant group. These 'fabulously well-qualified' migrant communities are 'a source of national competitive advantage in export markets' for Australia and also help 'show the way for large Australian companies' to invest in India because 'they have a higher tolerance for risk and are better able to navigate India.'[248] The doubling and tripling of Australia-India bilateral trade and investment that are on the cards will happen not just due to FTAs, but through vectors in the diaspora who are eager to capitalize on the official institutional arrangements and join the two countries at the hip through business.

Indian Australians have also become politically active in a way that enriches Australia's civic life and famed multiculturalism, while avoiding controversial behaviour associated with Chinese Australians, many of whom have been found to be Trojan Horses for Beijing as part of its infamous interference operations inside Australia. The

---

[247]DFAT, 'Joint Statement on a Comprehensive Strategic Partnership', op. cit.
[248]Charlton, Andrew, *Australia's Pivot to India*, 2023, Black Inc., Collingwoods, pp. 144, 150.

Australian scholar Clive Hamilton's chilling exposé of how the communist regime in Beijing systematically uses the Chinese diaspora to 'transform Australian society in a way that makes us all sympathetic to China and easy for Beijing to control,' and to compel Australia to 'assist China to become the hegemonic power in Asia and eventually the world,'[249] has no equivalent whatsoever with Indian Australians. India being a democratic country, there is no sinister ideological or systemic threat posed by the Indian diaspora to Australia's polity or freedoms. Some Sikh extremists based in Australia have riled India by abusing Australian liberal democracy and organizing anti-India secessionist activities in the name of an independent Khalistan. But these radicals do not represent the bulk of the Indian diaspora in Australia, nor have they succeeded in derailing the Australia-India strategic partnership.[250]

The overall benign and positive image of Indian Australians explains why Canberra signed a Migration and Mobility Partnership Arrangement (MMPA) with New Delhi in 2023, 'making it easier for students, academics and professionals to live, study and work in each other's countries.'[251] Higher education has been Australia's largest service sector export to India. The 2023 Mechanism for the Mutual Recognition of Qualifications (MMRQ), 'India's most comprehensive education agreement of its type with another country,' further boosted two-way student mobility, and spurred Australian universities to set up campuses in India to directly deliver

[249]Hamilton, Clive, *Silent Invasion: China's Influence in Australia*, 2018, Hardie Grant, Richmond, p. 26.

[250]Hall, Ian, 'India and Australia Can't Go the Canada Way Over Pro-Khalistan Activities', *The Print*, 27 September 2023, https://tinyurl.com/mrxv433y. Accessed on 17 June 2024.

[251]Mattoo, Shashank, 'India Signs Migration, Mobility Pact with Australia', *Mint*, 24 May 2023, https://tinyurl.com/4mmdt47k. Accessed on 17 June 2024.

degree programmes there.[252] When fee-paying Chinese students disappeared as a result of Coronavirus pandemic closures, Australian universities got a rude financial shock. The MMRQ with India was signed as part of a deliberate diversification strategy wherein 'Australia is seeking to reduce its reliance on China.'[253] With trendlines suggesting that Indian Australians will overtake Chinese Australians in numbers, the day when Indian students surpass Chinese students in Australian universities is not inconceivable. The 2023 Mobility Arrangement for Talented Early-Professionals Scheme (MATES), which opened ways for thousands of Indian students to remain and work in Australia after completing this tertiary education in Australian universities, was a harbinger.

The swelling Indian diaspora in Australia adds to Australia's salience in Indian eyes through its sheer demographic weight and presence. For India, which has made diaspora diplomacy a central feature of its foreign policy under Prime Minister Modi,[254] countries which host large and influential Indian diaspora communities get higher attention and prioritization (see Chapters 3 and 7). The spectacular televised showpiece addresses that Modi delivered to Indian Australians at the Allphones Arena (2014) and the Qudos Bank Arena (2023) in Sydney reverberated back home in India, and helped cement Australia's reputation as a welcoming place in the minds of ordinary Indians. Jodi McKay, National Chair of the Australia India Business Council (AIBC), a prominent Indian diaspora-led industry association in Australia, noted about ECTA that

[252]DE, 'Education Agreement Between Australia and India', Australian Government, Department of Education, 10 March 2023, https://tinyurl.com/yphc4mdx. Accessed on 17 June 2024.

[253]Argana, Carmell, 'Universities Race to Recapture Lucrative International Students', *Bloomberg*, 18 March 2023, https://tinyurl.com/52w57j6f. Accessed on 17 June 2024.

[254]Chaulia, Sreeram, *Modi Doctrine: The Foreign Policy of India's Prime Minister*, 2016, New Delhi, Bloomsbury.

'in the decisions that Prime Minister Modi made, the size of our diaspora, the power of our diaspora, certainly played a part in this agreement.'[255]

MANAGING RISE AND DECLINE

As the Australia-India friendship matures, it is worth revisiting Anna Michalski's point cited in the Introduction that strategic partnerships are 'role enhancing arenas', or ladders which help countries attain their desired status in the world order. Pardesi has observed that Australia and the USA have been in relative decline, while Asian powers like China, Indonesia and India are on the ascent. Since 'Australia is reaching out to India at the moment of "relative loss", while India is reaching out to Australia more self-assuredly,' Canberra 'will need to adjust to an Asia where the United States will be only one pole among many.'[256] The old belief that the USA will remain unassailable and firmly committed to Australia's security has receded in Canberra, and this realization definitely fuelled Australia's flurry of strategic partnerships, including that with India. Going forward, India will be indispensable for Australia to manage its relative decline, while Australia will be indispensable for India to navigate its relative rise as a leading power.

Australia will, of course, not give up on its alliance with the USA. The Australian Defence Minister Richard Marles' contention in 2023 that 'the alliance has never been in better shape than it is right now,' and Australia's willingness to host more American troops, submarines and fighter jets[257], indicate

---

[255]Luthra, Parikshit, 'Indian Diaspora in Australia Holds Significant Electoral Power, Says AIBC Chair Jodi McKay', *CNBC*, 23 January 2023, https://tinyurl.com/2bxupft4. Accessed on 17 June 2024.

[256]Pardesi, Manjeet, 'India-Australia Strategic Convergence', op. cit.

[257]Martinez, Luis, 'US and Australia Deepen Military Ties to Counter China', 29 July 2023, *ABC News*, https://tinyurl.com/mr3kmxs5. Accessed on 17 June 2024.

that Canberra is doubling down on its number one ally for security. The launch of the AUKUS trilateral alliance with the USA and the UK in 2021, to beef up Australia's maritime military muscle and deter China through hard balancing, left no ambiguity that Washington will still be the mainstay for Canberra's security. But what is also clear is that, like Japan, Australia is pursuing a USA-plus strategy in which India will take pride of place. Should the USA again retreat into isolationism and abandonment *à la* President Donald Trump, this diversified portfolio of friends with India in the middle would grow in salience. The debate about Australia being a 'dependent ally'[258] or an 'independent ally'[259] of the USA is a time-worn one, but its friendship with India and other like-minded partners holds more contemporary and future relevance for the Indo-Pacific.

It is instructive that India played a key hand in blocking China's resolution at the International Atomic Energy Agency (IAEA) which alleged that AUKUS' provision of nuclear-powered submarines to Australia violated the NPT through 'illegal transfer of nuclear weapon materials'.[260] Even though India is not party to AUKUS, and despite the rupture that AUKUS caused between Australia and India's best friend in Europe, France (*see* Chapter 5), New Delhi took the stand that AUKUS was in its national interests in overall terms, as it would increase military deterrence against China's expansionism. Likewise, Canberra has used its diplomatic capital to try and shoehorn New Delhi into

[258]Bell, Coral, *Dependent Ally: A Study in Australian Foreign Policy*, 1988, Oxford University Press, Melbourne.
[259]Tow, Shannon, *Independent Ally: Australia in an Age of Power Transition*, 2017, Melbourne University Press, Melbourne.
[260]Laskar, Rezaul, 'China Withdraws Anti-AUKUS Resolution at IAEA Due to Lack of Support', *Hindustan Times*, 1 October 2022, https://tinyurl.com/mthbps2h. Accessed on 17 June 2024.

important institutions like the APEC and the East Asia Summit (EAS) on grounds that India 'was essential to counter rising Chinese influence'.[261] The regional architecture is thus being co-constructed by Australia and India to burnish each other's image and stretch each other's zone of influence so that both get stronger to withstand shared adversaries. If the crux of Australia's legendary 'mateship' and India's customary '*maitri*' is 'friends looking out for each other,'[262] they are reifying it.

[261]Teo, Sarah, *Middle Powers in Asia Pacific Multilateralism: A Differential Framework*, 2023, Bristol University Press, Bristol, p. 119.
[262]O'Farrell, Barry, 'Realizing the Potential of '*Maitri*' and 'Mateship'', *The Hindu*, 22 March 2022, https://tinyurl.com/2vupjfhy. Accessed on 17 June 2024.

3

TWO GREAT POWERS: THE USA AND INDIA IN THE ASIAN CENTURY

[...] The relationship between the United States and India is one of the—will be one of the defining relationships of the 21st century [...] The challenges and opportunities facing the world in this century require that India and the United States work and lead together. And we are [...] two great nations, two great friends, two great powers that can define the course of the 21st century.[263]

—Joe Biden, President of the USA, 2023

The South Lawn of the White House was all decked up and looked immaculately green. Top functionaries of the USA's cabinet were standing and waiting alongside their Indian counterparts. Bands from the American military were ready for the cue to play their parts, and stood on alert with their colourful flags and insignia. Amid grand protocol, pomp

---

[263]TWH, 'Remarks by President Biden and Prime Minister Modi of the Republic of India at Arrival Ceremony', The White House, Washington, D.C., 22 June 2023, https://tinyurl.com/2p9t8cwp. Accessed on 17 June 2024.

and pageantry, the event commenced with the announcement of the arrival of President Joe Biden and the First Lady Jill Biden. Just as they walked out, an official black car bearing the flags of the USA and India drove by like clockwork. A man who had once been denied entry visa to the USA as Chief Minister of the western Indian state of Gujarat, got out, clasped hands with the Bidens, and waved triumphantly at a crowd of thousands of Indian diaspora supporters deliriously chanting his name. The two leaders stepped up to a podium and stood still as the national anthems played amid a 21-gun salute, and a full honour guard ceremony, with marchpasts by American troops in full regalia swaying to music. The phrase 'red carpet welcome' was an understatement.

Prime Minister Narendra Modi's first official state visit to the USA in June 2023 was a visual extravaganza. Quick to grasp the historic value of what was unfolding, Modi attributed his grand reception as 'a kind of honour for the 1.4 billion people of India' and 'for the over 4 million people of Indian origin living in America.' He reminded everyone about how far he himself, India and the Indian diaspora had come in the USA's order of priority. 'I embarked on a journey to America as an ordinary citizen nearly three decades ago and at that time, I only saw the White House from the outside. I have had the privilege of visiting here several times myself after becoming the Prime Minister. However, today marks the first time that the doors of the White House have been opened for the Indian American community in such a large number.'[264] The honours which followed in Modi's address to the Joint Sitting of the American Congress, the State Dinner and other high-profile engagements confirmed that Washington and New

---

[264]NM, 'PM Modi's Remarks During the Ceremonial Welcome at the White House', Narendra Modi, 22 June 2023, https://tinyurl.com/4xbcd3de. Accessed on 17 June 2024.

Delhi had indeed come a long way to finally lay claim to having become best friends.

NATURAL PARTNERS, NOT ALLIES

The progression of the USA-India friendship from 'strategic partnership' in 2004 and 'global strategic partnership' in 2009 to 'major defense partner' in 2016 and 'comprehensive global and strategic partnership' in 2020 (see Annexure, Tables I and III), tells a story of how the world's two leading democracies overcame hesitations, recalibrated their approaches, and built a defining relationship that holds the key to the balance of power in the Indo-Pacific, and to equilibrium in world politics as a whole. But before delving into the reasons for the friendship attaining high tide, it is worth rewinding to why it did not take off for decades. As some of the calculations and strains of that bygone era linger on, and keep cropping up in new avatars even now, a brief detour into the Cold War and early post-Cold War eras would help provide perspective on the present and future patterns of this consequential but complex partnership.

The role of global factors, including equations involving other countries, in keeping the USA and India at arm's length or taking a fresh look at each other during the 20th century is instructive. In the 1940s, the USA did nudge and prod its wartime ally, the UK, to decolonize and grant freedom to India, but it was a short-lived attempt. Washington eventually 'backed away' and chose not to risk the global benefits of its special relationship with the UK for the sake of the principle of India's self-determination.[265] In India's post-independence

---

[265]Clymer, Kenton, 'Franklin D. Roosevelt, Louis Johnson, India and Anti-Colonialism: Another Look', *Pacific Historical Review*, Vol. 57, No. 3, 1988, p. 283.

period, the USA was so consumed by the grand strategy of containment of Soviet Russia that it saw all developing countries through the prism of whether or not they will side with it to check the 'evil' of communism. As a great power that dreaded the prospect of losing key regions of the world to a rival great power, the USA did not have the sensitivity or the empathy to appreciate India's non-aligned stance or its socialist and post-colonial ethos. American policymakers dismissed India's leadership of a third neutral bloc that was equidistant from both the Washington-led Western bloc and the Moscow-led Eastern bloc as 'immoral and short-sighted', and believed that 'non-aligned countries were more dangerous than the communists because of their "veiled" function as "friends of communism".'[266]

Since Pakistan was pliant and willing to join the anti-communist crusade as a junior partner, the USA had no qualms about designating it as a formal ally and supplying weaponry to it, even though Islamabad would deploy them against New Delhi in its obsessive quest to wrest Kashmir. India's reading of the USA-Pakistan alliance was that it was an 'unfriendly act' wherein 'Pakistan becomes practically a colony of the United States' and a tool 'to bring India to her knees.'[267]

The irony of the USA alienating India, a democracy, and cultivating Pakistan, a miliary dictatorship, all the while claiming to be fighting a global battle for 'freedom' against authoritarianism, was unmissable in New Delhi and led it to forge closer strategic ties with Moscow. The line-up that formed by the 1970s was India and Soviet Russia in one camp against the USA, China and Pakistan in the other. The Indian view of the USA was bitter and cynical as the effect

---

[266]Male, Deelip, *Contribution of Pandit Jawaharlal Nehru to Indian Politics—A Critical Study*, 2015, Lulu, Morrisville, p. 172.
[267]Brands, H.W., *India and the United States: The Cold Peace*, 1990, Twayne Publishers, New York, p. 76.

of American policies was to check India's rise, especially by propping up Pakistan. As Triloki Nath Kaul, the then Indian Ambassador to the USA, put it in 1974, 'The US administration's policy towards the subcontinent is based on the concept of power, balance of power, of creating influence through supply of arms, a policy that has failed.' Kaul also decried the USA's 'cunning game of befriending China at the cost of India,' and fretted at Washington 'recognizing China as the predominant power in Southeast and East Asia.'[268] While the China factor will figure prominently throughout this chapter, here it suffices to note that there was a classic dissonance that led American diplomat Dennis Kux to label the USA and India of that time as 'estranged democracies' who shared the same political system, but not the same geopolitical friends or interests. They 'fell out because they disagreed on national security issues of fundamental importance to each,' wherein India was 'lined up with America's principal foe' while the USA was 'aligned with India's major enemy.'[269]

Even though the Cold War rigidities loosened up with the collapse of the Soviet Union, Washington was not happy that India and Russia still maintained a special friendship after 1991 (see Chapter 4). On the other hand, India chafed at the USA for sustaining its long transactional friendship with Pakistan under the GWOT. Today, leaders of the USA and India routinely hail the natural partnership between the world's 'largest democracy' and the 'oldest democracy', but both countries continue to have authoritarian allies or strategic partners to cater to their varied needs in different regions of the world. In some cases, the USA has endorsed

---

[268]Kaul, Triloki Nath, *A Diplomat's Diary (1947–99): China, India and USA (The Tantalising Triangle)*, 2000, Macmillan, New Delhi, pp. 146, 160.
[269]Kux, Dennis, *India and the United States: Estranged Democracies*, 2002, National Defense University Press, Washington, D.C., p. XIII.

and underwritten its authoritarian friends like the UAE to warm up to India (*see* Chapter 7), but in other cases the USA has tried in vain to wean India away from embracing its authoritarian adversaries such as Iran and Russia.

The most intriguing authoritarian country which played a key role in determining the ups and downs in USA-India relations both before and after the Cold War has been China. This strategic triangle, which refers to an interplay among three countries where ties between any two have a major impact on the third, took shape in the 1950s, and went through several twists and turns. From 1949 to 1956, when the USA was dead against communist China, and saw it as part of a monolithic authoritarian bloc, Washington 'hoped that India would play a critical role in the US strategic script as a geopolitical counterbalance and ideological democratic contrast to the Soviet Union's Asian ally.'

But India's socialist and post-colonial outlook meant it would not play along with Western imperialist designs in Asia. From 1956 to 1962, as China became more assertive and aggressive against India over Tibet and the disputed border, 'broad agreement on China was a significant reason for US-India engagement.' The American offer of military assistance to strengthen India's defences after its humiliating defeat to China in the 1962 war raised hopes of an alignment, but 'India's preferred strategy of diversifying its dependence with a partnership with the Soviet Union proved to be an obstacle to deeper US-India relations.' From the 1970s, once the USA entered into a long-term geopolitical alignment with China in order to trounce Soviet Russia, 'the US desire and need to seek an Indian role as a counterweight or contrasting model to China' waned and 'India's importance to the US decreased.'[270]

---

[270]Madan, Tanvi, *Fateful Triangle: How China Shaped U.S.-India Relations During the Cold War*, Brookings Institution Press, Washington, D.C., pp. 4–5.

In the immediate post-Cold War era, when the USA enjoyed a preponderance of power, and had no peer contestants, it was perceived that the need for permanent military alliances had declined. Since 'the problems of diplomacy and national security' had become complex and variegated, 'states (and organizations) that are useful and appropriate for the pursuit of one goal will not necessarily be the ones best suited for another.' In such an ambiguous environment, the USA was enjoined to adopt 'agile and creative statecraft', look beyond traditional allies, and seek 'new partners' like India.[271]

The Clinton administration (1992–2000) did not visualize China as a rival, and there was no conscious counterbalancing motive against China behind the USA's bid to improve relations with India. In fact, the USA announced a 'constructive strategic partnership' with China in 1997, four years prior to its 'commitment' to a strategic partnership with India and seven years before the USA and India formally announced 'next steps' for implementing their strategic partnership (*see* Annexure, Tables I, II and III). What particularly irked India was President Clinton's recognition of China as a leader in South Asia and his endorsement that China had a 'responsibility to contribute actively to the maintenance of peace, stability and security in the region.'[272] The then Indian government, with Atal Bihari Vajpayee as Prime Minister, shot back that 'the US-China "Joint Statement on South Asia" reflected the hegemonistic mentality of a bygone era in international relations, and is completely unacceptable and out of place in the present-day world.'[273] Coming at a time

[271]Menon, Rajan, 'The End of Alliances', *World Policy Journal*, Vol. 20, No. 2, 2003, pp. 16–17.
[272]APP, 'Joint Statement on South Asia', 27 June 1998, The American Presidency Project, https://tinyurl.com/mwxcv6c. Accessed on 17 June 2024.
[273]EI, 'Government of India's Response to the US-China "Joint Statement on South Asia"', Embassy of India, Washington, D.C, USA, 27 June 1998, https://tinyurl.com/bddfdb33. Accessed on 17 June 2024.

when the USA had imposed economic sanctions on India for conducting nuclear weapons tests, that row appeared to reconfirm to Indian minds that the USA was not trustworthy when it came to standing up to China.

Even after the friendship between the USA and India steadily blossomed in the new millennium, misgivings surrounding their respective different approaches to China did not vanish. What changed, though, was that prior to the onset of their strategic partnership, Washington and New Delhi used to disagree vehemently, and often suffered serious disruptions in bilateral ties owing to disputes about China and Pakistan. After their strategic partnership took off in 2004, the USA and India started to agree to disagree, while not terminating their friendship. They began 'de-hyphenating' or proofing their friendship from the vagaries of their shifting outlooks towards third and fourth countries.

As noted in the Introduction, strategic partnerships are not exclusive in character, but they do have a common adversary against which there is a soft or hard balancing intent. Strategic partnerships 'do not demand commitments to a partner's disputes with other countries,' and grant both partners 'the flexibility to continue political engagement and economic cooperation with their common adversary.'[274]

The USA-India friendship has grown in this climate of variable strategic partnerships. However, it must be mentioned that Washington has not easily or entirely switched from its habitual alliance mindset to a partnership mindset. Expectations that India should toe the line on a range of global crises and rivalries keep emanating from Washington, and limit the possibilities in the friendship. In the words of

---

[274]Basrur, Rajesh, and Sumitha Narayanan Kutty, op. cit.

Indian International Relations scholar Harsh Pant, 'Neither the United States nor India are used to partnerships among equals and India remains too proud, too argumentative, and too big a nation to reconcile as a junior partner to any state, including the United States.'[275] The former American diplomat Alyssa Ayres has echoed this sentiment by noting that 'in the United States, the mental model for positive international cooperation defaults to seeing "ally" as the ultimate endpoint. For India, that suggests a curtailment of independence. And with India, even as cooperation becomes more extensive than ever in the past, consequential differences remain.'[276]

This mismatch is unique because the USA is the only contemporary great power among India's closest friends. Structurally speaking, great powers behave in a certain manner, and approach lesser powers through a framework that is less egalitarian and more demanding of conformity. Great powers have a wider canvas of core national interests and they juggle competing foreign policy goals that can translate into impatience and unreliability vis-à-vis partners who are weaker. In 2023, President Biden rhetorically acknowledged that the USA and India were 'two great powers', but the history of the USA-India friendship suggests that asymmetry in power, and the related sensitivities it engenders, have been and will be a constraint.

What confuses perceptions further and adds to the mismatch is usage of the phrase 'natural allies' in popular parlance to describe the USA-India friendship. Although the two countries never signed any formal alliance, Indian and American politicians, diplomats and media commentators have

---

[275]Pant, Harsh, *Indian Foreign Policy: An Overview*, 2016, Manchester University Press, Manchester, p. 32.
[276]Ayres, Alyssa, 'India is Not a U.S. Ally—and Has Never Wanted to Be', *Time*, 21 June 2023, https://tinyurl.com/22rru298. Accessed on 17 June 2024.

frequently deployed this rhetorical term with the intention of elevating the bilateral friendship to higher levels. In 1998, Prime Minister Vajpayee labelled the USA and India 'natural allies in the quest for a better future for the world in the 21st century.'[277] This language stuck and was repeated by President George W. Bush in 2006, who praised India as 'a natural ally for us' in the context of the GWOT.[278] The Obama administration hailed the friendship as one between 'natural friends and natural allies' in 2009[279], and the Trump administration claimed in 2020 that the two friends were turning Vajpayee's vision of natural allies 'into a reality'.[280]

FOR BALANCE IN ASIA

What caused two erstwhile wary and alienated nations, the USA and India, to open a new page in history by committing to a strategic partnership in 2001 and operationalizing it in 2004? For New Delhi, it was the realization that accessing American markets and technology as well as getting the USA, which was then the sole superpower in the world, on its side in geopolitical matters would be beneficial for India's rise. On the American side, a rethink in grand strategy during the George W. Bush administration got the ball rolling. Bush's National Security Adviser and Secretary of State, Condoleezza

---

[277]AS, 'India, USA and the World: Let Us Work Together to Solve the Political-Economic Y2K Problem', Asia Society, 28 September 1998, https://tinyurl.com/4d8wavc2. Accessed on 17 June 2024.
[278]HT, 'Indo-US Partnership Can Transform World: Bush', *Hindustan Times*, 4 March 2006, https://tinyurl.com/yck9j8ew. Accessed on 17 June 2024.
[279]IE, 'India, US are Natural Friends and Allies: Obama', *The Indian Express*, 29 January 2009, https://tinyurl.com/2mvh9umy. Accessed on 17 June 2024.
[280]PTI, 'Trump, Modi to Outline Next Chapter of "Natural Alliance" Between America and India: Top US Diplomat', *The Times of India*, 14 February 2020, https://tinyurl.com/3phapjtz. Accessed on 17 June 2024.

Rice, warned as early as in 2000 that 'China is not a "status quo" power but one that would like to alter Asia's balance of power in its own favor.' In this light, she recommended that Washington should stop looking at India through the traditional prisms of Pakistan and nuclear non-proliferation, and instead 'pay closer attention to India's role in the regional balance.'[281]

Eyeing India as a 'swing state in international politics' which could tilt the scales and 'determine the ultimate outcome of the struggle between US and China' was 'one of the rationales behind the Indo-US rapprochement' under Bush.[282] The Bush team's 'more realist orientation than the Clinton administration's towards Asia' and its adoption of a 'dualist approach of economic engagement with China as well as balancing against its rise' played a big hand in kickstarting the strategic partnership with India, which began to be seen in Washington as 'a potential partner to balance against a rising China'.[283] The 'strategic generosity' which Washington displayed towards India by carving out exceptions to NPT rules and concluding a landmark civil nuclear deal that opened access to Western high-end technology for India, was not altruistic but the USA's 'investment in its own geopolitical well-being'.[284] When the USA promised a 'decisively broader strategic relationship' with India whose 'goal is to help India become a major world power in the 21st century,' and added

[281]Rice, Condoleezza, 'Promoting the National Interest', *Foreign Affairs*, Vol. 79, No. 1, 2000, p. 56.

[282]Pant, Harsh and Yogesh Joshi, *The US Pivot and Indian Foreign Policy: Asia's Evolving Balance of Power*, 2015, Palgrave Macmillan, New York, p. 24.

[283]Burgess, Stephen, 'The Evolution of India-US Relations and India's Grand Strategy', *UNISCI Journal*, No. 49, 2019, p. 83.

[284]Tellis, Ashley, 'New Delhi, Washington: Who Gets What?', *The Times of India*, 30 January 2010, https://tinyurl.com/mvpyujnh. Accessed on 24 April 2024.

that 'we understand fully the implications, including military implications, of that statement,' Beijing took notice.[285] India's signing of the first foundational defence agreement with the USA, General Security of Military Information Agreement (GSOMIA) in 2002, the launch of a New Framework for US-India Defense Relationship in 2005, and a Maritime Framework for Cooperation in 2006 had undertones of external balancing against China, as they increased the pace and intensity of intelligence sharing, joint exercises and consultations on the IOR.

Still, given that the USA itself was then hedging towards China, and was preoccupied with the GWOT, the strategic partnership was not consistently and single-mindedly focused on pushing back China. The USA-India joint communiqués and work agendas of bilateral summits in the Bush and early Obama presidencies harped more on jointly countering terrorism and jihadist extremism in the 'Af-Pak' (combined strategic space including Afghanistan and Pakistan) theatre than in checking China. The announcement to upgrade the USA-India friendship to a 'global strategic partnership' in 2009 'centred, *inter alia*, around countering international terrorism,' shared concern about 'the threat of terrorism emanating from India's neighbourhood,' and 'stability in Afghanistan.'[286]

But this aspect of the strategic partnership did not show much convergence of interests. It was fraught with misgivings in India, as the USA depended greatly on Pakistan for waging war in Afghanistan and negotiating with the Taliban. Behind the scenes, American pressure on India to exercise 'restraint' whenever it was brazenly attacked by Pakistan-sponsored jihadists rubbed Indian sensibilities the wrong way. Much

---

[285]CD, 'US to Help Make India a "Major World Power"', *China Daily*, 26 March 2005, https://tinyurl.com/4u8kcpkn. Accessed on 29 April 2024.
[286]Sibal, Kanwal, 'India-US Strategic Partnership: Transformation is Real', *Indian Foreign Affairs Journal*, Vol. 10, No. 2, 2015, p. 106.

to New Delhi's chagrin, Washington also pumped in at least $23 billion in military assistance to Islamabad between 2002 and 2016 in the name of counterterrorism,[287] a largesse that India loudly protested as effectively enabling Pakistan to counterbalance it and helping China to keep it bogged down so that it cannot emerge as a bigger player across Asia and the Indo-Pacific. India badly wanted the USA to apply maximum pressure, including launching direct military attacks, on Pakistan to shut down its jihad factories. But New Delhi could not convince Washington to crack down decisively on Islamabad. As long as the USA committed the 'gravest mistake' of pursuing the 'wrong enemy' in Afghanistan while letting the 'real enemy', Pakistan, off the hook[288], India had little to celebrate about this side of the strategic partnership.

The ghosts of the past, when American actions either intentionally or unintentionally suppressed India's rise, could not be exorcized until the Trump administration shut off the aid tap to Pakistan in 2018. But even after that fundamental break, the pell-mell manner in which the Biden administration made the American military pack its bags and exit from Afghanistan in 2021, and the subsequent fall of Kabul to the Pakistan-backed Taliban, left India fuming. The sudden collapse of the internationally recognized moderate Afghan government, which reminded the world of the humiliating retreat of the USA from Vietnam in 1974, put in jeopardy 20 years of patient Indian investment in the security and economic development of Afghanistan. Subrahmanyam Jaishankar, the External Affairs Minister, conveyed 'deep Indian unease' about the USA's fatal last act in Afghanistan and critiqued Washington's willingness

---

[287]CRS, 'Pakistan and U.S.-Pakistan Relations', Congressional Research Service, 22 May 2023, p. 3, https://tinyurl.com/yeyr3cxz. Accessed on 17 June 2024.
[288]Gall, Carlotta, *The Wrong Enemy: America in Afghanistan 2001–2014*, 2014, Penguin Books, New Delhi.

to sacrifice hard-fought gains 'at the expediency of politics of the day'.[289] The shadow of past perceptions about the selfishness, unreliability and uncertainty of the USA, and its security guarantees came back to haunt India as a result of the catastrophic failure of the Western-led nation-building project in Afghanistan. After 2021, New Delhi did coordinate and consult with Washington to form joint positions on terrorism and human rights in Taliban-ruled Afghanistan[290], but the overall performance of the strategic partnership on the Af-Pak and terrorism issues has been less than optimal.

On the plus side of the ledger, what has worked for the friendship is that New Delhi and Washington have converged and coordinated far deeper for balancing China in the Modi era. Prior to the advent of Modi, Indian leaders were wary about how far to go with the USA to check China, owing to a mix of domestic political and international considerations. A non-proactive strategic culture and unwillingness to take risks by aligning with friends against adversaries were typical traits of the pre-Modi period. Indian scholars Harsh Pant and Yogesh Joshi observe that during the prime ministership of Manmohan Singh, India's stance towards the USA's attempted 'rebalance' or 'pivot' to Asia to counterbalance China was 'punctuated by reluctance and caution', owing to uncertainty about Washington's determination to stay the course against Beijing, 'residual anti-Americanism and nostalgia for non-alignment' in New Delhi, and India's fears of incurring China's retaliatory wrath.[291]

[289]Raj, Yashwant, 'Jaishankar Reiterates Unease Over US Pullout from Afghanistan', *Hindustan Times*, 27 May 2021, https://tinyurl.com/2z3bn2hk. Accessed on 17 June 2024.
[290]DOS, 'Joint Statement on the Fifth Annual India-U.S. 2+2 Ministerial Dialogue', 10 November 2023, U.S. Department of State, https://tinyurl.com/mtk9pa6t. Accessed on 17 June 2024.
[291]Pant, Harsh, and Yogesh Joshi, op. cit., pp. 45, 48.

Readers will recall from Chapter 2 how multinational Malabar joint naval exercises hosted by the USA and India were aborted in 2008, owing to such considerations. The USA-India Defense Technology and Trade Initiative (DTTI), signed in 2012, also stuttered with no spectacular deliverables in defence co-production and co-development due to India's doubts as well as the USA's apprehensions about sharing cutting-edge sensitive dual-use technologies with an India that still had robust military ties with Russia. Impressions in India that 'the US is not interested in sharing the latest defence technologies despite all the rhetoric of shared values, strategic convergence, and comprehensive partnership,'[292] and that Washington preferred to keep selling more weapons to New Delhi instead of empowering it with the wherewithal to become a top defence manufacturer, held back the friendship from realizing its full military potential. The long-time American refusal to part with nuclear submarine technology, for instance, incurred dismay in New Delhi.[293]

THE DECISIVE TURN

Blaming each side for not living up to expectations completely is par for the course in the USA-India friendship, on which there is limitless commentary and an abundance of strong opinions in both countries. But finding the way forward has required decisive political leadership. Defence cooperation grew significantly under Prime Minister Modi, who has been credited by American officials for 'a foreign policy

---

[292]Bajpai, Siddhant, 'India-US Defence Technology Cooperation: Promises and Pitfalls', CeSCube, 22 February 2022, https://tinyurl.com/52cs5k44. Accessed on 17 June 2024.
[293]Unnithan, Sandeep, 'Why the US Won't Give India Nuclear Submarines', *India Today*, 23 September 2021, https://tinyurl.com/mrydrbsb. Accessed on 17 June 2024.

that overcomes the hesitations of history and embraces the convergence between our two countries and our shared interests.'[294] Unencumbered by Left-wing ideological shackles, and driven by nationalistic conviction that India must become a leading power by harnessing its bilateral friendships to the maximum possible extent, Modi aimed for greater strategic dividend from the USA-India partnership and got it. Even though he tried personal summit diplomacy with President Xi Jinping to stabilize relations with China and manage India's territorial disputes with its menacing northern neighbour, he came around to the firm conclusion that India's friendship with the USA must have a sharper strategic edge to sustain pressure on China.

The linear advances made under Modi with three very different presidents—Obama, Trump and Biden—read like a relentless march of milestones in the friendship. In 2016, India received the bespoke status of 'major defense partner' of the USA and signed the second foundational defence agreement— the Logistics Exchange Memorandum of Agreement (LEMOA), after 14 long years. In 2017, India and the USA revived the Quad with Australia and Japan after a decade of dormancy. In 2018, India signed the third foundational defence agreement— the Communications Compatibility and Security Agreement (COMCASA). In 2020, the USA-India friendship was upgraded to 'comprehensive and global strategic partnership' (first mooted in 2013 but enacted in 2020)[295], the Malabar naval exercises were permanently turned into quadrilateral format, and the last and final foundational document—Basic

---

[294]PTI, 'US Christens PM's Vision of Indo-US Ties as "Modi Doctrine"', *The Economic Times*, 10 June 2016, https://tinyurl.com/4s2peju4. Accessed on 17 June 2024.

[295]Basu, Nayanima, 'Comprehensive Global Strategic Partnership: What Modi-Trump Just Formalised is 2013 Concept', *The Print*, 26 February 2020, https://tinyurl.com/4e4b583t. Accessed on 17 June 2024.

Exchange and Cooperation Agreement (BECA)—was inked. To understand the sea change, it is worth recalling that BECA 'had been pending for over a decade-and-a-half after the earlier United Progressive Alliance (UPA) government [under Manmohan Singh] did not sign it because Left parties, which were part of the coalition, were strongly opposed to close ties with the US.'[296]

All these landmarks in the bilateral friendship and its broader regional application in the Indo-Pacific were goaded by India's worsening relations with China, and the USA's move away from 'congagement' and shift to overt counterbalancing or containment of China. For example, BECA was signed just four months after the deadly Galwan Valley clash between the Indian Army and China's PLA. It ushered in a new era of geospatial intelligence sharing to boost the Indian military's deterrence capabilities against China.

Reports (not denied by India) that the USA had 'for the first time provided real-time details to their Indian counterparts on the Chinese positions and force strength in advance of a PLA incursion' into Tawang at the LAC in December 2022, helping India thwart China's expansionist designs[297], show how operationally effective the USA-India friendship has become on the ground. In the Indo-Pacific, Washington's vow to 'steadily advance our Major Defense Partnership with India and support its role as a net security provider'[298] has advanced through major weapons sales and greater interoperability. The

[296]Philip, Snehesh, 'The 3 Foundational Agreements with US and What they Mean for India's Military Growth', *The Print*, 27 October 2020, https://tinyurl.com/4yntvp5u. Accessed on 17 June 2024.

[297]Kumar, Ankit, '"They Were Waiting...:" Intel Shared by US Helped Thwart Chinese Incursion in Tawang | Report', *India Today*, 21 March 2023, https://tinyurl.com/36wp9bj2. Accessed on 17 June 2024.

[298]WH, 'Indo-Pacific Strategy of the United States', February 2022, The White House, p. 13, https://tinyurl.com/5bcx97eb. Accessed on 17 June 2024.

USA's sale in 2024 of the General Atomics-manufactured MQ-9B Predator drones to India worth $4 billion promised to significantly boost the Indian Navy's surveillance and attack capabilities across the IOR and beyond. This 'hunter-killer' capacity could enable India to not only deter the Chinese PLA Navy's encroachment, but also strike at wanted jihadist terrorist targets in Pakistan, Afghanistan and beyond.[299]

Apart from weaponry, the Pentagon's strategy of 'places not bases', i.e. 'pursuing access to more sites where the United States has no military installations of its own,' has found a willing friend in India which has opened the 'door for a U.S. military trying to stretch out across the Indo-Pacific and counter Chinese power'.[300] Proposals from veterans of the two navies for combined operations and 'interchangeability', wherein the Indian Navy could 'relieve the U.S. Navy of its maritime security responsibilities in the Persian Gulf and Horn of Africa' and let Washington train its guns on China in the Pacific[301] are no longer unthinkable flights of fancy. The emergence of the USA as India's largest military exercise partner augurs well for this kind of sophisticated defence diplomacy since the armed forces of the two sides are learning from and mingling with each other so much more today than ever before.

Cynicism expressed in some quarters in Washington, that India will sit out any collective fight to save Taiwan if China invades the self-governed island, or that India will not deploy its

---

[299]De, Abhishek, 'India to Get "Hunter-Killer" Predator Drones. What Makes them so Lethal?' *India Today*, 5 February 2024, https://tinyurl.com/fyatzzn9. Accessed on 17 June 2024.

[300]Cave, Damien, 'U.S. Pursues Defense Partnership with India to Deter Chinese Aggression', *The New York Times*, 17 October 2023, https://tinyurl.com/3jcsbv7j. Accessed on 17 June 2024.

[301]Singh, Karambir, and Blake Herzinger, 'Partnership, Not Threats: How to Deepen U.S.-Indian Naval Cooperation', *War on the Rocks*, 12 January 2023, https://tinyurl.com/mvcdfkc6. Accessed on 17 June 2024.

limited assets to the East or South China Seas to augment the USA's firepower in the West Pacific, misses out on the 'division of labour' formula, for the USA-India friendship to have a strategic effect. India's military may not be ready for large-scale presence and deterrence missions east of the Malacca Strait, but as Lieutenant General Anil Ahuja, former Co-Chair of the India-US DTTI Inter-agency Task Force, has pointed out, 'The Indian Navy, with the support of the US and partners, can provide the nucleus for the maritime security architecture in the Indian Ocean, relieving the burden of deployment of scarce US military assets in the region.'[302] In Chapter 1, we saw that Japan and India have a double act to apply simultaneous pressure on China from different fronts. Australia and India also have such a burden-sharing game to play. Whatever India can pitch in to enable the US Indo-Pacific Command to concentrate on China's eastern seaboard is worth its weight in gold. There is also the huge commercial benefit to American defence manufacturers, who have gained substantial access to the gargantuan Indian arms market, and accounted for 11 per cent of India's total military imports between 2017 and 2022.[303] Suggestions that the USA has been naively charitable or overly generous to India are misguided. These two friends are unequal in capabilities, but their exchanges have become fair and equal.

With defence taking a lion's share in the multifaceted USA-India friendship in the Modi era, analysts have argued that 'if India has formally not entered into a "quasi-alliance" with the U.S. yet, certainly it is on the threshold of one.' Despite this 'quasi-alliance', India is expected to not lose sight of its

---

[302]Ahuja, Anil, 'India and the US are Indispensable Partners', *The Tribune*, 7 June 2023, https://tinyurl.com/mu7pexuj. Accessed on 17 June 2024.
[303]Pandit, Rajat, 'India Remains World's Largest Importer, with Russia, France & US as the Biggest Suppliers', *The Times of India*, 14 March 2023, https://tinyurl.com/4wp9yy6e. Accessed on 17 June 2024.

eternal goal of strategic autonomy 'to avoid being labelled as a "deputy sheriff" to the USA and pursue its ambition to become a leading power in Asia.'[304] Whether the USA-India friendship will indeed morph into an alliance will depend on China's behaviour in years and decades to come. What we can be certain of is that the USA-India strategic partnership has crossed the Rubicon and come a long way from its early hesitant baby steps. China's aggression and India's mounting self-confidence to manage different types of strategic partnerships have put to rest old shibboleths and opened the door to new possibilities.

STRATEGIC ECONOMICS

In 2006, when India was hotly debating the merits and demerits of the civil nuclear deal with the USA, the doyen of India's national security thinking, Krishnaswamy Subrahmanyam, made an observation that proved clairvoyant.

> [...] India has a lot to gain from the partnership with the US and it will accelerate Indian growth as it did Chinese growth in the 1980s and '90s. If India does not do it and China overtakes the US, will that be preferable from the Indian point of view? If India nurtures its partnership with the US in the next two to three decades, it could become the third economy in the world in a position to influence the ranking of the US and China. After that, it will take several decades for India to move further to the second place [...] Therefore, India should confidently approach the future Indo-US relations as a partner.[305]

---

[304]Muraviev, Alexey, Dalbir Ahlawat and Lindsay Hughes, 'India's Security Dilemma: Engaging Big Powers While Retaining Strategic Autonomy', *International Politics*, Vol. 59, No. 6, 2022, p. 1135.
[305]Subrahmanyam, Krishnaswamy, 'Partnership, Not Alliance', *Indian Foreign Affairs Journal*, Vol. 1, No. 1, 2006, p. 6.

Tapping India's growing and reforming market economy for business opportunities has been a tremendous source of attraction for USA Inc., which covets India as the final frontier for global capitalism to make inroads. Corporate America has not been entirely disappointed in the past two decades. When the strategic partnership was operationalized in 2004, bilateral trade in goods and services stood at $30 billion. As of 2023, it had risen to around $200 billion and was projected to cross $500 billion by 2030.[306] In 2023, the USA beat all other friends of India to become the largest foreign investor there, bringing in $103 billion, 'representing a 17.2 per cent share of the total FDI' India had received.[307] Of course, from a macro perspective, India was only the ninth largest trading partner of the USA and the twentieth largest recipient of American FDI by 2023. But with strategic considerations of diversifying Western capital and supply chains away from China taking centre stage in Washington, India is destined to climb up the ranks to be among the USA's top five most valued economic partners in trade and investment.

The USA's singling out of India as an 'indispensable partner for friend-shoring as part of the overall "de-risking strategy" for the American supply chain,'[308] coupled with India's desire to deepen economic linkages with 'like-minded countries, particularly countries with a rules-based order, transparent

---

[306]ET, 'India, US Looking at Four-Fold Rise in Trade: Piyush Goyal', *The Economic Times*, 5 May 2023, https://tinyurl.com/bdcf2kb7. Accessed on 17 June 2024.
[307]IT, 'US Largest Source of India's Foreign Direct Investment in FY23: RBI Data', *India Today*, 13 September 2023, https://tinyurl.com/mtrv8jxz. Accessed on 17 June 2024.
[308]TNN, 'Yellen: India Indispensable for Friendshoring', 17 July 2023, *The Times of India*, https://tinyurl.com/5e8z72bb. Accessed on 17 June 2024.

economic systems,'[309] has set up a conducive bilateral policy environment for private sectors of both sides to aim higher and break records. The prediction by John Chambers, the former Chief Executive Officer of the American technology giant Cisco Systems and a hitherto bullish investor in China, that India will be the 'number one economy in the world' and 'the preferred alternative for trade and tech partnerships with the U.S. [...] as tensions with China and Russia continue,'[310] indicates what the future holds.

Historically, India had disappointed Western business communities due to its trade protectionism and unfriendly attitudes to FDI. But with geopolitical competition between Washington and Beijing intensifying, and as bolder economic reforms are undertaken by New Delhi, one can foresee India's stock rising to unprecedented levels in American estimates. Certitude that 'Indo-optimism' and 'Inevitable India' are for real this time around rests on the 'more distinctive geopolitical positioning for India, triggered, most significantly, by the growing rift between China and Western economies, particularly the U.S.'[311] With more American trade wars and divestments from China on the cards, even those American capitalists who were not convinced by India will give it a relook and reassess the distribution of their portfolios.

As Krishnaswamy Subrahmanyam had foreseen, the key to India's quest to become a manufacturing and innovation power lies in its friendship with advanced industrialized

---

[309]PIB, 'Structural Reforms Taken in Last 8 Years Will Help India Emerge Among the Top Three Economies in the World: Shri Goyal', Press Information Bureau, 7 January 2023, https://tinyurl.com/4yrpk25e. Accessed on 17 June 2024.

[310]TI, 'John Chambers' 2024 Predictions', *The Innovator*, 14 November 2023, https://tinyurl.com/39jbjpad. Accessed on 17 June 2024.

[311]Chakravorti, Bhaskar, and Gaurav Dalmia, 'Is India the World's Next Great Economic Power?' *Harvard Business Review*, 6 September 2023, https://tinyurl.com/2re28atv. Accessed on 17 June 2024.

economies. The multi-dimensional economic partnership which India enjoys today with the USA has no parallel with any of its other friends. Official pronouncements like 'no corner of human enterprise is untouched by the partnership between our two great countries, which spans the seas to the stars'[312] reflect the broad-based nature of the economic relationship. But the most strategic and futuristic of the varied branches of business between the two friends is the field of critical and emerging technologies. The 2023 Initiative on Critical and Emerging Technologies (iCET), and the India-US Strategic Trade Dialogue (IUSSTD) to co-develop 'in critical domains such as semiconductors, space, telecom, quantum, AI [Artificial Intelligence], defense, bio-tech and others'[313] have placed this bilateral friendship in a league of its own. The USA's anxieties about overdependence for chips on Taiwan, which has been in China's crosshairs, have opened pathways to invest in India and enable India to become 'an electronics hub' and a solution-provider to the 'demand-supply gap in semiconductors'.[314]

It is informative that the National Security Advisors of the two sides were tasked to manage iCET since its inception. Careful guidance by governments is necessary to steer cutting-edge business cooperation between democratic countries where free markets reign, and monetary calculations of individual firms can diverge from national objectives. India and the USA have long had a mutually beneficial business-to-business partnership in civilian information technology (IT) services, spearheaded by

---

[312]WH, 'Joint Statement from the United States and India', The White House, 22 June 2023, https://tinyurl.com/4n4mf8mt. Accessed on 17 June 2024.
[313]IE, 'Launch of India-US Strategic Trade Dialogue', Embassy of India, June 6 2023, https://tinyurl.com/32f7xy9n. Accessed on 17 June 2024.
[314]Das, Yudhajit, 'India to Chip in After Pact with US, May Fill World's Semiconductors Gap', India Today, 11 March 2023, https://tinyurl.com/bdd5ztsj. Accessed on 17 June 2024.

Indian software whizz-kids. What iCET and the India-United States Defense Acceleration Ecosystem (INDUS-X) are doing is injecting dual-use and military dimensions to endow explicit strategic elements into commercial ties. For example, the 2023 agreement for the American aerospace giant General Electric (GE) under the Roadmap for U.S.-India Defense Industrial Cooperation to co-produce advanced jet engines for fighter aircraft in India included transfer of technology (ToT). India hailed it as belonging to 'a different level and scale [that] has never happened anywhere in the world in terms of military technology.'[315]

With technology and geopolitics inextricably intertwined amid the USA-China 'new Cold War', the avenues for the USA-India friendship to shine in emerging fields have broadened. It has even reached outer space, with the USA's National Aeronautics and Space Administration (NASA) and the Indian Space Research Organisation (ISRO) jointly launching an observatory mission called NISAR (NASA-ISRO Synthetic Aperture Radar) to monitor and photograph changes in the entire earth's land and ice surfaces. Today, Washington is more eager than ever before to lift export controls and share its latest proprietary know-how with New Delhi. Future progress on this front will determine the outcome of fierce competition for balance of power in the Indo-Pacific.

THE *DESI* HAND

While geopolitics and economics are cementing factors propelling the India-USA strategic partnership, there is a powerful human element which makes this friendship a

---

[315]Singh, Dalip, 'GE-HAL Deal to Co-Produce 99 Jet Engines to Cost Less than $1 Billion', *The Hindu Business Line*, 24 June 2023, https://tinyurl.com/3343m5wu. Accessed on 17 June 2023.

living reality. The USA is a household name among ordinary Indians and vice versa, as a result of the extraordinary success of Indian students pursuing higher education in the USA, and Indian immigrants chasing the famed American Dream. In 2023, American universities had enrolled a whopping '269,000 students from India, more than ever and second only to China,'[316] making the USA the most sought-after foreign destination for skilling and training young Indians in scientific fields. With more USA-educated young Indians choosing to return home for nation-building, the old 'Brain Drain' theory has been replaced by 'Brain Gain', and also created a reservoir of social goodwill in India about all things American. In a deep and emotionally resonant way, Indians can palpably see an American hand in India's rise through the human resource development route. When every second middle-class home's daughter, and its neighbour's son have both been to the USA, and this phenomenon extends to entire localities and communities, especially in South India, there is a little bit of America throbbing in India's heart.

By 2023, the USA hosted more than 4.4 million people of Indian origin, who overtook Chinese-Americans as the 'most populous Asian-alone group in the United States'.[317] Among India's global diaspora of over 32 million, Indian Americans constitute the largest, wealthiest and best-organized groups. They comprise less than one-and-half per cent of the USA's population, but make up six per cent of its taxpayers. Colloquially known as *Desis*, Indian Americans have risen to top governmental and corporate positions across the USA,

[316]PTI, '35% Increase in Number of Indian Students in US: Report', *The Indian Express*, 13 November 2023, https://tinyurl.com/395f663f. Accessed on 17 June 2024.
[317]Venkatraman, Sakshi, 'Indians Surpass Chinese as Largest "Asian-Alone" Group in U.S.', *NBC News*, 27 September 2023, https://tinyurl.com/3k3ku3ma. Accessed on 17 June 2024.

and are acknowledged as a key voting bloc and a high-net-worth community that fundraises for both the Democratic and Republican parties.

The USA-based Indian journalist Seema Sirohi's insider account of the milestones in the bilateral friendship which had a distinct Desi hand is worth citing. From the 1990s, the Desis began 'slowly chipping away at the entrenched Pakistan lobby' in Washington, trying to reverse its decades-long pro-Islamabad policies. The 2006 USA-India civil nuclear deal cleared political hurdles in the American Congress, partly due to persuasive canvassing by the Desis that 'a growing Indian economy presented opportunities, and supporting the nuclear deal would open doors in New Delhi for more business.' The 2016 designation by the USA of India as a 'major defense partner' was enabled in part by Desis who worked the political class in the USA to grant India status equal to NATO allies and others like Israel, Japan and Australia. Indian Americans networking with key senators, representatives and executive branch officials at that time had 'created "a lot of ferment and discussion" on Capitol Hill and in the White House on how to give India better access to defence technology,' culminating in the one-of-its-kind declaration of India as a major defence partner.[318]

Coordinated efforts involving professional lobbying firms in Washington hired by New Delhi, the bipartisan Congressional India Caucus and Desi associations pack a punch, and have been compared to the well-oiled Israel lobby. Indian political scientist Ashok Sharma has shown that Desis were trained and mentored by the Jewish lobby to become more effective in the USA. His finding that 'the Indian lobby has been working in coordination with the Israel lobby not only in terms of their

---

[318]Sirohi, Seema, *Friends with Benefits: The India-US Story*, 2023, HarperCollins, New Delhi, pp. 49, 212, 352.

shared concern about terrorism, but also due to the growing and deepening strategic partnership between India and Israel that encompasses almost all areas of bilateral relations,'[319] is significant and we will revisit this special diaspora connection in Chapter 6. Here, it suffices to state that the Desis are undeniable force multipliers for New Delhi to ensure that India's national interests are not harmed by willful or inadvertent policies or laws passed in the USA. The election of more Indian Americans to both houses of Congress and the nomination of hundreds of Indian Americans to serve in important offices under both Republican and Democratic presidents[320] keep anti-India forces on the backfoot in the USA. The prospect of the USA ever again imposing economic sanctions on India over policy divergences is effectively foreclosed due to the power of the Desis, not to mention the overriding need in Washington to counterbalance Beijing.

There have been some roadblocks involving fundamentalist Khalistan Sikh activists carrying out separatist anti-India activities on American soil, and also Left-leaning Desis agitating against alleged undemocratic trends in Prime Minister Modi's India. But these critics have not succeeded in derailing the strategic partnership, as American elites know they are ideologically motivated and do not represent the majority of the Indian diaspora in the USA. Moreover, the very definition of a strategic partnership entails overlooking domestic political matters and coordinating to face international threats and challenges. One of the obligations of strategic partnerships is a 'commitment to promoting stable relationships and extensive economic intercourse, muting disagreements about domestic

---

[319]Sharma, Ashok, *Indian Lobbying and Its Influence in US Decision Making: Post-Cold War*, 2017, SAGE Publications, New Delhi, p. 234.
[320]PTI, 'Record 130-Plus Indian-Americans at Key Positions in Biden Administration', *The Hindu*, 24 August 2022, https://tinyurl.com/5yrf8358. Accessed on 17 June 2024.

politics in the interest of working together on matters of shared concern in international diplomacy.'[321] Washington would do well by heeding USA-based Indian foreign policy expert Aparna Pande's advice that Indians are sensitive to real or perceived slights and 'care deeply for, what may appear to others, symbolism.'[322]

GOING GLOBAL

Since the 2020 upgrade to a 'comprehensive and global strategic partnership,' the USA and India have sought to maximize the 'global' component. As two pillars of Quad and the Indo-Pacific, they have a special responsibility to jointly deliver regional public goods in areas like physical and digital infrastructure, healthcare, clean energy and connectivity. India's participation in the USA-led Indo-Pacific Economic Framework (IPEF) and in the Quad's Partnership for Cable Connectivity and Resilience are institutional vehicles for pushing back China's hegemony in non-military domains. Bilaterally, the 'US India Global Digital Development Partnership' to enable joint delivery of Digital Public Infrastructure (DPI) in developing countries, and joint projects in Asia and Africa where American and Indian institutions combine to impart skills, agricultural techniques, dairy management, healthcare best practices, etc., are stretching the 'global' impact of the strategic partnership to distant shores. Initiatives like Feed the Future and the Agriculture Innovation Partnership in Africa, as well as the South Asia Regional Initiative for Energy Integration, augur more extensive

[321]Goldstein, Avery, 'An Emerging China's Emerging Grand Strategy: A Neo-Bismarckian Turn?' in Ikenberry, John, and Michael Mastanduno, eds., *International Relations Theory and the Asia-Pacific*, 2003, Columbia University Press, New York, p. 75.
[322]Pande, Aparna, 'Natural Allies? The India-US Relations from the Clinton Administration to the Trump Era', Center for Asian Studies, 2018, p. 14.

triangular cooperation so that the oft-stated proclamations of the strategic partnership as a 'force for the global good'[323] are realized. Triangulating with each other's strategic partners like Vietnam and Indonesia can strengthen the regional architecture in the Indo-Pacific. External Affairs Minister Jaishankar's quip that 'you ain't seen anything yet' in the USA-India friendship and his vow that 'we are going to take this relationship to a different level'[324] should include creative third and fourth country collaborations beyond the Quad.

A USA-India tango for geopolitical integration in South and Southeast Asia is also required. Despite the shared threat perception about China's menacing threat in India's neighbouring countries, and the intent to coordinate policies, Washington and New Delhi often back different political horses and implement policies that are at odds with each other. For example, the USA's opposition to Prime Minister Sheikh Hasina's regime in Bangladesh, which had been strategically close to India, made no broader regional or global sense.[325] India was left scratching its head as to why the USA undermined Hasina's hold on power in the name of promoting democracy and human rights when it had no such moral compunctions while befriending authoritarian allies in other parts of the world. American economic sanctions on Myanmar also did not find concurrence with India, which worried that pushing the military junta with its back to the wall would hand over

[323]ANI, 'PM Modi Meets Blinken, Austin, Says "India-US Partnership Force for Global Good"', *Hindustan Times*, 10 November 2023, https://tinyurl.com/4v4rbuzf. Accessed on 17 June 2024.

[324]Jha, Prashant, 'India-US Ties are at All-Time High: Jaishankar', *Hindustan Times*, 2 October 2023, https://tinyurl.com/2cv9ec2b. Accessed on 17 June 2024.

[325]Das, Yudhajit, 'Why India and China are in Same Camp in Bangladesh's "Battle of Begums"', *India Today*, 2 December 2023, https://tinyurl.com/23j8t7wx. Accessed on 17 June 2024.

this geopolitically crucial country to China on a platter.[326] As sovereign states and strategic partners, the USA and India can indeed disagree on what they prefer in certain countries. The fact that the USA is a great power, with a larger set of international balls to juggle, as opposed to a rising or leading power like India that is possessive about strategic autonomy and concerned mainly about Asia, places limits on agreement on all and sundry. But with China breathing down the neck, the need of the hour is to live up to the 'global' part of the partnership, especially in vital sub-regions of the Indo-Pacific like the Bay of Bengal. Allies invariably line up on the same side in critical spaces. The task for the USA and India is to prove that strategic partners can do so too. The U.S. International Development Finance Corporation (DFC)'s decision in 2023 to pour in $553 million in the mega infrastructure project helmed by India's Adani Group to build the deep-water West Container Terminal in Colombo, Sri Lanka, is a harbinger of the potential that needs to be tapped, for Washington and New Delhi to integrate and repel Chinese regional influence.

The core China-India-USA strategic triangle deserves a last word here. The turning point after which Washington and New Delhi fast-forwarded their friendship was the decision by both sides to stop hedging or 'congagement' towards Beijing. Could there be future global circumstances when the USA steps back from counterbalancing China, and instead decides to accommodate or 'meet it halfway'?[327] Structurally, a modus vivendi or 'G-2' between the USA and China is impossible, as both sides are steeling themselves for a long struggle amid the global power transition. The USA's explicit commitments

[326]Parashar, Sachin, 'India Doesn't Follow National Sanctions: Jaishankar on Myanmar at Quad Meet', *The Times of India*, 12 February 2022, https://tinyurl.com/bdfze2fy. Accessed on 17 June 2024.
[327]Goldstein, Lyle, *Meeting China Halfway: How to Defuse the Emerging US-China Rivalry*, 2015, Georgetown University Press, Washington, D.C.

to support India's permanent membership in the UN Security Council, and help India become a great power presumes that China can never be trusted with the keys to the 'Asian century'.

But one must watch out for domestic political currents of foreign policy isolationism and escapism from balance-of-power responsibilities in the USA. The temptation to pull away from alliances and strategic partnerships, and let regional actors manage their local affairs, is not a theoretical proposition in an era of extreme domestic political polarization in the USA. Another possibility is that the USA again gets sucked into distracting wars involving its allies in West Asia/ the Middle East and Europe, losing sight of the primary goal of countering China. American entanglements in the Israel-Palestine and the Russia-Ukraine conflicts raised legitimate concerns that a concerted rollback of China in the Indo-Pacific might be put on the backburner.[328]

Conversely, we need to also ask if India might find it prudent to one day distance itself from the USA to secure concrete territorial concessions from China along the disputed LAC or even re-engage China as a partner. Given the totalitarian nature of the regime in Beijing and its expansionist designs, this seems unlikely. Any unwinding of the strategic partnership with the USA could be interpreted by China as a sign of Indian weakness, and would magnify Chinese demands and pressures on India to kowtow further. Still, the spectre of opportunistic abandonment or soft-pedalling lurks in a strategic partnership between a great power like the USA and a rising power like India, whose different positions in the international system can produce dissonance in national interests. Avoiding this worst-case scenario requires will, wisdom and patience to play the long game in Washington and New Delhi.

---

[328]Greene, Andrew, 'Israel-Gaza and Ukraine Conflicts Risk "Strategic Distraction" for United States in Indo-Pacific', *ABC News*, 31 October 2023, https://tinyurl.com/4f257enw. Accessed on 17 June 2024.

4

THE LONG BEAR HUG: RUSSIA AND INDIA AGAINST ALL ODDS

They [the West] try to portray those who are not willing to blindly follow Western elite groups as enemies. They have used this approach with various countries, including the People's Republic of China, and they tried to do this to India in certain situations. They are flirting with it now, as we can see very clearly. We are aware of and see the scenarios they are using in Asia. I would like to say that the Indian leadership is independent and strongly nationally oriented. I think these attempts are pointless, yet they continue with them.[329]

—Vladimir Putin, President of Russia, 2023

It was early summer in 2020. The Red Square in Moscow was spruced up for an extravaganza to commemorate the 75th anniversary of the Soviet Union's World War II victory over Germany. The Victory Day Parade featured a dazzling display of Russia's latest advanced weaponry, fly-pasts by the

---

[329]Madhava, Vibha, '"Indian Leadership Independent, Nationally Oriented": Putin Says West's Attempts to Sway New Delhi "Pointless"', *The Indian Express*, 6 October 2023, https://tinyurl.com/4tzpj956. Accessed on 17 June 2024.

Air Force in special formations, rows of soldiers of various wings of the Russian military standing to attention, marching bands in finest regalia, and contingents of foreign troops from 13 friendly countries. Despite opt-outs due to the prevalent Coronavirus pandemic, ten heads of state and government, eight ministers and several top diplomats of countries that had been allies during the Great Patriotic War were present at that moment of Russia's historic pride and glory. Among them was Rajnath Singh, India's Defence Minister, who applauded appreciatively, especially when the tri-services contingent of the Indian military goose-stepped in all its vigour, and the sacrifices of Indian troops (serving under the banner of the colonial British Indian Army) fighting alongside Soviet forces were recalled by announcers.

The most interesting fact about Singh's attendance was that it had not been on the cards until a few days prior to the Victory Day Parade on June 24. New Delhi confirmed to Moscow only on June 19 that he would be representing India even though Russia had issued invitations way back in February 2020.[330] A grave episode on June 15 had made the minister's visit not only possible, but absolutely imperative. In the Himalayan heights of Galwan Valley at the LAC, Indian and Chinese soldiers had engaged in deadly clashes over disputed territory and suffered many casualties. Russia's intelligence, which was well networked in both India and China, assessed that 'at least 20 Indian soldiers and 45 Chinese servicemen were killed during the clashes,'[331] making it the bloodiest confrontation between the two Asian giants in more

---

[330]Unnithan, Sandeep, 'Rajnath Singh Goes Arms Shopping to Russia', *India Today*, 17 August 2020, https://tinyurl.com/38y6uxje. Accessed on 17 June 2024.

[331]Krishnan, Revathi, '45 Chinese Soldiers Killed in Galwan Clash June Last Year, Russian News Agency TASS Says', *The Print*, 11 February 2021, https://tinyurl.com/4mt42j25. Accessed on 17 June 2024.

than four decades.

Singh's visit to Moscow took place within days of this peace-shattering incident, amidst India's massive mobilization and build-up of troops along multiple sectors of the LAC as part of the 'mirror deployment' to face down the Chinese PLA, and deter it from further aggressive actions. His mission in Moscow was to request timely implementation of all ongoing contracts for military hardware and faster supply of spare parts for fighter jets, battle tanks and submarines. Also on the agenda was 'advanced delivery of the Russian S-400 Triumf anti-aircraft missile defence system and the purchase of Russian-made Su-30MKI jet fighters,'[332] that would be critical to push back Chinese expansionism, using quicker means than had been originally scheduled. Singh sang paeans to 'our special friendship', announced 'all our proposals have received positive response from the Russian side,' and declared 'I am fully satisfied with my discussions.'[333] It was one more litmus test of the long-standing Russia-India 'special and privileged strategic partnership', which Moscow again passed with flying colours. In spite of the industrial shutdowns and slowdowns in production of materiel at the heights of the pandemic, Russian supplies, spares and new weapons arrived in India without major delays, and added to India's capabilities to block China's adventurism.

That Russia came to the rescue during an acute emergency faced by India even though the former had upgraded its relations with China to a 'comprehensive strategic partnership of coordination for a new era' in 2019, and viewed China

---

[332]SNS, 'With Rajnath Singh in Moscow, India Pushes Russia to Speed up Defence Contracts Amid Tensions with China', *The Statesman*, 24 June 2020, https://tinyurl.com/fvbk7hm7. Accessed on 17 June 2024.

[333]PIB, 'Raksha Mantri Shri Rajnath Singh's Press Statement at Media Interaction in Moscow', Press Information Bureau, 23 June 2020, https://tinyurl.com/3rvy3dz3. Accessed on 17 June 2024.

as a vital friend to counter the West, was nothing less than remarkable. Just as Singh was acing defence diplomacy in Moscow in 2020, Chinese state-run media mouthpieces publicly warned Russia not to oblige Indian requests. Reminding Moscow that the 'two Asian powers are Russia's very close strategic partners,' China's *People's Daily* advised that 'if Russia wants to soften the hearts of the Chinese and Indians, it is better not to deliver arms to India in such a sensitive moment.'[334] One can imagine how much more bluntly Chinese officials may have conveyed this message to their Russian counterparts behind closed doors. Yet, to Beijing's chagrin and New Delhi's relief, Moscow did not pay heed to any external pressure to water down its commitments to a friend in need.

AN ANCHOR OF STABILITY

It was not the first instance when the Russia-India friendship got a new lease of life in military, diplomatic and geopolitical terms after a sharp deterioration in India's relations with China. If one were to flashback to 1963, just months after China inflicted a crushing defeat on an unprepared and under-defended India, Moscow supplied the first squadron of MiG-21 bombers for New Delhi to deploy along the border with China. At that time, the PLA Air Force had no comparable fighter jets, and Russian hardware was instrumental for India to repel Chinese offensive conduct.

As the Sino-Soviet split widened in the 1960s and 1970s, Moscow kept a close eye on clandestine nuclear weapons programmes of both China and its junior partner Pakistan,

---

[334]Mohan, Geeta, 'Chinese Government Mouthpiece People's Daily Urges Russia Not to Sell Arms to India', *India Today*, 23 June 2020, https://tinyurl.com/4kxekt4n. Accessed on 17 June 2024.

and provided India with 'detailed intelligence information on the progress and problems of both programmes, including satellite imagery and human-derived intelligence.'[335]

Soviet Russia's consistent understanding of India's necessity to possess nukes despite international pressure on New Delhi to sign the NPT, was premised on empathy— India had to have a deterrent against a hostile recognized nuclear weapons power, China. In principle, Russia favoured 'a very tough great-power interpretation of NPT,' but when it concerned India, 'concrete political considerations' of 'India's special strategic position vis-à-vis China' had outweighed non-proliferation goals.[336] Even after the demise of the Soviet Union, the successor state of Russia which was weakened, dependent and friendly to the USA, did not comply with the USA's push to impose collective economic sanctions on India as punishment for its testing of nuclear weapons in 1998. After India explicitly cited the China threat as its motive for going nuclear, Yevgeny Primakov, the then Prime Minister of Russia, assured New Delhi that Russia-India civil nuclear energy and wide-ranging military cooperation would continue unabated, and defended this position saying 'our special relationship with India, and our influence there' was at stake.[337]

Numerous other examples abound from the past and present where Russia acted in ways that ensured India remained a capable and strong power centre in the sub-regions of Asia so that China did not become predominant. During the 1971 Bangladesh Liberation War, Soviet Russia blocked Chinese-sponsored anti-India moves at the UN,

[335]Parthasarathi, Ashok, 'Forty Years of the Indo-Soviet Treaty: A Historic Landmark at the Global Level', *Mainstream*, Vol. 49, No. 34, 2011, https://tinyurl.com/5n8knw6u. Accessed on 17 June 2024.
[336]Quester, George, 'Soviet Policy on the Nuclear Non-Proliferation Treaty', *Cornell International Law Journal*, Vol. 5, No. 1, 1972, pp. 31–32.
[337]Topychkanov, Petr, 'US-Soviet/Russian Dialogue on the Nuclear Weapons Programme of India', *Strategic Analysis*, Vol. 42, No. 3, 2018, p. 258.

warned China from entering the fray as it would risk direct hostilities with Russia, and tied down the PLA through timely troop movements along China's northern borders so that it had no bandwidth to intervene on behalf of Pakistan. India's greatest geopolitical triumph under the leadership of the then Prime Minister Indira Gandhi, which gave it preeminent status in South Asia, was achieved thanks to Russia blocking and frustrating not only the USA but also China. At that time, 'Russia's partisan role was a part of her international strategy, her primary concern being containment of China.'[338]

If India was a useful counterweight for Soviet Russia against both China and the USA during the Cold War era, this logic did not disappear entirely during the less polarized post-Cold War period. Security studies scholar Lavina Lee argued in 2014 that the Russia-India friendship had been sustained and unbroken despite earth-shaking shifts in the international system due to 'shared apprehension about the impact a rising China might have on their respective spheres of influence in Central and South Asia.' She added that 'just as Russia presently bristles against a United States-led unipolar order, so it does against the future prospect of becoming a junior partner to a regionally hegemonic China.'[339]

Russia's approval of the establishment of India's first overseas military bases in Farkhor and Ayni in Tajikistan, its abiding interest in operationalizing the International North-South Transport Corridor (INSTC) linking India to Europe through Central Asia, and its sustained campaign for India to be granted full membership of the Shanghai Cooperation Organisation (SCO), can all be interpreted as part of the

---

[338]Mahmood, Safdar, 'The Role of the Super Powers in the 1971 Conflict', *Strategic Studies*, Vol. 5, No. 2, 1982, p. 52.
[339]Lee, Lavina, 'Russia's Engagement of India: Securing the Longevity of a "Special and Privileged" Strategic Partnership', in Hall, Ian, ed., *The Engagement of India*, op. cit., pp. 62,70.

broader Russian strategy to ensure China is balanced by means of India so that Russia's 'near abroad' in former Soviet spaces does not get overwhelmed by Chinese money and power. Russia is also concerned about Islamist extremism and terrorism spilling out of Afghanistan and Central Asia, a threat which Moscow seeks to blunt through strategic coordination with New Delhi. But the Chinese shadow is in the back of Russia's mind as it appraises India. Elsewhere, I have shown that India too sees Russia's presence in the RIC and BRICS as invaluable for soft balancing of China.[340] Be it through direct military cooperation or coordination in softer multilateral platforms, Russia and India matter to each other due to the China factor.

The China-balancing angle is often shrouded in analyses that highlight giant strides in the Russia-China friendship to jointly combat the West. It is true that Moscow brandishes its 'no limits partnership' with Beijing in the context of the former's all-out confrontation with Washington and its allies. But Russia's structural weakness and vulnerability vis-à-vis China are not lost on the status-conscious and restorationist Kremlin, which aims to re-establish Russia as a great power by regaining control over former Soviet spaces and maintaining a favourable balance of power in Eurasia. India is an indispensable friend for fulfilling these aims. The more powerful India becomes, the easier it is for Russia to breathe in terms of its strategic anxieties of overdependence on China.

A recurring theme in Russia-India bilateral summits and 2+2 ministerial dialogue is the declared objective of working together for a 'more representative, democratic, just and multipolar world order.'[341] It is obsolete to interpret Moscow

---

[340]Chaulia, Sreeram, 'In Spite of the Spite: An Indian View of China and India in BRICS', *Global Policy*, Vol. 12, No. 4, 2021, pp. 519–523.

[341]Kremlin, 'Partnership for Peace, Progress and Prosperity. India-Russia Joint Statement Following the Visit of the President of the Russian Federation', President of Russia, 6 December 2021, https://tinyurl.com/3uh2tjza. Accessed on 17 June 2024.

and New Delhi's repeated emphasis on multipolarity as revisionist intent to whittle down the USA's power because China too is a great power today, and Russia is acutely aware of its own inferiority to China.

Bilateral communiqués between Moscow and Beijing do use the language of jointly achieving a fairer multipolar world order free from Western neo-colonial exploitation and diktats, but their positioning in the world order is miles apart. China's economic heft, military spending and geographical reach are far ahead of those of Russia, whose GDP shrank to around $2 trillion by 2024. The range of instruments China has at its disposal for power projection and influence peddling worldwide, dwarfs Russia's limited means. China specialist Patricia Kim's point that 'Beijing's and Moscow's conflicting priorities and the latter's generally dismal prospects limit the pair's ability to revise the existing global order in a truly coordinated and radical way,'[342] will become more pronounced as the Russia-China power gap keeps widening.

On the other hand, Russia and India have thus far been closer in their material circumstances and positioning in the middle rungs of the international power configuration. The Russia-India friendship's ultimate purpose is to diffuse power from the duopoly of the top two—the USA and China—and bring in more players (including themselves) to the high table of world politics. In the Introduction of this book, we characterized Russia as a former great power that is declining while India was portrayed as a rising or would-be great power. The friendship between Moscow and New Delhi has outlasted seminal global changes and remained 'an anchor of stability in

---

[342]Kim, Patricia, 'The Limits of the No-Limits Partnership: China and Russia Can't be Split but They Can be Thwarted', *Foreign Affairs*, Vol. 102, No. 2, 2023, p. 95.

a complex international situation'[343] owing to this fundamental complementarity.

The Indian International Relations analyst Chandra Rekha has underlined the structural compatibility argument by observing that 'both Russia and India cannot be expected to be treated as equal partners or perhaps will be given a limited role' by China and the USA. That is why there is 'a trust deficiency between India and the US, and between Russia and China, while in the traditional and strategic partnership between India and Russia, there has been no such antipathy towards each other.'[344] A friendship of equals sounds clichéd but fits the Russia-India reality.

THE FRIEND'S ENEMY

In December 2021, as President Vladimir Putin and Prime Minister Narendra Modi extended the Russia-India bilateral military technical cooperation pact for another ten years, and announced a flurry of new defence and civilian commercial deals, the first units of the Russian S-400 Triumf surface-to-air missile defence system began arriving in India. Deemed the most advanced anti-aircraft, anti-missile and anti-drone weapon, with operational ranges of up to 400 kilometres, it got caught in the crosshairs of sharply deteriorating ties between Moscow and Washington, and became a Rorschach test for India's strategic autonomy. Ever since India chose the S-400 as the most suitable for its national security needs vis-à-vis growing threats from China and to a lesser extent from Pakistan, and signed the contract worth $5.5 billion

---

[343]MEA, 'India-Russia Joint Statement During Visit of Prime Minister to Vladivostok', Ministry of External Affairs, Government of India, 5 September 2019, https://tinyurl.com/2bta92cu. Accessed on 17 June 2024.
[344]Rekha, Chandra, *India-Russia Post Cold War Relations: A New Epoch of Cooperation*, 2017, Routledge, Abingdon, p. 210.

in 2018, the prospect of American retaliation hung like the sword of Damocles over the agreement.

Warnings from the USA's legislative and executive branches that India might be punished under the Countering America's Adversaries Through Sanctions Act (CAATSA), an American law aimed at countries engaging in 'major transactions' with the Russian military and intelligence, raised questions about whether the Russian weaponry was worth it for India to antagonize its number one economic partner and 'natural ally' in the Indo-Pacific. Already, China and Turkey, which had ordered the S-400 from Russia, had been subjected to CAATSA sanctions by the USA. In March 2021, Lloyd Austin, the USA's Defense Secretary, publicly warned New Delhi that 'we certainly urge all our allies and partners to move away from Russian equipment […] and really avoid any kind of acquisitions that would trigger sanctions on our behalf.'[345] Parallelly, Washington also played the card of weaning India away from the S-400 by offering USA-made alternatives such as the THAAD (Terminal High Altitude Area Defense) and Patriot systems, neither of which met the gold standard of the S-400.

In spite of the multi-dimensional pressure campaign from the USA, India did not yield and stuck to its sovereign right to acquire the S-400, which was crucial for its national security. New Delhi firmly rebutted Western nods and pushes by holding that while 'India and the US have a comprehensive global strategic partnership,' India also had 'a special and privileged strategic partnership with Russia' and 'has always pursued an independent foreign policy.'[346] Through a combination of

---

[345]Seligman, Lara, 'Austin Hints India's Purchase of Russian Missile System Could Trigger Sanctions', *Politico*, 20 March 2021, https://tinyurl.com/w82mmkp5. Accessed on 17 June 2024.

[346]Miglani, Sanjeev, 'India's Friction with U.S. Rises Over Planned Purchase of Russian S-400 Defence Systems', *Reuters*, 15 January 2021, https://tinyurl.com/4fkeswas. Accessed on 17 June 2024.

diplomatic persuasion and lobbying by pro-India politicians and Indian American legislators in the American Congress, New Delhi eventually rode out the CAATSA storm and more or less secured a waiver from American sanctions in 2022. The argument that won in Washington was that a waiver was 'in the "best interests" of the US since India needs to maintain its Russian weapon systems as it faces "immediate and serious" threats from China along the border.'[347] The USA, which had painted Putin's Russia as a global villain and an archenemy of democracies, had to acknowledge during the S-400 sanctions drama that Russia did concretely help India in hard-balancing China. It was an oblique admission that while Russia never uttered one word of criticism of China, it was quietly and undeniably assisting India to defend itself against Chinese aggression.

But if India successfully deflected American wrath over its military ties with Russia, another controversy erupted about Indian oil purchases from Russia after Putin's fateful decision to invade Ukraine in February 2022. So shocking to NATO's security calculus and Western sensibilities was Russia's war in Ukraine that it triggered an avalanche of economic sanctions on Moscow from Washington and Brussels. With European markets shutting doors to Russian exports, a desperate Moscow pivoted to Asia with cut-price discount offers to lap up Russia's vast quantities of coal, oil and gas. In a span of one year, Russia's export profile altered from dependence on Europe to dependence on China and India as the primary markets for selling its fossil fuels. By the end of 2023, as the devastating war in Ukraine raged between Russia and NATO-backed Ukraine, China became the largest buyer of Russian oil,

---

[347]Sirohi, Seema, 'US House Recommends CAATSA Waiver for India', *The Economic Times*, 15 July 2022, https://tinyurl.com/2jzzskya. Accessed on 17 June 2024.

accounting for 52 per cent of Russia's crude exports, followed by India at 34 per cent, and the EU at merely 8 per cent.[348] Since China was anyway an inveterate authoritarian rival of the West and an ideological bedfellow of Russia, its willingness to absorb Russian fossil fuels simply invited more Western sanctions, and did not raise many eyebrows in the USA and Europe. But democratic India's newfound oil-based dealings with Russia kicked up a furore.

In 2023, Russia had become India's number one oil supplier, single-handedly surpassing the combined volume of oil India received from its traditional trading partners in West Asia/the Middle East—Iraq, Saudi Arabia, the UAE, Kuwait, Oman and Qatar. Western barbs began to be fired thick and fast as to why India, a 'natural ally' of the USA, was 'funding' Russia's horrific war on Ukraine and choosing to stay on 'the wrong side of history'.[349] India responded with what I have described as 'counterpunch diplomacy', reminding the West of the fact that it had filled Russia's coffers for decades by doing the maximum business in oil and gas with it, and deploying logical reasoning and factual narratives to politely but firmly unmask the double standards of the Western liberal establishment.[350] External Affairs Minister Subrahmanyam Jaishankar's plain speak that 'quite honestly, we have seen that the India-Russia relationship has worked to our advantage [...] So, if it works to my advantage, I would like to keep that going,'[351] struck Western elites and

[348]Levi, Isaac, 'October 2023—Monthly Analysis on Russian Fossil Fuel Exports and Sanctions', Centre for Research on Energy and Clean Air, 23 November 2023, https://tinyurl.com/3tce48dd. Accessed on 17 June 2024.
[349]BT, 'India's Decision to Buy Russian Oil Would Put Them On "Wrong Side of History": US', *Business Today*, 18 March 2022, https://tinyurl.com/vvcazz2. Accessed on 17 June 2024.
[350]Chaulia, Sreeram, 'Counterpunch Diplomacy', *The Week*, 19 June 2022, p. 33.
[351]Patel, Shivam, and Krishna Das, 'India Says Russia Oil Deals Advantageous as Yellen Visits Delhi', *Reuters*, 8 November 2022, https://tinyurl.com/4sxjnvzj. Accessed on 17 June 2024.

commentators as immoral and ungrateful for all the 'strategic generosity' that the USA had been showing to India. But New Delhi did not budge one inch on compromising its energy security. It used the stand-off over Russian oil, and the broader Western criticism of major developing countries for not adequately condemning Russia's invasion of Ukraine, to burnish its credentials as a leader of the Global South whose basic needs cannot be compromised to satisfy proxy wars of great powers.

Not for the first time, Russia was the touchstone for India to demonstrate its strategic autonomy and stature as a rising or leading power in the world, with a steadfastly independent foreign policy. The Modi government's stance on the Russia-Ukraine War unleashed a wave of nationalistic pride and multi-partisan endorsement domestically in India, and also earned gratitude from Moscow, which direly needed to counter Western attempts to isolate it internationally. Putin's frequent public remarks wondering how India managed to adhere to its core national interests in the face of Western pressure to dissociate itself from Russia, were expressions of genuine thankfulness and also stratagems to goad India to stay the course. They deserve full citation here.

I cannot imagine that Modi could be intimidated or forced to take any actions, steps and decisions that are contrary to the national interests of India and the Indian people. And there is such pressure, I know. By the way, he and I never even talk about this. I just look at what is happening from the outside, and sometimes, to be honest, I'm even surprised at his tough position on defending the national interests of the Indian state […] Relations between Russia and India are developing progressively in all directions, and the main guarantor of this is the policy pursued by Prime Minister Mr. Modi.[352]

From Moscow's perspective, New Delhi is ushering in a multipolar world order by thumbing its nose at the West and proving that it has the guts to defy Washington. Russia's best-case scenario is that India distances itself from the West, and joins a troika with itself and China to 'democratize' the international order. Through RIC and BRICS, Russia has tried to soften and manage the China-India rivalry from spilling over into an all-out war. The Russian Foreign Minister Sergey Lavrov's remarks that 'we are interested in these two great nations [India and China] to be friends,' and that 'Russia is trying to be helpful' in reconciling the two Asian rivals, clearly conveyed Moscow's wish.[353] But returning to the halcyon days when emerging powers congregated in minilaterals to form counter-hegemonic coalitions for soft balancing against the USA is no longer possible because the world order has shifted, and China has climbed to the rank of a great power that is bellicose towards India. Moscow has grudgingly come to terms with New Delhi's acute threat perceptions about Beijing, and is now content as long as India does not abandon Russia. In one sense, Russia does not also mind China-India conflict, given that hundreds of its defence manufacturing units have thrived on sales of weaponry to India and China—its first and second biggest defence markets.

India's careful balancing act of extracting benefits from

---

[352]ANI, 'PM Modi Can't be Forced to Take Actions Contrary to Indian Interests: Russia's Putin', *Hindustan Times*, 8 December 2023, https://tinyurl.com/27tdub6n. Accessed on 17 June 2024.

[353]Chaudhury, Dipanjan, 'Want India and China to be Friends, Can Help Reduce Tensions: Russian Foreign Minister Sergey Lavrov', *The Economic Times*, 4 March 2023, https://tinyurl.com/bdzm785c. Accessed on 17 June 2024.

the USA and Europe in one set of issue areas, while also notching up concrete gains from Russia in other domains is not guaranteed to have smooth sailing forever, particularly if Russia opens more fronts to literally and figuratively fight the West. Ideally, India would prefer that Russia and the USA get along and have a functional relationship, if not become best friends, so that New Delhi does not have to worry about situations where it is under duress to choose between Moscow and Washington. Given Russia's potential to undercut Chinese hegemony in Eurasia, India would also welcome Washington and Moscow striking a grand bargain so that Beijing is cornered, and its strategic space is constricted. But the no-holds-barred conflict in one form or the other that characterizes Russia's ties with the West has escalated year over year, and is unlikely to thaw as long as Putin and his brand of geopolitics prevail in the Kremlin.

Russian foreign policy did have a brief pro-Western slant when the 'Atlanticist' school of thought had the upper hand in the early 1990s under President Boris Yeltsin. But this did not last. NATO's military intervention in Russian-allied Serbia to carve out a de facto independent state in Kosovo (1999) was interpreted by Russians as 'shattering the dream that the West would accept Russia as an equal partner,' and confirmed their fears that the arrogant USA believed 'Russia had "lost" the Cold War and Washington was free to dictate terms to the loser.'[354] Under Putin's long rule, there were phases when Russia extended tactical cooperation to the USA. After the 11 September 2001 (9/11) terrorist attacks, Moscow enthusiastically endorsed the USA-led military coalition to access Central Asian countries as launchpads to invade and overthrow the Taliban in Afghanistan. At

---

[354]Pedraja, René De la, *Putin Confronts the West: The Logic of Russian Foreign Relations, 1999–2020*, 2021, McFarland, Jefferson, p. 57.

that time, Putin floated the possibility that Russia and the USA 'can be partners and, in the more distant future, even allies.'[355] But this optimism faded because Washington did not keep the implicit bargain to 'continue to take Russian security concerns seriously and to treat Russia with the status befitting a great power in return for Russian support of or acquiescence to US actions.'[356] The fifth and sixth rounds of NATO's eastward enlargement in 2004 and 2009 confirmed to Putin and nationalistic Russians longing for a return to great power status that the USA was 'a malicious, devilish superpower that aims to destroy the Russian essence,' and revived the old historical 'paranoid fear of being surrounded by enemies.'[357]

Domestic politics in Russia and the USA have also poisoned ties beyond repair. The Russian elite's foreboding that Washington would use 'colour revolutions' and other kinds of subterfuge to erode Russia's sphere of influence in Eastern Europe and Central Asia and unseat Putin from power has been a source of unending friction. In Washington, claims that Putin meddled in the 2016 presidential election to tip the balance in favour of Donald Trump, and sensational allegations of Russian agents carrying out hit jobs against dissidents in Western countries, meant that all bridges with Moscow were burnt. The full-scale war in Ukraine from 2022 was a culmination of bad blood that had accumulated for decades.

The more Russia's ties with the West have soured, the greater has been Moscow's inclination to see China and India

[355]House, Karen Elliott, and Andrew Higgins, 'Putin Says Bush Shouldn't Go It Alone When Deciding How to Deal with Iraq', *The Wall Street Journal*, 11 February 2002, https://tinyurl.com/28k3p7pn. Accessed on 17 June 2024.
[356]Ambrosio, Thomas, *Challenging America's Global Pre-eminence: Russia's Quest for Multipolarity*, 2005, Ashgate, Aldershot, p. 143.
[357]Nalbandov, Robert, *Not by Bread Alone: Russian Foreign Policy Under Putin*, 2016, Potomac Books, Sterling, pp.118, 128.

as its two primary strategic partners and fallback options to create a multipolar or polycentric world. When relations with the USA and Europe were tense but not irretrievably ruptured, Moscow adopted a 'multivector foreign policy approach' of establishing 'constructive relations with all potential poles of the world,' and maintaining a 'balance between various partners and their specific interests.'[358] This meant pursuing friendships with China, India and Brazil, and simultaneously cooperating on specific issue areas with the EU and the USA.

The multivector policy's geopolitical implication in Asia was that Russia did 'not at all intend to take sides or be involved in any schemes to "contain China", while it also did "not intend to build an alliance relationship with China that would be directed against any party".'[359] The 2000 Declaration announcing the Russia-India strategic partnership clarified that it was 'not directed against any other State or group of States, and does not need to create a military-political alliance.'[360] Moscow's multivector policy had dovetailed with India's 'multi-alignment' strategy (*see* Introduction), wherein both pragmatically kept their doors open to the West, while deepening bilateral cooperation. That era of countries being friends with everyone has, however, come to a close. Russia no longer has any 'vector' going towards the West, following its 2022 invasion of Ukraine, and India has little reason to see

[358]Streltsov, Dmitri, 'The National Interests of Russia in the Asia Pacific Region', in Kundu, Nivedita, ed., *India-Russia Strategic Partnership: Challenges and Prospects*, 2010, Academic Foundation, New Delhi, pp. 138, 141.

[359]Trifonov, Victor, 'Triangle of Russia-India-China: Current Situation and Future Prospects', in Singh, Jasjit, ed., *India-Russia Relations*, 2012, KW Publishers, New Delhi, p. 97.

[360]MEA, 'Declaration on Strategic Partnership Between the Republic of India and the Russian Federation', Ministry of External Affairs, Government of India, 3 October 2000, https://tinyurl.com/33jy3256. Accessed on 17 June 2024.

any alignment with China whatsoever after the 2020 Galwan Valley clash.

CONVERGENCE TO DISSONANCE?

The radical reorganization of the Russia-USA-China-India quadrangle has major implications for the future of the Moscow-New Delhi friendship. Russia's 'new foreign policy concept' of 2023 slammed the Western 'policy of confrontation and hegemonic ambitions,' and hailed the advent of a multipolar world order, which is presented as an inevitability that cannot be stopped by the West's 'neocolonialism' and 'logic of global dominance.' It also recommitted Moscow to 'comprehensive deepening of ties and enhancement of coordination with friendly sovereign global centres of power which are located on the Eurasian continent and committed to approaches which coincide in principle with the Russian approaches to a future world order and solutions for key problems of the world politics,' namely China and India. It presented these two Asian countries as key to Russia's quest to overturn the unfair Western-made international system.[361]

Although the new concept was a crystal-clear elucidation of Putin's core beliefs and preferences, it faced serious headwinds due to the widening fissures in world politics. The Russian invasion of Ukraine led to Moscow burning all bridges with Washington and Brussels, where the very word 'Russia' evoked extreme negative feelings. In earlier times, Russia had a grand strategic goal of dividing Europe from the USA, and thereby weakening the threat posed by NATO. Once the USA and Europe coalesced around defending Ukraine's

---

[361]MID, 'The Concept of the Foreign Policy of the Russian Federation', 31 March 2023, The Ministry of Foreign Affairs of the Russian Federation, https://tinyurl.com/44k4fu3z. Accessed on 17 June 2024.

sovereignty, Russia was compelled to look at China and India as its main go-to to push back against the West as a whole.

The problem here is that Moscow continues to club Beijing and New Delhi together as part and parcel of a united front to counterbalance the West. But Beijing and New Delhi have developed distinct policies towards the West that do not coincide with Moscow's worldview. China still enjoys humongous trade and investment links with the USA and Europe. Beijing has not yet given up on wanting to access Western technology and capital despite growing Western restrictions on transfers of sensitive materials to China. India's economic and military ties with the USA, France (*see* Chapter 5), Britain, Germany, Italy and Australia (*see* Chapter 2) are booming.

India wants to leverage its Western partnerships to push back against Chinese expansionism. Russia's hope that its 'two great friends'—China and India—can get along well with each other and join hands with it to check Western influence, is not based on an objective reading of the contemporary configuration of forces, and the insecurity that India feels vis-à-vis China's coercion. The 2023 Russian foreign policy concept vowed that Moscow would work with New Delhi to develop 'resistance to destructive actions of unfriendly states and their alliances,'[362] which suggested that Russia believed Western powers were unfriendly and unnecessary for India's rise.

The fundamental Russian misreading is that it assumes China to be a benign and non-hegemonic actor, an assessment that India and the USA do not share. During the Trump administration, when a top American official showed Chinese maps depicting Russian territories as part of China 'to underscore the threat China posed,' Putin's confidante

---

[362]Ibid.

had scoffed and retorted 'we know who our enemies are.'[363] Russia's refusal to even accept the validity of the term Indo-Pacific, while India's entire grand strategy rests on the success of this construct, is a core difference that cannot be wished away. Moscow's repeated critiques of Quad as an Asian NATO, and a military containment alliance that is part of a 'bloc architecture against Russia and China'[364] mean that Russia feels it has been pushed to the wall by the West, and has no option but to accept China's version of what is happening in Asia. Worrisome from an Indian and Quad perspective are joint naval and aerial military patrols and exercises by Russia and China in the Sea of Japan, the East China Sea and the West Pacific as a tit-for-tat to Quad and AUKUS manoeuvres targeting China.[365] Although Russia's force posture and military asset deployment are primarily aimed at pushing back NATO in Eastern Europe, token Russian joint operations with China in the Indo-Pacific are, to say the least, awkward for India. Moscow did intervene forcefully in West Asia/the Middle East and Africa to displace the USA and France from their spheres of influence, but in the Indo-Pacific, there is neither intent nor capability that Russia can bring to bear to challenge China.

In light of the intensifying fault lines in Eurasia, as well as the economic, technological and military degradation of Russia due to Western sanctions imposed since the Russia-

[363]Grove, Thomas, Alan Cullison and Bojan Pancevski, 'How Putin's Right-Hand Man Took Out Prigozhin', *The Wall Street Journal*, 22 December 2023, https://tinyurl.com/52czp8tv. Accessed on 17 June 2024.

[364]PTI, 'Russian FM Lavrov Accuses NATO Making "Overtures" to India to Create "Additional Problems" in Ties with China', *The Indian Express*, 20 January 2023, https://tinyurl.com/y8a9hj6p. Accessed on 17 June 2024.

[365]Xuanzun, Liu, and Guo Yuandan, 'China, Russia to Hold Third Joint Naval Patrol in West, North Pacific', *Global Times*, 26 July 2023, https://tinyurl.com/5have6bc. Accessed on 17 June 2024.

Ukraine War, there is also a practical question mark about how Russia and India can sustain their 'special and privileged strategic partnership' in the future. Can a Russia that has no access to Western components and know-how still remain a world leader in manufacturing and co-producing advanced weapons systems which bolster India's military deterrence against China? The phenomenal BrahMos supersonic cruise missile, which was co-developed by Russia and India in the first decade of the 21st century when Russia could tap into Western components and technology, may not be repeatable thanks to Russia being cut off from the West, and its reliance shifting to China for future innovation.

Delays in Russian deliveries of the S-400 components and of the Chakra-3 nuclear-powered Akula class submarine to India due to the Russia-Ukraine War and Western sanctions have raised doubts in Indian minds about Moscow's capability, albeit not its political will, to keep meeting India's crucial military needs. In 2022, the American and Indian scholars Spenser Warren and Sumit Ganguly argued that Western 'sanctions on the Russian economy, combined with increased demand for parts and weapons by the Russian military, have already hampered Russian arms sales and transfers to India and other arms recipients.' They predicted that 'if sanctions continue to affect the Russian arms industry, and/or the war in Ukraine becomes a long-term, protracted conflict, and the Russian military's demand for parts and weapons remains high, Russian arms exports could be hampered for several years,' and 'India may be forced to find alternative sources of weapons, including from Russia's traditional rivals.'[366] If India looks to Russia's rivals for arms, Moscow could pay it back in the same coin by selling more advanced weapons

---

[366]Warren, Spenser, and Sumit Ganguly, 'India-Russia Relations After Ukraine', *Asian Survey*, Vol. 62, No. 5–6, 2022, pp. 818, 823.

to Pakistan, a red line that has in the past ruffled feathers in the Russia-India friendship.

In the decade from 2013 to 2022, prior to the Russia-Ukraine War, Russia's share of arms exports to India fell from 64 per cent to 45 per cent, while France's share rose to 29 per cent and that of the USA went up to 11 per cent. According to the Stockholm International Peace Research Institute (SIPRI), between 2014 and 2018, and 2019 and 2023, Russia accounted for only 36 per cent of weapons that India bought, while France closed in with as much as 30 per cent. SIPRI observed that 'Russia's position as India's main arms supplier is under pressure due to strong competition from other supplier states, increased Indian arms production and since 2022, the constraints on Russia's arms exports related to its invasion of Ukraine.'[367]

In Chapters 5 and 6, the reader will see how France and Israel became protagonists in India's diversification strategy from Russian military hardware. Here, it is worth noting that the Indian Navy and Air Force have considerably lowered their reliance on Russian weaponry. Between 2000 and 2020, the Russian-made share of India's total aircraft fell from 81 to 67 per cent, and the share of Russian-made Indian naval ships declined from 58 to 44 per cent. On the other hand, Russian-manufactured armoured vehicles still accounted for 98 per cent of the Indian Army's stocks by 2020.[368] From a war-fighting lens, if these trends hold, it means that India's power projection and counterbalancing in the maritime spaces of the crucial Indo-Pacific theatre will

---

[367]Pandit, Rajat, 'India Remains World's Largest Arms Importer, with Russia, France & US as the Biggest Suppliers', *The Times of India*, 14 March 2023, https://tinyurl.com/4wp9yy6e. Accessed on 17 June 2024.
[368]TE, 'India is Cutting Back its Reliance on Russian Arms', *The Economist*, 14 April 2022, https://tinyurl.com/5335dc3p. Accessed on 17 June 2024.

depend less on Russia. Russia's aircraft carrier and nuclear submarines were once the pride of the Indian Navy, but that is a bygone era.

Apart from the hiccups and headwinds in the core area of defence cooperation, there is the geopolitical question mark on whether a Russia that is progressively leaning on China can really give India strategic space to ensure a balance of power in Asia, or if the Russia-India strategic partnership will dilute into a purely transactional one of buying and selling products for monetary gains. Putin has been cognisant of the risk of over-dependence on China. He remarked in 2023 that 'if our trade turnover with China this year is close to 200 billion [dollars], it would be right for us to increase it with India [which had reached $45 billion].'[369] Operationalization of the INSTC and the Chennai-Vladivostok Eastern Maritime Corridor hold out promise for Russia-India economic exchanges to be scaled up, albeit not matching the volumes of Russia-China trade and investment.

We can safely assume that India will remain 'special and privileged' for Russia as it enables the latter to sustain its balance or hedge for strategic autonomy vis-à-vis China. One of the core rationales of the Russia-India friendship has been that 'both sides intended their mutual relationship to offset the growing role of China,' and this was the reason why 'the elite in Moscow was convinced of the full convergence between Russia's and India's interests on the international arena.'[370] For the moment, this calculation holds. Thus far, Russia has continued to share with India whatever it asked for in the domains of military, energy security, outer space exploration,

---

[369]ANI, 'PM Modi Can't be Forced to Take Actions Contrary to Indian Interests', op. cit.

[370]Rodkiewicz, Witold, 'The Twilight of the Russian-Indian Strategic Partnership', Centre for Eastern Studies, 10 August 2023, https://tinyurl.com/4t8mhhs7. Accessed on 17 June 2024.

etc., without succumbing to Chinese remonstrations. India, in turn, has stuck to a balanced position on the Russia-Ukraine War and NATO's eastward expansion, instead of falling in line with the USA. Russia's self-image as a former great power, a proud power centre, and independent pole in a multipolar order offers some assurance that it will endeavour to never turn into a puppet of China.

Still, given the declining fortunes of Russia and the enlarging geostrategic cracks of the 'new Cold War', it is obvious that Moscow's dream of an RIC axis to counter the West is not viable. Applying the realpolitik logic of Kautilya's *Rajamandala* or Circle of Kings, the enemy's enemy is supposed to be a friend. If China is India's enemy, what exactly is Russia going to mean for India in time to come? One cannot shy away from reckoning with this question, at least in the interest of the longer term. The International Relations scholar Rajan Menon and the former American intelligence officer Eugene Rumer have sketched two possibilities for the future. In the first scenario, Russia becomes a vassal state of China and grows vulnerable to Chinese demands that 'Russia significantly curtail or even end its arms sales to India,' culminating in Russia being 'supplanted in the Indian arms market by the United States and its European allies.' The alternative scenario is the continuation of Russia's balancing act between India and China, wherein Moscow offers New Delhi 'more advanced weapons systems, especially on favorable financing terms; long-term energy deals at discounted prices [...] and a steadfast refusal to takes sides on the issues that divide China and India.' And New Delhi, 'facing an increasingly hostile and powerful China [...] will not want to abandon its long-standing security relationship with Russia, and will work hard to preserve it, in part because of a lack of confidence that the United States can be counted upon as a reliable security partner.'[371]

The accumulated historical goodwill and elite bureaucratic understandings between Russia and India could ensure the second scenario wins out. A look at the Russia-India relationship in the past reveals that there have been patches when it stagnated, but it was again purposefully revived by leaders on both sides. Writing in the mid-1990s, when the 'special' nature of Russia-India friendship had disappeared owing to tectonic shifts after the end of the Cold War, Vidya Nadkarni was sanguine that 'since Russia and India appear to have no conflicting "vital interests", neither acrimony nor bellicosity is imaginable.' She forecasted that the friendship 'will remain pragmatic, having neither the seeds of an alliance nor the germs of total rupture.'[372] But once Putin arrived and deliberately reinvested energy into the relationship by declaring a strategic partnership in 2000, there was a concerted effort for wilful revival of the 'special' friendship.

Current trends are not unlike those of the 1990s, with question marks and doubts on India's ability to prolong the bear hug with a weakening Russia. Shakespeare's maxim, 'What's past is prologue,' may well apply again, and the pulls and pressures of the emerging multipolar world order could cyclically push leaders in Moscow and New Delhi to once again prioritize and push the Russia-India friendship back on an upswing. Compared to India's other close friendships, the Russia-India strategic partnership stands on few legs and is not broad-based. But those few legs have been hefty and their salience in global power rebalancing cannot be understated. External Affairs Minister Jaishankar's observations in 2023

---

[371]Menon, Rajan, and Eugene Rumer, 'Russia and India: A New Chapter', Carnegie Endowment for International Peace, 20 September 2022, https://tinyurl.com/43c5e3nz. Accessed on 17 June 2024.
[372]Nadkarni, Vidya, 'India and Russia: The End of a Special Relationship?' *Naval War College Review*, Vol. 48, No. 4, 1995, p. 29.

about the eternal nature of the friendship indicated what lay ahead. 'There is an understanding in both countries that as big powers in the Asian continent, there is a kind of structural basis for having to get along, wanting to get along. And so we take great care to make sure the relationship is working.'[373]

[373] Atri, Pawan, '"Very, Very Steady": EAM Jaishankar on Russia-India Relationship', *Sputnik*, 27 September 2023, https://tinyurl.com/ycyj9ycu. Accessed on 17 June 2024.

5

INDEPENDENT AND ALIGNED: FRANCE AND INDIA IN A MULTIPOLAR WORLD

France and India are moving ahead based on a historic trust [...] Our strategic interests converge in the Indo-Pacific because we have the same viewpoint about it. We want to combat hegemony and keep the Indo-Pacific an area open and free from all forms of domination. Our militaries are consulting in a regularized manner and are making full contributions to maintain peace and security in the Indo-Pacific and sustain respect for international law.[374]

—Emmanuel Macron, President of France, 2023

O n 14 July 2023, the Champs-Élysées was the epitome of pageantry and grandeur. The who's who of French politics and officialdom had assembled to witness the annual Bastille Day parade, featuring 6,500 marching soldiers, 94 airplanes and helicopters, 219 ground vehicles and

---

[374]ANI, 'PM Modi, French President Macron Hold Joint Press Conference in Paris', *Asian News International*, 14 July 2023, https://tinyurl.com/4rjry3t5. Accessed on 18 June 2024.

200 horses. Apart from the customary showcasing of France's military prowess, the parade's tradition of honouring 'certain people and causes', and bolstering diplomatic ties with friendly countries, whose troops are 'invited to join the parade as a gesture of friendship and alliance,'[375] was on full display. On the VIP viewing deck, amidst a sea of mostly Western dark-suited attendees, a man in white ethnic Indian attire with a blue trademark jacket stood out as he mingled with France's First Lady Brigitte Macron and cabinet members. Once President Emmanuel Macron arrived, and was ceremonially escorted to the dais, the man in ethnic Indian attire stepped forward, clasped his hands and embraced him warmly, patting him on the back. It was the highest symbolic gesture for a notable foreign leader by France since 2017, when President Donald Trump of the USA had been the show-stopper at Bastille Day.

Prime Minister Narendra Modi's presence as Guest of Honour for France's most important national event, coinciding with the 25th anniversary of the France-India strategic partnership, was widely covered in the country's news media. *Le Monde* reported that Macron had 'awarded the country's highest honour, the Grand Cross of the Légion d'Honneur (Legion of Honour), to Modi [...] to salute the role of the prime minister in the excellent relations of friendship and confidence that unite France and India.'[376] While mentioning that French Left-wing activists were fuming at Modi's so-called illiberal rule in India, *Le Parisien* termed his presence 'an opportunity to consolidate the strategic relationship with this key international actor,' and reminded readers that India

[375]F24, 'Bastille Day: A Brief History of France's July 14 National Holiday', *France 24*, 13 July 2023, https://tinyurl.com/cmc4mbvb. Accessed on 19 June 2024.
[376]LM, 'France Honours India's Modi During Bastille Day Celebrations', *Le Monde*, 14 July 2023, https://tinyurl.com/yc6yf3jk. Accessed on 19 June 2024.

had approved plans to purchase 26 additional Rafale fighter jets in their naval variant for India's aircraft carrier, as well as more French submarines.[377] *Time* observed that 'about 240 Indian troops led the march down the Champs-Élysées before thousands of French forces, and French-made Indian warplanes joined the traditional fly-by above the event,' and concluded that 'the choice of India comes as France looks to further strengthen cooperation on fighting climate change, military sales and the strategic Indo-Pacific region.'[378]

THE REALPOLITIK BOND

The prioritization of pragmatism and geopolitical considerations over partisan value judgements about domestic politics was also evident in the way the leaderships of the two countries presented the essence of the bilateral friendship during Modi's 2023 visit to Paris. The Indian leader told the French financial daily *Les Echos* that 'our partnership aims to advance a free, open, inclusive, secure and stable Indo-Pacific region, working together and with others in the region who share our vision.' He referred to 'a strong defence and security component that extends from seabed to space' that 'also seeks to help other countries in the region and strengthen the regional institutions for security cooperation and norm setting.' He emphasized the strategic intent of the friendship by saying, 'we are working together not just to strengthen India's defence industrial base and our joint operational capabilities,' but also to 'collaborate to support the security needs of other countries, including on defence equipment.' He also spoke

---

[377]LP, 'July 14 Ceremonies, Arms Contracts...What Indian Prime Minister Modi Will Do in Paris', *Le Parisien*, 13 July 2023, https://tinyurl.com/2654a83d. Accessed on 19 June 2024.

[378]Chartlon, Angela, and Youcef Bounab, 'France Celebrates Bastille Day with Pomp, Extra Police—and a Tribute to India', *Time*, 14 July 2023.

about congruence with France 'to safeguard our economic and security interests, ensure freedom of navigation and commerce, advance the rule of international law in the region [...and] work with other countries to develop their capabilities and support their efforts to make free sovereign choices.'[379]

Statecraft and statist considerations were also reflected by Macron, who tweeted in both Hindi and English, describing India as 'a giant in the history of the world that will have a determining role in our future, a strategic partner and friend.'[380] Earlier in 2018, when Macron was received with fanfare in India, he had declared, 'India is our priority and has always been. India has been France's first ally in the region. It is the entry point for France in the region, and my aim is to make France the entry point for India to Europe.'[381] Notwithstanding demands from the political Left in France to take up domestic human rights concerns in Modi's India, Paris rarely raised such issues with New Delhi and never veered from the strategic calculus. French scholar Jean-Luc Racine explained this approach as follows: 'French foreign policy is set by the president. The Élysée [presidential palace] does consider human rights from time to time, but basically the position is the world is what it is, it's a matter of realpolitik.'[382] Little wonder then that French leaders have been chief guests at India's Republic Day parades for a record six times, the latest

---

[379]Barré, Nicolas, and Clément Perruche, 'EXCLUSIVE—Narendra Modi: <<I See India as a Strong Shoulder for the 'Global South'>>, *Les Echos*, 13 July 2023, https://tinyurl.com/f3d2k9z8. Accessed on 18 April 2024.

[380]ANI, 'French President Emmanuel Macron Tweets in Hindi', *Asian News International*, 14 July 2023, https://tinyurl.com/2avv9jf4. Accessed on 19 June 2024.

[381]TAA, 'India Is, Has Always Been Our Priority: French Prez Emmanuel Macron', *The Asian Age*, 10 March 2018, https://tinyurl.com/4par89y2. Accessed on 19 June 2024.

[382]Jacinto, Leela, 'Arms, Not Democratic Values, On Parade as Macron Hosts India's Modi on Bastille Day', *France 24*, 13 July 2023, https://tinyurl.com/47ncyuad. Accessed on 19 June 2024.

being in 2024, when Macron graced the occasion where India's full military might and national strength were on display for the world to take note.

The feeling that France respects India for what it is, rather than hectoring it with a condescending and hypocritical attitude the way some liberal Western allies of France periodically do about threats to religious tolerance and civil society, is one of the many intangible factors that has gone into making this a deep and mutually respectful friendship. With France remaining 'relatively quiet' about controversial political topics in India[383], India has reciprocated by maintaining a studied silence about periodic outbreaks of racial violence, riots and debilitating labour unrest in France, deeming them internal affairs. As democratic republics with social and ethnic diversity, both countries have flaws and problems. But one cannot build an international friendship if the urge for finger-pointing and fault-finding is not restrained. In Chapter 3, we cited Avery Goldstein's parameters of a strategic partnership as involving 'muting disagreements about domestic politics'. France and India have abided by this golden rule by keeping their eyes on the ball of regional and global coordination, thereby reaping the full dividends of a thriving strategic partnership.

CONFLUENCE OF AUTONOMIES

That France is an atypical member of the rich Western countries' club is obvious not only from its hands-off approach to India's domestic politics, but also from its conscious attempt over decades to pursue an independent foreign policy line

---

[383]RFI, 'Arms Deals Overshadow Rights Concerns as France Welcomes India's PM Modi', *Radio France Internationale*, 14 July 2023, https://tinyurl.com/2x76rsbd. Accessed on 19 June 2024.

towards India. The beginning of France's strategic partnership with India in 1998 was a manifestation of its much-touted strategic autonomy principle that harked back to the legacy of President Charles de Gaulle, founder of the Fifth Republic. De Gaulle had 'twin goals of disengaging France from Washington's hegemony and of building a European Europe' that is liberated 'from the American colossus.'[384] His grand vision for France 'to lead Europe as a "balancing third force" in a world suffering under the hegemony of the two superpowers—the United States and the Soviet Union'[385] may not have been practical, and did not find concurrence with fellow European powers, but it seeded a rebellious tradition of French foreign policy that sought to set itself apart from 'the Anglo-Saxons', i.e. the USA and the UK, and pursue its own interests.

During the Cold War, France's decisions to recognize communist China, enter into a rapprochement with Soviet Russia, withdraw from NATO's integrated military command, place its nuclear arsenal outside NATO structures, and expel American troops from French bases, were markers of an adamantly autonomous mindset, coupled with a nostalgic great-power mentality. Years after De Gaulle exited the scene, political theorist Philip Cerny noted that 'the presidentialist style and symbolic primacy of the assertion of French independence and *grandeur* have become institutionalised.'[386] Arguably, these traits continue to this day, no matter who the occupant of the Élysée Palace is.

[384]Kuisel, Richard, 'De Gaulle's Dilemma: The American Challenge and Europe', *French Politics & Society*, Vol. 8, No. 4, 1990, p. 14.
[385]Larson, Scott, 'Charles De Gaulle and the Break with Atlanticism', National Defense University, 1995, https://tinyurl.com/4wu62sa9. Accessed on 19 June 2024.
[386]Cerny, Philip, *The Politics of Grandeur: Ideological Aspects of de Gaulle's Foreign Policy*, 1980, Cambridge University Press, Cambridge, p. 5.

In earlier chapters, we saw how the USA and its allies reacted harshly and imposed economic sanctions and suspended aid when India conducted nuclear weapons tests in May 1998. In the months before the Pokhran-II nuclear explosions, Washington and other Western capitals had begun issuing warnings to deter India from going nuclear. But true to its unique Gaullist pedigree, France under President Jacques Chirac decided to break ranks with its American ally, and took an empathetic stand. Instead of pressurizing India, Chirac landed in New Delhi in January 1998, and announced the launch of 'a global partnership grounded on our complementarities and our common interests,' dangling cooperation in defence, energy, space, and environmental protection. What stood out at that time was Chirac's offer to focus on India's energy security by bringing French nuclear power experts and finding practical workarounds to the NPT 'rules of the game' so that France, as the world's leading nuclear energy power, could assist India's renewables future.[387] After Pokhran-II, as the West came down on India like a ton of bricks, Chirac doubled down on civil nuclear cooperation, and helped India avoid complete international isolation. In the mid-1990s, France itself had been braving barbs from allies for conducting nuclear tests 'to guarantee the reliability of its nuclear deterrent force,'[388] and hence did not see any point in adopting double standards when it came to India's national security. Mohan Kumar, a former Indian Ambassador to France, recalled that Chirac 'was keen to deepen ties with India at a time when we were seen as a pariah nation' because 'he viewed India as a major and emerging superpower and

[387]JC, 'Discours de M. Jacques CHIRAC, Président de la République, à Vigyan-Bhavan', Jacques Chirac, 25 January 1998, https://tinyurl.com/8kncasjb. Accessed on 19 June 2024.
[388]Drozdiak, William, 'France Defends Nuclear Test', *The Washington Post*, 3 October 1995, https://tinyurl.com/ef5vcse3. Accessed on 19 June 2024.

at par with China' and 'took a bet on India that paid off.'[389]

The historian Jayita Sarkar has shown that France's exceptional treatment of India goes back a long time. Right since the 1950s, France had defied its Western allies, who were 'keen on maintaining high censorship and control over nuclear technology and information,' and developed 'nuclear proximity' with India by sharing know-how, expertise and eventually nuclear fuel for the Tarapur nuclear power plant. When India conducted its first nuclear test, Pokhran-I, in 1974, there had been 'hostile reactions from Canada, Australia, Japan, surprise from the United States, and silence from the Soviet Union,' but France openly congratulated India for its 'scientific feat', making it 'the only Western country that expressed encouragement.' Sarkar attributes this French *noblesse oblige* to Paris' willingness to see New Delhi as an 'almost equal' and the absence of 'neocolonial exploitation'[390], which mattered a lot to a sensitive developing country like India.

The comradeship that naturally comes to a middle power and a rising power that treasure strategic autonomy, and see each other as ushering in a multipolar world order, is a cornerstone of the France-India friendship. In Racine's words, France presents 'an interesting profile' for India as it is 'strong enough to have something to offer; not strong enough to put too much pressure in search of grand strategy games.'[391] The Indian author Abhinayan Iyer has echoed this compatibility

---

[389]Basu, Nayanima, 'Late French President Jacques Chirac Saw India as a Power, not a Land of Snake-Charmers', *The Print*, 27 September 2019, https://tinyurl.com/28ay6wdh. Accessed on 19 June 2024.

[390]Sarkar, Jayita, '"The Middle Powers" Congruence: India, France, and Nuclear Technology', Center for the Advanced Study of India, 29 June 2015, https://tinyurl.com/4x5jzt4f. Accessed on 19 June 2024.

[391]Racine, Jean-Luc, 'India's Foreign Policy Toward France: A Strategic Partnership First', in Ganguly, Sumit, ed., *Engaging the World: Indian Foreign Policy Since 1947*, 2015, Oxford University Press, Oxford, p. 267.

factor by writing that 'India's institutional hesitations are plausibly less intense in relation to France, a middle power that comes with much less political baggage than the United States.'[392]

In Chapter 3, we analysed debates about the USA's 'strategic generosity' towards India from the first decade of the 21st century. France does not brag about being generous, but its munificence and respect for India far predated that of any Western country, thanks to its autonomous identity and hard-nosed pursuit of its own national interests. As French and Indian scholars have observed, 'shared understanding that strategic autonomy and sovereignty is only possible with strong indigenous capacities in key sectors has led to Indo-French cooperation in nuclear and space research since the 1950s.' Further, India's growing kitty of defence contracts with France also illustrates 'New Delhi and Paris' common aim at maximizing their strategic autonomy.'[393] This thread runs all the way from the official launch of the France-India strategic partnership in 1998 until today, with every milestone in cooperation reflecting the underlying mutual capacity-building motive.

There are differences in what France considers to be strategic autonomy and a multipolar world, and what India means by these terms. France remains a NATO member and an ally of the USA, while India refrains from formal alliances. Hubert Védrine, the former Minister for Europe and Foreign Affairs of France, once clarified that 'France's call for a multipolar world has nothing to do with any anti-

---

[392]Iyer, Abhinayan, *France and India: Defence and Security in Indo-Pacific*, 2023, HOW Academics, New Delhi, p. 104.
[393]Droin, Mathieu, Rajesh Basrur, Nicolas Blarel and Jyotsna Mehra, 'France and India: Two Nuances of "Strategic Autonomy"', Center for Strategic and International Studies, 13 July 2023, https://tinyurl.com/5fpjxx6r. Accessed on 19 June 2024.

Americanism,' and that 'we are friends and allies, but not aligned.'[394] In the case of India, the converse holds. It is aligned with the USA in the Indo-Pacific but not an American ally. Paris and New Delhi must understand these nuances, and find new ways to advance their friendship by aligning against common threats.

A NATIONAL SECURITY SHIELD

In July 2020, as the first consignment of the state-of-the-art 4.5 Generation French-made Rafale fighter jets arrived in India, Prime Minister Modi hailed them by evoking a Sanskrit hymn that translates as follows: 'There is no greater blessing than protecting the nation, protecting the nation is a virtuous deed and protecting the nation is the best *yagna* [sacrifice]. There is nothing beyond this. Touch the sky with glory. Welcome.'[395] The touchdown of the Rafales at that moment aroused national cheering in India because the Galwan Valley clash with the Chinese PLA had occurred just a few weeks ago. France had honoured India's urgent need for beefing up its offensive capabilities by delivering the 'beauty and beast' flying machines to the Indian Air Force on an accelerated time-frame.[396]

So strategically impactful was the speedy induction and deployment of the Rafale aircraft near the LAC, where Indian forces were engaged in a stand-off with the PLA, that the

---

[394]RF, 'Entretien de M. Hubert Védrine, Ministre des Affaires Étrangères, Avec le Quotidien Allemand "Handelsblatt"', République Française, 13 March 2001, https://tinyurl.com/mtxwecfx. Accessed on 19 June 2024.

[395]HT, '"Touch the Sky with Glory": PM Narendra Modi Welcomes Rafale Fighter Jets with a Sanskrit Tweet', *Hindustan Times*, 29 July 2020, https://tinyurl.com/4af8nnh7. Accessed on 19 June 2024.

[396]HT, 'Rafales, "Beauty and Beast", are Home. A Look at Their Journey in Pics', *Hindustan Times*, 29 July 2020, https://tinyurl.com/mrx5dutf. Accessed on 19 June 2024.

Chinese scrambled to bring their most advanced J-20 fighter aircraft to areas close to eastern Ladakh the moment Indian Rafales were in the vicinity. China even made an attempt to contain the strategic impact of the French induction into the Indian Air Force by spinning the narrative that 'the Rafale is only a third-plus generation fighter jet, and does not stand much of a chance against a stealth, fourth generation one like the J-20.'[397] R.K.S. Bhadauria, the then Chief of Air Staff of India, publicly responded with confidence: 'Rafale fighter jets had caused worries in the Chinese camp.'[398]

While the Rafales may not have altered the overall balance of power between India and China, they have been battlespace game-changers, and one cannot underestimate their deterrent effect in preventing further Chinese aggression at the LAC. French aircraft like Rafale and Mirage have partially addressed the shortage of squadrons of advanced jets in the Indian Air Force. French combat aircraft have also remade India's defence matrix through their massive valuation in the recipient country's foreign defence procurements. The order for 36 Rafale jets for the Indian Air Force, which was initially placed in 2016, cost $8.8 billion. The 2023 order for 26 additional Rafales (marine version) for the Indian Navy amounted to approximately $6 billion more. Acquisition of Scorpene diesel-electric submarines for the Indian Navy to be manufactured in India would generate contracts worth around $5 billion for French defence companies. Many other sophisticated French-manufactured and co-developed weapons

---

[397]Qiang, Li, and Liu Xuanzun, 'India's Rafale Fighter Jets Have No Chance Against China's J-20: Experts', *Global Times*, 30 July 2020, https://tinyurl.com/599tvbte. Accessed on 19 June 2024.

[398]WION, 'India-China Standoff: "China Moved J-20 Fighters the Moment Rafales Were Stationed at LAC," says IAF Chief Bhadauria', *World Is One News*, 4 February 2021, https://tinyurl.com/2nz6er93. Accessed on 19 June 2024.

are expected to come into play to boost India's national
security capabilities in years to come, and keep the French
defence industry humming.

France is well aware that the Indian arms bazaar is a
competitive buyer's market, and knows that it has to respond
to India's aim to move away from buyer-seller relationships to
co-designing and co-producing. The 'Horizon 2047' roadmap,
which set goals for the strategic partnership until the centenary
of bilateral relations in 2047, mentioned 'building sovereign
defence capabilities together' and committed to 'cooperation
in advanced aeronautical technologies by supporting the joint
development of a combat aircraft engine'.[399] Reportedly, if the
USA had agreed to 80 per cent transfer of technology (ToT) in
the joint production of jet engines for fighter aircraft, France
had offered 100 per cent ToT for a more powerful engine.[400]
The 2024 Roadmap for Indo-French Defence Industrial
Partnership went further and laid the foundation for 'not
only fulfilling the defence needs of the Indian armed forces
but also to provide a reliable source of defence supplies to
other friendly countries.'[401]

As mentioned in Chapter 4, France stormed the Indian
defence market and grabbed the second spot with 30 per
cent of India's total arms imports, just behind the traditional
supplier Russia, which commanded 36 per cent of the
market share during the periods ranging from 2014–18 to

[399]MEA, 'Horizon 2047: 25th Anniversary of the India-France Strategic
Partnership, Towards A Century of India-France Relations', Ministry of
External Affairs, Government of India,14 July 2023,
https://tinyurl.com/3h483jf9. Accessed on 19 June 2024.
[400]Pandit, Rajat, 'India, France Seal Deal on Making 3 Scorpene
Submarines', The Times of India, 15 July 2023,
https://tinyurl.com/p6bw3jms. Accessed on 19 June 2024.
[401]Kumar, Mohan, 'The M&M Factor in Indo-French Relations', Hindustan
Times, 29 January 2024, https://tinyurl.com/4dwrbe8z. Accessed on 19 June
2024.

2019–23. What gives France an edge as a defence partner is its undeniably high quality of weapons, combined with relatively lower costs, flexibility of terms, willingness to transfer know-how, and membership of the Western alliance system that insulates it from international pressures and economic sanctions. It is not uncommon for Western policymakers and commentators from France's allied nations to applaud France-India defence cooperation on grounds that it is reducing India's dependence on Russia and slowly drawing India closer to the West. Recommendations from American think tanks that the USA should 'quietly discuss best practices for effective defense cooperation with India with like-minded mutual partners like France, Israel, and the UK' and formulate a joint Western strategy to wean India away from Russia[402], indicate how France's status as a NATO member and a Western power redounds to its defence partnership with India.

Characteristically, France itself has not chastised India for failing to denounce Russia's invasion of Ukraine or to join Western sanctions against Russia. In 2022, General Stéphane Mille, Chief of the French Air and Space Force, even flew in an Indian Russian-origin Sukhoi jet fighter while his Indian counterpart flew in a French Rafale during joint military exercises to showcase the interoperability of the two militaries. Given the legacy value and separate importance of Russia to India, France has no qualms about military cooperation with India that will inevitably involve some Russian weaponry or the other.

Bilateral trust does play a role in India's choice of France as a main vector for its military modernization and diversification away from Russia. But the deal-clincher has been technical

---

[402]Kalyankar, Akriti, and Dante Schulz, 'Continental Drift? India-Russia Ties After One Year of War in Ukraine', Stimson Center, 9 March 2023, https://tinyurl.com/msc6hu2f. Accessed on 19 June 2024.

superiority of French weapons in specialized domains. India's armed forces have picked France over its competitors after conducting test trials. For example, France's Dassault, the maker of Rafale, beat the Russian Mikoyan, the American Boeing and Lockheed Martin, the multinational European Eurofighter, and the Swedish Saab in technical evaluations to bag the lucrative fighter jet contract for the Indian Air Force. The Rafale's marine version also outcompeted *inter alia* Boeing's F/A 18 Super Hornet for the Indian Navy because France gave 'all the necessary clearances and modifications to integrate stand-off nuclear weapons' on the Rafales, while 'there is no way that the Americans would allow the integration of any nuclear weapons delivery system with the Super Hornet.'[403] If supreme national interests mean something, then France often fits the bill for India compared to its other friends.

Ultimately, it boils down to similarity of national circumstances and goals under the common umbrella of an independent foreign policy. In 2022, India's External Affairs Minister Subrahmanyam Jaishankar lauded France as a key partner in defence and security and 'a trusted collaborator in countering security challenges from the seabed to space, from cyber to oceans.' He praised France as 'among the foremost countries as India seeks to build industrial self-reliance in the defence sector, with a sense of urgency and priority.' He added that in this pursuit, 'we draw inspiration from the national self-sufficiency France has itself built.'[404] A year later, the French Finance Minister Bruno Le Maire talked up 'France's

---

[403]Iyer-Mitra, Abhijit, 'Why India Chose Rafale-M over F/A-18 Super Hornet', *India Today*, 17 July 2023, https://tinyurl.com/ydutkunf. Accessed on 19 June 2024.
[404]PTI, 'Indo-French Ties Free from Sudden Shifts and Surprise: Jaishankar', *The Indian Express*, 23 February 2022, https://tinyurl.com/5t4htuv5. Accessed on 19 June 2024.

commitment to being India's foremost partner for investing in the sectors of the future.' He declared that 'developing together the technologies that will anchor our nations' independence tomorrow, such as artificial intelligence or supercomputers, is the new frontier for our strategic partnership.'[405] Be it past, present or future, the vision of strategic autonomy has been the guiding light in the France-India friendship.

TWO RESIDENT POWERS

While France's inputs in military hardware and defence industrial modernization are beefing up India's hard-power capabilities, the two sides have also made strides in realizing a shared vision for regional order in maritime spaces of Asia. In 2023, Paris and New Delhi announced a landmark 'India-France Indo-Pacific Roadmap' to signal that they would ramp up geopolitical coordination not just in their traditional zone of the IOR, but also in the Pacific. Calling themselves 'strategically located resident powers and key partners with vital stakes in the Indo-Pacific region,' they vowed not only to 'secure our own economic and security interests,' but also to 'build partnerships of prosperity and sustainability in the region; advance the rule of international law; and, working with others in the region and beyond, build a balanced and stable order in the region, with respect for sovereignty and territorial integrity.'[406] This vision stretched the previous boundaries of France-India maritime cooperation, which

---

[405]Chaudhury, Dipanjan, 'French Cos Positioned to Support India Towards Achieving Strategic Goals in Multiple Sectors, says French Finance Minister', *The Economic Times*, 23 February 2023, https://tinyurl.com/58yzm55r Accessed on 19 June 2024.

[406]MEA, 'India-France Indo-Pacific Roadmap', Ministry of External Affairs, Government of India, 14 July 2023, https://tinyurl.com/mjvvn67t. Accessed on 19 June 2024.

had concentrated on the South-West IOR. It drew a wider canvas for joint development works and security coordination, ranging from French facilities and territories in the UAE, Djibouti, Seychelles, La Reunion, Mayotte, Madagascar and the east coast of Africa in the west, all the way up to Singapore and the French Pacific territories of New Caledonia and French Polynesia in the east.

In Chapter 1, we saw how Japan's expanded conception of the Indo-Pacific that included the western IOR aided the positioning of India as a major power far beyond its immediate maritime spaces. Likewise, what France has done is to invite and set up a platform for the Indian Navy and its civilian institutions to play a more substantive role in the Pacific by gaining access to French overseas bases there.

Already, the reciprocal logistics agreement between France and India, which was operationalized in 2019, had 'helped the Indian Navy to operate freely and far away from its shores' and 'fulfill its mandate of being the first responder and security provider' in the IOR.[407] The France-India bilateral strategic dialogue on outer space cooperation and space-based Maritime Domain Awareness (MDA) is a promising new area that could turbo-charge the Indian Navy's reach and monitoring capacities when China's PLA Navy is prowling the waters of the two oceans, and pressurizing established regional powers.

The 2024 France-India Defence Space Agreement is committed to jointly developing and launching military satellites, and promises to expand India's capabilities to comprehensively track and counter Chinese moves. With the remit of bilateral military interoperability redefined as

---

[407]Dubey, Ajit, 'Indian Navy Benefits from Strategic Logistics Pacts with US, France', *Business Standard*, 16 June 2019, https://tinyurl.com/aftrn75v. Accessed on 19 June 2024.

including French territories east of the Strait of Malacca, India's aspiration to be a full-fledged Indo-Pacific power and exert influence in the Pacific Island nations that seek alternatives to China, has received a boost. New Delhi's 'Act East' policy could not have found a more conducive catapult.

Drawing India into the Pacific is part of a larger French strategy to preserve its influence in its far-flung oceanic territories from Chinese encroachment. A sovereign state in the IOR and the Pacific thanks to its colonial-era possessions, France has more than 1.65 million citizens and 93 per cent of its Exclusive Economic Zone (EEZ) in the two oceans to defend from adversarial powers. France has pre-positioned large numbers of troops in these distant Indo-Pacific territories but nurses deep fears of China's lengthening shadow by means of the BRI and the PLA Navy's 'two-ocean strategy'. Since France's mainland is thousands of miles away, and it lacks a blue-water navy of the scale of the USA for sustained power projection in multiple theatres globally, strategic partnerships with like-minded countries are critical for Paris to hold on to its islets from the Chinese juggernaut.

France's announcement of an 'enhanced strategic partnership' with Australia in 2017 and the signing of the France-Australia mutual logistics support agreement in 2018 were steps towards firming up this coalition of friends. It was in Australia in 2018 that Macron floated the concept of a 'Paris-Delhi-Canberra' axis, and justified it by asserting, 'we are not naïve and if we want to be seen and respected, as a partner by China, as an equal partner, we have to organise ourselves.'[408]

By 2023, French alarm bells about China were ringing louder. In Vanuatu, a former French colony in the Pacific,

---

[408]SP, 'Speech of the President of France at the Sydney Naval Base, Garden Island', 2 May 2018, Sciences Po, https://tinyurl.com/3mafvyb8. Accessed on 19 June 2024.

Macron flagged a 'new imperialism' and 'a power logic that is threatening the sovereignty of several states—the smallest, often the most fragile,' apparently referring to China. His answer to Chinese hegemony was to 'defend through partnerships, the independence and sovereignty of all states in the region that are ready to work with us.'[409] In Chapter 2, we have shown how the India-France-Australia (IFA) trilateral that was floated with great expectations, almost foundered due to the AUKUS alliance, and was again revived due to the sober reality check that Paris, Canberra or New Delhi cannot singly counterbalance Chinese expansionism. All three partners have been on the defensive to protect their respective turfs from China in the Indo-Pacific. There is thus a natural synergy for the three to cast aside other differences and pool resources to check Chinese advances.

The Indian analyst Shairee Malhotra and French researcher Thibault Fournol have argued that the trilateral mechanisms established by France and India with Australia (IFA) and with the UAE (IFU) (more on this in Chapter 7) underscore 'the importance of moving beyond the traditional self-centred approach to foster a more outward-looking dynamic.'[410] This refers to a proactive approach for geopolitical rebalancing where Paris and New Delhi transcend the focus on their respective sub-regions of influence, and look to bolster each other through a systemic vision of the Indo-Pacific as one undivided whole. The logic of 'you scratch my back and I'll scratch yours' is a compelling one for friendship between a

---

[409]F24, 'Macron Denounces "New Imperialism" in the Pacific During Landmark Visit', *France 24*, 27 July 2023, https://tinyurl.com/4fjj42cp. Accessed on 19 June 2024.
[410]Malhotra, Shairee, and Thibault Fournol, 'India-France Trilaterals in the Indo-Pacific: Imperatives, Interests, Initiatives', Observer Research Foundation, 4 December 2023, https://tinyurl.com/4prkbm84. Accessed on 19 June 2024.

middle power that is desperate to cling to its former imperial glory, and a rising power that seeks to push the boundaries of its footprint. Paris basically compensates for its long-distance existence and medium-sized military and economic instruments by casting the net wide for friends, to be effective in the Indo-Pacific.

Since India and Australia are the two nearest regional power centres to French overseas territories which face pressures and inducements from Beijing to break away from Paris and accept Chinese suzerainty, France has naturally invested much in its friendships with these two countries. But Paris has also diversified its Indo-Pacific strategy by forging strategic partnerships with Japan, Indonesia and Vietnam, and criticizing China's unilateral violations of the rule of law in the South China Sea.

France's participation in joint naval exercises in the Indo-Pacific with all four Quad countries under the La Perouse banner, and its steering role in the EU to conceive and implement an Indo-Pacific outlook for the entire European bloc, reveal its multi-pronged approach. Since France's Indo-Pacific strategy 'is more oriented towards hard security,' while the EU's Indo-Pacific stance 'emphasizes values, connectivity, soft security issues such as sustainable development and environmental protection,' Paris has worked to 'bring the EU's Indo-Pacific strategy closer to its own strategy.'[411] There was a French hand in nudging individual European countries like Germany, Italy and the Netherlands to have naval presence in the Indo-Pacific, and also in the EU considering permanent military deployment in the Indo-Pacific through the Coordinated Maritime Presences (CMP).

---

[411] Cabestan, Jean-Pierre, 'France's Ambitious Indo-Pacific Goals for its EU Presidency', The German Marshall Fund of the United States, 8 February 2022, https://tinyurl.com/r5eemnyh. Accessed on 19 June 2024.

India values France for this shepherding role in the EU. In 2021, Prime Minister Modi 'welcomed the European Union's Indo-Pacific Strategy [...] and thanked the French President for France's leadership role in the same.'[412] India looks up to France as a magnet that will pull more European partners to join a counterbalancing coalition in the Indo-Pacific. Even when it comes to non-military components of the France-India friendship like the Indo-Pacific Triangular Cooperation (IPTDC) fund, India has sought to link them to bigger European pathways like the EU-India Connectivity Partnership and the Global Gateway. France's expression of confidence that India would 'receive a chunk' of the €300 billion fund announced by the EU under its Global Gateway scheme, a soft balancing counter to China's BRI,[413] raised hopes in India. France's co-founding with India of the International Solar Alliance (ISA) also helped mobilize EU funding for transfer of knowledge and capacity-building in solar energy businesses and technology to ISA members from the Global South.

TOWARDS STRATEGIC CLARITY

Despite convergences among India, France and the EU to unite for a rules-based Indo-Pacific, differences exist and need to be addressed for the friendship to extract higher dividends. France's Gaullist penchant to steer a middle path for Europe as a 'third force' between two great powers has not gone away, and it perpetuates strategic confusion about how far Paris

---

[412]EI, 'Prime Minister Narendra Modi Meets President of France on the Sidelines of the G20 Leaders Summit', Embassy of India in Moscow, 30 October 2021, https://tinyurl.com/55zmjwh5. Accessed on 19 June 2024.
[413]PTI, 'India Could Get a Chunk of EU's Euro 300 Billion Fund Under Global Gateway Scheme: French Envoy', The Times of India, 9 October 2022, https://tinyurl.com/ye29cvpb. Accessed on 19 June 2024.

and Brussels will realistically go to counterbalance China. As previously mentioned, France's notion of strategic autonomy has been with reference to sustaining its independence vis-à-vis the USA. Under Macron, this tendency has manifested itself in efforts for Europe to develop its own 'autonomous operating capabilities' and doctrines in defence[414], and to implement an endogenous European 'Strategic Compass' that would enhance 'the EU's capacity for action in an increasingly brutal and unpredictable world'.[415] Although Macron qualified his autonomy agenda by saying it was meant not to compete with the USA and NATO, but to complement them, Paris has mined every opportunity to differentiate Europe as much as possible from the USA on a range of foreign policy issues, such as how to handle a revanchist Russia and how to manage industrial policies and subsidies that impact trade competitiveness.

In the Indo-Pacific, France's strategic autonomy has translated into a chaotic and incoherent West, whose countries work at cross-purposes. When AUKUS was launched and resulted in France being deprived of a lucrative submarine contract with Australia due to what Paris called a 'stab in the back' by Canberra and a 'huge breach of trust' by Washington[416], it rekindled French distaste for 'the Anglo-Saxons' and delighted Beijing. Always eager to divide adversaries and rule, China's leadership egged France on to maintain its strategic autonomy line, and praised Macron

---

[414]OF, 'Sorbonne Speech of Emmanuel Macron', *Ouest-France*, 26 September 2017, https://tinyurl.com/yfypp9zr. Accessed on 19 June 2024.
[415]FD, 'A Strategic Compass to Strengthen the Security and Defence of the European Union by 2030', France Diplomacy, January 2022, https://tinyurl.com/mr33uw4v. Accessed on 19 June 2024.
[416]Chrisafis, Angelique, and Daniel Boffey, '"Stab in the Back": French Fury as Australia Scraps Submarine Deal', *The Guardian*, 16 September 2021, https://tinyurl.com/234hyea4. Accessed on 19 June 2024.

as 'highly regarded in China' for his refusal to be 'a vassal of the US' on the global stage.[417]

Following a controversial visit in 2023 to China to boost bilateral business and diplomatic ties, Macron's remarks that Europe must not get 'caught up in crises that are not ours,' and that 'the worse thing would be to think that we Europeans must become followers on this topic [Taiwan] and take our cue from the U.S. agenda and [risk] a Chinese overreaction,'[418] raised doubts about the EU's Indo-Pacific intent, and won loud ovation in Beijing. The state-owned Chinese media gushed that 'Macron's statement signals the US strategy of luring Europe to contain China is coming to a dead end.'[419] Beijing had the additional satisfaction of witnessing Russia's war in Ukraine totally consuming European attention and rendering containment of Russia, not China, the top priority for the EU.

In New Delhi, analysts lamented that France's vouching for 'a close and solid global strategic partnership' with China had the 'possibility of denting its earlier stand on [the] Indo-Pacific,' and recommended that 'India needs to moderate emerging French posturing on China,' and ensure that India is 'suitably accommodated in the French Gaullist worldview.'[420] It is indeed worthwhile for India and France to review and reassess through their bilateral dialogue channels how China can simultaneously be a 'systemic rival', as Paris and

---

[417]Sheng, Wen, 'Strategic Autonomy Will Enable Europe to Stand Equally Among Major Powers', *Global Times*, 24 April 2023, https://tinyurl.com/y8a9rfx8. Accessed on 19 June 2024.

[418]Anderlini, Jamil, and Clea Caulcutt, 'Europe Must Resist Pressure to Become "America's Followers," says Macron', *Politico*, 9 April 2023, https://tinyurl.com/mtcexmdp. Accessed on 19 June 2024.

[419]GT, 'US' Uneasiness Over Macron's "Strategic Autonomy" Statement Shows Washington's Declining Ability to Maintain Hegemony', *Global Times*, https://tinyurl.com/3m82xj3u. Accessed on 19 June 2024.

[420]Srichandan, Sakti Prasad, 'India-France Relations in Changing Times', *Financial Express*, 5 December 2023, https://tinyurl.com/2z8jx5ea. Accessed on 19 June 2024.

Brussels call it, and also a 'strategic partner'. Whatever be the unease in Paris about Washington's unreliable or overbearing nature, this should not translate into a continuation of the old European fuzziness towards China. If France and Europe cannot break out of their old mindset of 'congagement' or hedging with China, then there is a real risk that their Indo-Pacific commitments to partners like India, Japan, Australia and Southeast Asian nations can be diluted or traded for concessions from Beijing.

It is understandable that France and the EU can only afford to 'de-risk' but not 'decouple' economically from China due to their enormous interdependence. Yet, the realization that China has abused global free trade rules by unfairly subsidizing its solar power and electric vehicle manufacturers to decimate French and European competitors, is not lost on Paris and Brussels. The likelihood that the competitive and 'systemic rivalry' parts of the EU-China relationship will gradually overshadow the 'strategic partnership' part is high in the wake of the 'China Shock 2.0' that buffeted Western economies in 2024.[421]

Whatever be the long-term prognosis for the France-China and EU-China economic equations, India is keen to forestall a scenario where Paris or Brussels thaws or abandons counterbalancing of China in the realms of security and defence. The Indian scholar of European affairs, Swasti Rao, has pointed out that French defence policy documents are 'undoubtedly anything but pro-China'. They raise alarms about 'China threatening to destabilize the Indo-Pacific, while reiterating concern for the security of France's territories in the region,' and emphasize 'deepening ties with NATO and

---

[421]Douglas, Jason, and Dave Sebastian, 'China Shock 2.0 Sparks Global Backlash Against Flood of Cheap Goods', *The Wall Street Journal*, 5 April 2024, https://tinyurl.com/2d538322. Accessed on 19 June 2024.

the criticality of France's strategic cooperation with the US.'[422]

India's meagre trade volumes with France ($13.4 billion in 2022) and France's modest FDI in India ($10.49 billion between 2000 and 2022) mean that New Delhi cannot replace Beijing as a commercial opportunity for Paris anytime soon. On the other hand, France does not sell any weapons to China, while its defence portfolio in India has grown by leaps and bounds. Keeping the focus of the bilateral friendship on national security, especially enhanced military coordination in the Indo-Pacific, as well as on counterterrorism, where the two sides feel a strong camaraderie as victims of Islamist fundamentalism, would be prudent as that puts the friendship's best foot forward. Like India's friendship with Russia (*see* Chapter 4), its partnership with France is skewed in the direction of hard security. That itself is a treasure to preserve and advance by narrowing gaps in mutual perception and understanding, both bilaterally and with Quad partners. We would echo American trans-Atlantic affairs commentators Chloe Laird and Jason Moyer, who noted aptly that the France-India strategic partnership 'does not exist in a vacuum', and 'how France and India navigate other major powers—namely the United States and China—will determine their ability to alter the current international order and better exercise their shared definitions of strategic autonomy.'[423]

[422]Rao, Swasti, 'Macron's Gaffes in China Open a Door for India—Unwavering French Support at the UNSC', *The Print*, 21 April 2023, https://tinyurl.com/3u8xbzud. Accessed on 19 June 2024.

[423]Laird, Chloe, and Jason Moyer, 'France and India's Strategic Partnership in a Contested World', Wilson Center, 30 November 2023, https://tinyurl.com/3nbm7mn9. Accessed on 19 June 2024.

6

BROTHERS IN ARMS: ISRAEL AND INDIA TAKE ON COMMON DANGERS

We receive you with open arms. We love India. We admire your culture, we admire your history, your democracy, your commitment to progress. We view you as kindred spirits in our common quest to provide a better future for our peoples and for our world [...] The ties between our talented innovative peoples are natural [...] so natural that we could ask what took so long for them to blossom? Well, it took a meeting of minds and hearts, it took a commitment of our governments. We have that today.[424]

—Benjamin Netanyahu, Prime Minister of Israel, 2017

O ctober 7, 2023, was a black-letter day in the history of Israel. From the early hours, a complex coordinated cross-border terrorist attack by Hamas and its allied jihadist groups from the Gaza Strip through land, sea and

---

[424]GOVIL, 'Statements by PM Netanyahu and Indian PM Narendra Modi', Government of Israel, 4 July 2017, https://tinyurl.com/tjwx353d. Accessed on 17 June 2024.

air took the Jewish state by utter surprise. Timed to coincide with the Jewish holidays of Shemini Atzeret and Simchat Torah, and with the completion of the 50th anniversary of the 1973 Arab-Israeli Yom Kippur War, the assault involved as many as 3,000 armed Palestinians attacking Israel from multiple directions.[425] In all, over 1,200 people, the majority of them civilians, were killed. Around 250 more were taken hostage, and forcibly transported to the Gaza Strip to be used as human shields and bargaining chips. The methodical brutality and deliberately cold-blooded manner in which the attack was executed was spine-chilling, even for a region of the world where violence and warfare are endemic. It left a deep trauma in the recesses of Israel's consciousness and memory, and came to be remembered as the Black Sabbath.

Within days, Joe Biden, President of the USA, Israel's number one ally and supporter, landed in Tel Aviv on an emergency mission and deplored the 'pure unadulterated evil' of the Hamas attacks that were reminiscent of 'atrocities that recall the worst ravages of ISIS [Islamic State]'. He promised Israeli Prime Minister Netanyahu that the USA would make sure 'you have what you need to protect your people, to defend your nation,' and announced an 'unprecedented support package for Israel's defense,' plus deployment of American military assets in the region 'to deter further aggression against Israel and to prevent this conflict from spreading.' Yet, in the same breath, Biden advised an anguished and revengeful Israel that 'while you feel that rage, don't be consumed by it.' He reminded his hosts that the USA had 'made mistakes' after the 11 September 2001 (9/11) terrorist attacks, cautioned Israel to play by the 'rule of law' and the 'law of wars', and added

---

[425]Fabian, Emanuel, and Gianluca Pacchiani, 'IDF Estimates 3,000 Hamas Terrorists Invaded Israel in Oct. 7 Onslaught, *The Times of Israel*, 1 November 2023, https://tinyurl.com/yju9dfrt. Accessed on 19 June 2024.

'what sets us apart from the terrorists is we believe in the fundamental dignity of every human life—Israeli, Palestinian, Arab, Jew, Muslim, Christian—everyone.'[426]

As a bloody war unfolded, the USA spelt out more of its concerns that Israel was losing the support of the West due to its 'indiscriminate bombing' and that Jerusalem 'can't say no to a Palestinian state.'[427] This was followed by American pressure on Israel to agree to humanitarian pauses, ceasefires and a post-Hamas settlement that would leave the Gaza Strip under Palestinian control. At one point in 2024, the USA even withheld shipments of certain munitions to Israel as a pressure tactic to force it to reconsider its heavy-casualty counter-attack deep inside Gaza. However, critics of Washington's habitual bias towards Israel saw in the whole saga a repetition of what they considered to be play-acting by a disingenuous USA shedding crocodile tears for unfortunate Palestinians, while not definitively terminating the supply of lethal weapons to the Israeli Defence Forces (IDF), who were accused of reducing Palestinian infrastructure to rubble and carrying out 'genocide crimes'.[428] But the reality was that the devastating 2023–24 Israel-Hamas war once again revealed the limits of the USA-Israel exceptional alliance. Contrary to critics who believe that the USA's special relationship with Israel enables it to use disproportionate force and act with unfettered impunity against its opponents, Jerusalem has often bristled, huffed and puffed at the lack of a *carte blanche* from Washington, and

[426]TWH, 'Remarks by President Biden on the October 7th Terrorist Attacks and the Resilience of the State of Israel and its People', The White House, 18 October 2023, https://tinyurl.com/36xwscn6. Accessed on 17 June 2024.
[427]AJ, 'Biden Warns Israel Risks Losing Support Over "Indiscriminate" Gaza Bombing', *Al Jazeera*, 12 December 2023, https://tinyurl.com/49nd7e93. Accessed on 17 June 2024.
[428]Rjoub, Awad, 'Palestinian President Charges US of Being Accomplice to Israel's Genocide Crimes by Using Veto in UNSC', *Anadolu Ajansi*, 9 December 2023, https://tinyurl.com/mryv6fx9. Accessed on 17 June 2024.

at the conditionalities and constraints that the USA imposes on Israel's freedom to use force.

Still, since the USA is the undisputed guarantor of Israel's 'qualitative military edge' over its rivals in West Asia/the Middle East, the saviour of last resort which invariably uses its veto power in the UN Security Council to shield Israel from international enforcement actions, and host to the largest concentration of Jewish people outside Israel, Jerusalem has learnt to grudgingly live with a less-than-perfect but absolutely necessary Washington. As Biden quipped about the alliance, 'we love one another and we drive one another crazy.'[429] Given the hugely controversial and polarizing nature of the Israel-Palestine conflict, Jerusalem understands that it cannot get everything it ideally wants from its friends. As long as Israel secures something valuable out of them, it is seen as good enough to guarantee its right to existence, its survival and growth as a Jewish state.

THE DUAL TRACK

Foremost among such friends is India. The dualistic approach of having Israel's back through concrete military and economic cooperation, but balancing it by diplomatically pushing for human rights and a political solution to the aspirations of the Palestinian people, is not uniquely American. There are echoes of it in India, a strategic partner that has come to be seen in Jerusalem as a crown jewel in its 'Go East' or 'pivot to Asia' strategy. The historical origins of Israel's pivot to the East, especially India and China, lay in the 'garrison state' mindset of seeking to 'bypass the hostile Arab states by establishing

---

[429]Baker, Peter, and Lisa Lerer, 'U.S. Confronts Tight but Turbulent Relationship with Israel', *The New York Times*, 23 July 2023, https://tinyurl.com/bd22c655. Accessed on 17 June 2024.

diplomatic relations with the nations of Asia, and thereby combat the political and economic boycott imposed by the Arab world.'[430] Over time, with Israel gradually gaining diplomatic recognition from Arab neighbours, its need for powerful friends like China and India transcended the original motive of breaking free from isolation in West Asia/the Middle East. Jerusalem began looking to Asia to 'go to the fastest-growing markets' where the future of the global economy lay, and to diversify trade and investment links from its traditional markets of the USA and Western Europe.[431] Israeli scholar Mordechai Chaziza has argued that Jerusalem also courted Beijing in particular, as part of a limited strategic hedging 'to gain latitude in foreign-policy decisions and economic independence' and reduce the 'leverage for the US and other Western nations to pressure Israel over the Palestinian and settlement issues.'[432]

Be that as it may, the intensifying 'new Cold War' between the USA and China, as well as the geopolitical churn after the 7 October 2023 terrorist attacks showed the limits of how far Israel could proceed with China. Beijing did not condemn Hamas' terrorist attacks, deepened its 'comprehensive strategic partnership' with Hamas' benefactor Iran, and backed Arab and Muslim countries demanding an immediate halt to Israeli military operations. The anti-American axis of China-Iran-Russia also fanned propaganda in support of Hamas[433],

---

[430]Abadi, Jacob, *Israel's Quest for Recognition and Acceptance in Asia: Garrison State Diplomacy*, 2004, Routledge, London, p. XIV.

[431]Shapiro, Ahron, 'Naftali Bennett: Israel's Pivot to Asia', *Australia/Israel Review*, 18 December 2013, https://tinyurl.com/2ydfn5vb. Accessed on 17 June 2024.

[432]Chaziza, Mordechai, 'Israel-China Relations Enter a New Stage: Limited Strategic Hedging', *Contemporary Review of the Middle East*, Vol. 5, No. 1, 2018, p. 11.

[433]Myers, Steven Lee, and Sheera Frenkel, 'In a Worldwide War of Words, Russia, China and Iran Back Hamas', *The New York Times*, 3 November 2023, https://tinyurl.com/y5dpp3rz. Accessed on 17 June 2024.

causing deep disappointment in Jerusalem about Beijing's bias and insensitivity.

It is noteworthy that despite the sizeable economic and technological linkages Israel has forged with China, no robust military component has developed (or has been allowed to develop by the USA). The Israel-China friendship goes by the curious name 'innovative comprehensive partnership' (*see* Annexure, Table II), as opposed to the straightforward Israel-India 'strategic partnership' (*see* Annexure, Table III). Both these partnerships were declared by Israel in the same year—2017—but the different nomenclatures convey a lot. The oft-cited optimism of Israeli and Indian leaders that the 'sky is no longer the limit' in their strategic partnership[434] is more than rhetorical, and has a fairly good chance of realization, especially as the post-7 October 2023 situation raised India's strategic salience for Israel to its highest level.

India's responses to the 2023 Hamas attacks, and the subsequent war, were closer to the USA's positions and contrasted with those of China. Within hours of the launch of the daring 'Operation Al-Aqsa Flood' by Hamas, Prime Minister Modi was one of the first world leaders to convey that he was 'deeply shocked by the news of terrorist attacks,' and declared that 'we stand in solidarity with Israel at this difficult hour.'[435] As Israel launched a full-scale war with the goal of uprooting Hamas from Gaza, New Delhi coordinated with Jerusalem to evacuate thousands of its stranded citizens under 'Operation Ajay'. Two weeks into the war, India abstained from the UN General Assembly resolution drafted by Jordan,

---

[434]DNA, 'Modi in Israel: Even the Sky Isn't the Limit, Says Netanyahu on Indo-Israel Ties', *Daily News and Analysis*, 4 July 2017, https://tinyurl.com/2u9274aw. Accessed on 19 June 2024.
[435]TOI, 'India Stands in Solidarity with Israel at this Difficult Hour, says PM Modi after Hamas Attack', *The Times of India*, 7 October 2023, https://tinyurl.com/56nmt8fy. Accessed on 17 June 2024.

calling for an immediate and durable humanitarian truce, and justified its abstention on grounds that the resolution did not name Hamas as the perpetrator of despicable terrorist attacks or condemn terrorist violence. The USA debunked that resolution as an 'omission of evil', and India voiced a similar viewpoint that the world must 'unite and adopt a zero-tolerance approach to terrorism' and 'should not buy into any justification of terror acts.'[436] Jerusalem publicly expressed thanks and said 'we appreciate India's support.'[437]

But as the post-7 October 2023 war dragged on, with record numbers of Palestinian casualties, and as Arab countries that were strategic partners of India and the USA besides being friends of Israel fell in an extremely uncomfortable tight spot, New Delhi subtly altered its messaging. External Affairs Minister Subrahmanyam Jaishankar continued to reiterate to Israeli counterparts 'our firm commitment to countering terrorism,' but stressed that India wanted respect for 'international humanitarian law and for a two-state solution'—the long-unfulfilled UN-mandated bid to create an independent Palestinian state alongside Israel. Jaishankar explained, 'the conflict can't be the normal of the region' and that 'we have to find a balance between different issues.' He went on that 'if there is issue of terrorism, and we all find terrorism unacceptable, we have to stand up. But there is also an issue of Palestine. There has to be solution for the problems faced by the Palestinian people.'[438]

---

[436]OI, 'Explained: Why did India Abstain from Voting on UN Resolution for Humanitarian Truce in Gaza Strip, Does it Mark Shift in Policy?' *Outlook*, 28 October 2023, https://tinyurl.com/5faff7e2. Accessed on 17 June 2024.
[437]IT, 'Appreciate India's Support: Israel after New Delhi Abstains from UN Vote', *India Today*, 30 October 2023, https://tinyurl.com/38xs3anm. Accessed on 17 June 2024.
[438]ANI, 'Israeli Foreign Minister Thanks India for Support Amid War on Hamas', *NDTV*, 5 November 2023, https://tinyurl.com/2796xbcb. Accessed on 17 June 2024.

The longer the war went on, the more India plied the mixed message that 'you have these three broad sets of issues (terrorism, humanitarian crisis and future of Palestinians) [...] we have to find a way by which all of them are addressed.'[439] By December 2023, India even voted in favour of a UN General Assembly resolution introduced by Egypt, demanding an immediate humanitarian ceasefire in Gaza and release of all hostages being held by Hamas and its sister outfits. Here too, a fine balance of competing strategic interests was struck. India insisted on the need to 'find a peaceful and lasting two-state solution to the long-standing Palestine question,' but also voted in favour of a USA-sponsored amendment to the resolution that the UN 'unequivocally rejects and condemns the heinous terrorist attacks by Hamas that took place in Israel.'[440] In May 2024, with the prospect of endless onslaught testing everyone's patience, India voted in favour of a UN General Assembly resolution, calling for a sovereign Palestinian state and advocated for a 'two-state solution where the Palestinian people are able to live freely in an independent country with secure borders, with due regard to the security needs of Israel.'[441]

India's dual track of standing shoulder to shoulder with Israel against jihadist terrorists, whom both countries consider to be threats to national security and enemies of humanity, while reiterating India's traditional preference for a political settlement involving creation of a Palestinian state, was interpreted by some as a fig leaf or cover behind which India

---

[439]Singh, Rahul, 'India, Australia Back Two-State Solution to Resolve Israel-Palestine Conflict', *Hindustan Times*, 21 November 2023, https://tinyurl.com/mt2e2csb. Accessed on 21 May 2024.
[440]IT, 'India Votes in Favour of UN Resolution Demanding Immediate Ceasefire in Gaza', 13 December 2023, https://tinyurl.com/yw9xdzk6. Accessed on 17 June 2024.
[441]TOI, 'India Backs Full UN Membership for Palestine, Stresses on Two-State Solution', *The Times of India*, 14 May 2024, https://tinyurl.com/bdhh7b7u. Accessed on 17 June 2024.

had decisively tilted towards Israel in the Modi era. One can read too much into India abstaining or voting this way or that way on non-binding UN resolutions, but the concrete reality on the ground of India's ever-increasing pragmatic cooperation with Israel in strategically crucial domains, irrespective of the periodic flare-ups and wars between Israel and the Palestinians, is undeniable and predates Modi's advent to power. Since the new millennium, long before the strategic partnership was brought out of the closet and magnified by Prime Minister Modi in 2017, Indian governments of different political persuasions had been de-hyphenating bilateral convergence of interests with Israel from differences in opinion over the Israel-Palestine dispute and the elusive peace process.

As the Indian scholar of Israel studies, P.R. Kumaraswamy, has pointed out, the willingness of the government headed by Prime Minister Manmohan Singh to expand defence cooperation and promote joint missile research with Israel in 2007 signalled that 'disagreement over the Palestinian issue does not impede both countries from pursuing converging interests.'[442] Kumaraswamy added pertinently that 'by expressing its reservations over the peace process, India is contributing to the consolidation of domestic support for bilateral relations [with Israel].'[443] Another Indian academic specializing in Israel, Khinvraj Jangid has observed that under Prime Minister Modi since 2014, 'the ideological alignment between India and Israel around cultural-religious nationalism coupled with neo-liberal free market economy' elevated the Israel-India partnership to a much higher level than before.[444]

---

[442]Kumaraswamy, P.R., *India's Israel Policy*, 2010, Columbia University Press, New York, p. 249.
[443]Ibid., p. 273.
[444]Jangid, Khinvraj, 'Growing Ideological Convergence, Not Just Business, is Driving India-Israel Relations', *Hindustan Times*, 7 July 2017, https://tinyurl.com/mrxnea2m. Accessed on 17 June 2024.

While it is true that kinship of Modi's Bharatiya Janata Party (BJP) for Israel has taken the bilateral friendship to new heights, a remarkable bipartisan consensus prevails in India that no matter what happens in Israel's endless tussles with its adversaries in West Asia/the Middle East, India needs Israel and will not abandon or dilute its strategic partnership come what may.

WIN-WIN BILATERALISM

Of all the areas in which the Israel-India friendship has taken root, none is more strategically vital than defence cooperation. Israel's readiness and promptness to help India with its military needs is extraordinary as it predates 1992, the landmark year in which a Congress Party-led Indian government ended 44 years of Left-liberal ostracism of the Jewish state, and established full diplomatic relations with Israel, paving the way for official embassies to be opened in Tel Aviv and New Delhi. Under the rubric of a 'secret friendship', India secured limited quantities of arms and ammunition from Israel during its wars with China and Pakistan in 1962, 1965 and 1971.[445] After the collapse of the Soviet Union, which had been India's predominant weapons supplier, New Delhi felt an urgent need to find alternative sources, and found in Jerusalem an eager and ever-ready partner. When the USA and most of its allies imposed sanctions on India following the Pokhran-II nuclear tests (see Chapter 3), Israel did not waver. It sold advanced electronic equipment (AEE) for warplanes to India. Jerusalem even 'resisted American pressure to cancel the sale of AEE to India' and 'assured New Delhi that contracts

---

[445]Swamy, Subramanian, 'The Secret Friendship Between India and Israel', *Sunday*, 28 November 1982.

negotiated over the past year would be honoured.'[446]

In 1999, during the India-Pakistan Kargil War, as 'New Delhi was facing a technological, economic and arms embargo by countries, led by the US,' Israel again defied American pressure and 'helped India with mortars and ammunition [...] providing the Indian Air Force with laser-guided missiles for its Mirage 2000H fighter jets.' Jerusalem also gave New Delhi 'photographs from its military satellites to locate the Pakistan Army's strategic locations,' earning gratitude and trust from the national security establishment and the general public in India.[447]

By the 2000s, Israel emerged as the go-to country for India's requirements in niche military areas like drones, surveillance systems, anti-missile defence, airborne early warning systems, radars, avionics and electronic sensors. As of 2003, Israel became India's second largest supplier of weapons, behind only the traditional defence partner, Russia. As explained in Chapters 3 and 5, the USA and France also made inroads into India's diversifying military basket at the cost of Russia. But Israel's willingness to brave American objections and live up to the billing of a limitless friendship with India cemented the special bond. This unique attribute of Israel can be understood from the varying fates of two weapons systems—the Arrow-2 anti-tactical ballistic missile system and the Phalcon airborne warning and control system (AWACS). India had sought the former from Israel since 1999 but the USA, which jointly developed it with Israel, vetoed the sale in 2002 on grounds that it would violate the Missile Technology Control Regime (MTCR), and exacerbate tensions

[446]Naaz, Farah, 'Indo-Israel Military Cooperation', *Strategic Analysis*, Vol. 24, No. 5, 2000, p. 975.

[447]Sharma, Rishabh, 'How Israel Stood as India's Brother in Arms', *India Today*, 13 October 2023, https://tinyurl.com/5an2rp74. Accessed on 17 June 2024.

in South Asia, i.e. make India more aggressive against Pakistan, or tilt the balance of power in the subcontinent in favour of India. Because the USA had been the major funder of Arrow-2, and Israel needed American clearance for sale to third parties, Jerusalem was compelled to shelve that deal with New Delhi.[448] But on the AWACS, since it was indigenously made by Israel, Jerusalem persisted and succeeded in persuading Washington to relent, thereby handing New Delhi a game-changing means to deal with threats from both Beijing and Islamabad. Foreign and defence policy scholar Nicolas Blarel observed that 'since most of Israel's sophisticated weapons have been developed indigenously, there are fewer risks of external pressures to stop supplying India [...] during military crises' and, therefore, Israel is 'perceived positively by politicians across the political spectrum as a way to preserve India's strategic autonomy.'[449]

In 2019, and subsequently, as India's border tensions with Pakistan and China rose, the Indian Army and Indian Air Force procured Israel's Spike anti-tank guided missile rather than the USA's Javelin missile because the Israelis, unlike the Americans, were more willing to share technology and manufacture the missiles in India. Joint ventures between Indian and Israeli defence manufacturers like the Kalyani Rafael Advanced Systems (KRAS) have produced effective weapons such as the Barak 8 surface-to-air missile and the Spice 2000 air-to-surface bombs, which were made in India and used by the Indian Air Force during the 2019 Balakot airstrike inside Pakistan.

Integrating Israel's technological prowess with India's

---

[448]Rajghatta, Chidanand, 'US Blocks Israeli Arms Sales to India', *The Times of India*, 15 January 2002, https://tinyurl.com/bp9fbmpz. Accessed on 17 June 2024.
[449]Blarel, Nicolas, *The Evolution of India's Israel Policy: Continuity, Change and Compromise Since 1922*, 2015, Oxford University Press, New Delhi, p. 328.

manufacturing base holds out immense potential for advancing the strategic partnership in future. In 2023, Eli Cohen, the then Israeli Foreign Minister, reminisced that with 'well-synchronized defence cooperation, Israel was among the first countries to take up the call for the Make in India initiative and start joint projects with a manufacturing base in India.' His declaration that 'we are willing to create more platforms of joint R&D to pinpoint shared challenges, discuss and find solutions together, and even manufacture them together,'[450], was not rhetorical in light of Israel's proven keenness to do business with India on transfer of technology (ToT) basis.

With Russia, France and the USA also dangling ToT in order to maintain their competitive positions in India's defence market, Israel is not the type of player to easily concede ground. As a destination for Israeli arms, India accounted for only 15 per cent at the turn of the millennium but climbed to 42 per cent by 2021.[451] As the largest purchaser which spends an average of $2 billion per annum on Israeli arms, India helps sustain thousands of Israeli jobs and meet the corporate bottom lines of the Israeli defence-industrial complex. It is win-win bilateralism at its best that is based on mutual benefit.

Apart from commercial revenues and national security gains, there are also positive implications of Israel-India defence-industrial partnerships for regional coordination involving both countries. In 2021, the American analyst Caroline Rose described the planned 10-year roadmap in bilateral defence cooperation as 'an attempt by both Jerusalem and New Delhi to diversify their alliance system outside of existing

---

[450]PTI, 'Indo-Israeli Defence Relationship a Key Pillar of Growing Partnership: Foreign Minister Cohen', *The Economic Times*, 20 September 2023, https://tinyurl.com/2td8hwjp. Accessed on 7 June 2024.
[451]Essa, Azad, 'India and Israel: The Arms Trade in Charts and Numbers', *Middle East Eye*, 31 May 2022, https://tinyurl.com/yckbtr3z. Accessed on 17 June 2024.

relations with the US, Russia, and others,' and as 'an attempt to build a new, capable security system' and an 'emerging multilateral security framework from the Mediterranean to the Indian Ocean, a development being pushed by GCC [Gulf Cooperation Council] countries as well.'[452]

HARD STATE AND ASSERTIVE STATE

Earlier in this chapter, we saw how India stood by Israel's right to defend itself against the scourge of jihadist terrorism after the 7 October 2023 attacks. Counterterrorism and intelligence-sharing have been major glues binding Israel and India for decades. India's external intelligence agency, the Research and Analysis Wing (R&AW), had a 'secret liaison relationship' with Israel's Mossad since 1968 'to benefit from Israel's knowledge of West Asia and North Africa, and to learn from its counterterrorism techniques.'[453] Owing to the deep-rooted anti-Semitism and radically anti-Israel attitude of Pakistan, Jerusalem always perceived Islamabad as a threat (though not as big as Iran or Palestinian extremists) to its interests, and looked to partner with India to curb the menace of global jihadist extremism emanating from Pakistan. This equation came to light in 1991, when Israeli tourists were attacked, killed and abducted by Pakistan-backed terrorists in Kashmir Valley. By 2001, it was reported that 'Israeli intelligence agencies had "several teams" now in Kashmir, training Indian counter-insurgency forces and getting "heavily involved" in

[452]Cited in Siddiqui, Sabena, 'Inside India and Israel's 10-Year Military Roadmap', The New Arab, 11 November 2021, https://tinyurl.com/457995tw. Accessed on 17 June 2024.
[453]Raman, B., The Kaoboys of R&AW, 2007, Lancer, New Delhi, pp. 127–128.

helping New Delhi combat Islamic militants.'[454] In 2003, a senior Israeli official was quoted during a Joint Working Group meeting that 'we find ourselves in the same camp that fights terrorism and we have to develop our relationship according to that,' while his Indian counterparts seconded him that 'India finds it increasingly beneficial to learn from Israel's experience in dealing with terrorism since Israel, too, has long suffered from cross-border terrorism.'[455]

Israel-India counterterrorism cooperation grew exponentially after the terrorist attacks in Mumbai in 2008, when Pakistan-based jihadists infiltrated India's commercial megapolis, and committed mass carnage, killing not only Indians but also Israeli citizens. The cold-blooded and deliberate killing of Jews by Pakistani terrorists on Indian soil during the 26/11 attacks ensured that the Israel-India strategic partnership grew exponentially after that traumatic episode. Since then, 'Israel has provided India with satellite photo imagery, unarmed vehicles (UAVs), handheld thermal imagers, night-vision devices, long-range reconnaissance and observation systems (LORROS), and detection equipment for counterterrorism purposes.'[456] In 2018, India set up 'smart border fences' along its militarized Himalayan frontier with Pakistan, using an Israeli 'first-of-a-kind high-tech surveillance system that will create an invisible electronic barrier on land, water and even in air and underground.'[457]

---

[454]Rajghatta, Chidanand, 'Israeli Teams Training Forces in Kashmir: Jane's', *The Times of India*, 16 August 2001, https://tinyurl.com/umdcw9kv. Accessed on 17 June 2024.

[455]Chengappa, Bidanda, 'India-Israel Relations: Politico-Military Dimensions', *CLAWS Journal*, Summer 2010, p. 252.

[456]Karmon, Ely, 'India's Counterterrorism Cooperation with Israel', *Perspectives on Terrorism*, Vol. 16, No. 2, 2022, p. 5.

[457]Khajuria, Ravi, 'Rajnath Singh Inaugurates 2 Pilot Projects of "Smart" Border Fence in Jammu and Kashmir', *Hindustan Times*, 17 September 2018, https://tinyurl.com/39adymax. Accessed on 17 June 2024.

After the 7 October 2023 attacks, when an army of Hamas jihadists easily breached Israel's 'Iron Wall' fence with Gaza, and went on a rampage for hours inside Israeli territory, Indians were shell-shocked at the stunning Israeli intelligence failure. One of the lessons learnt from it was that hi-tech fences could be useful to curb cross-border terrorist infiltration, but must not be left unmanned, the way Israel had done prior to the 7 October attacks 'because of the ideological priorities of its political leadership.'[458] It is instructive that within weeks of the collapse of Israel's Iron Wall fence, India was reportedly negotiating with two Israeli companies for anti-drone technology 'to arm Border Security Force (BSF) to fight against drones coming from Pakistan, as the neighbouring country has started using Chinese made high quality drones to smuggle drugs, arms and ammunition into India.'[459]

Neither Israel nor India has a foolproof record in successfully preventing all cross-border jihadist terrorism. Also, the primary sources of threats that Israel and India perceive are different. Being located in West Asia/the Middle East, Israel considers Iran, the state sponsor of Hamas and Hezbollah, to be its number one adversary, and the fountainhead of terrorism. Residing in South Asia, India sees Pakistan as its everlasting terrorist challenge. India's strategic partnership with Iran (see Chapter 7) even rankles with Israel, although Jerusalem understands New Delhi's geopolitical calculus for befriending Tehran, and has never applied any meaningful pressure on New Delhi to dissociate itself from Tehran. Jihadist attacks aimed at Israeli diplomats in India in 2012 and 2021

[458]Swami, Praveen, 'Israel's Border Defence Collapse Should Make India Think How it Manages LOC in Kashmir', *The Print*, 1 November 2023, https://tinyurl.com/3ac334fr. Accessed on 17 June 2024.
[459]IDN, 'Israel-Made Anti-Drone System to be Installed Along India-Pakistan Border', *Indian Defence News*, 25 November 2023, https://tinyurl.com/yc84vpj5. Accessed on 17 June 2024.

were blamed on Iran, but those incidents did not lead to India downgrading ties with Iran, nor did they derail the Israel-India friendship.

Despite differences, Israel and India share collective fears about global jihadist collusion, coordination and inspiration that bring Islamists of various hues together to think and act in the name of a universal *Ummah* (community). One can see the *Ummah*-based linkages at play in many theatres. In June 2023, Mossad claimed to have thwarted an Iranian terrorist plot to assassinate Jewish businesspersons in Cyprus, wherein a senior Iranian intelligence officer was referred to as boasting that he had hitmen from Pakistan whom he trusted and who 'carried out very important activity' for him.[460] In November 2023, Hamas leaders met Pakistani Islamist politicians in Qatar and proclaimed that 'the lingering Kashmir and Palestine [issues] have been a slap in the face of those calling themselves as the advocates of human rights.'[461] Equating India's rule in Kashmir with Israel's occupation of Palestine and glorifying 'freedom struggles' of Muslims against 'infidels' in Kashmir and Palestine, are commonplace in Pakistan and get deployed in motivation, recruitment and training of hardened jihadists.

In overall anti-terrorism strategy, Israel and India do diverge. The 'Dahiya doctrine' of Israel that involves use of disproportionate force against adversaries goes 'well beyond defeating an opponent in a brief conflict,' and extends 'to the destruction of the economy and state infrastructure with many civilian casualties, with the intention of achieving a sustained

[460]PTI, 'Mossad Discovers Pakistani Involvement in Yet Another Plot to Kill Jewish Business People', *The Times of India*, https://tinyurl.com/243yp46m. Accessed on 17 June 2024.
[461]ET, 'Hamas Chief Appeals for Ummah Support', *The Express Tribune*, 5 November 2023, https://tinyurl.com/yc544dv8. Accessed on 17 June 2024.

deterrent impact.'[462] As a classic national security state or 'hard state', where the military and intelligence agencies have an inordinate influence on foreign policy, Israel has not hesitated to use force against its opponents with overwhelming might. Since it enjoys a nuclear asymmetric superiority over its rivals (although Iran may be developing nuclear weapons), Israel can also afford to go hammer and tongs at its foes. India is not a hard state but has become what I described elsewhere as an 'assertive state', with a counter-offensive strategic culture in the Modi era.[463] As a leading power or would-be great power in the world that needs a range of friendships and partnerships, India cannot afford a Dahiya doctrine of its own because it cares much more about maintaining its international image as a rule-abiding good global citizen than Israel. Moreover, India faces two nuclear-armed adversaries, Pakistan and China, and lacks the asymmetrical leverage to deploy stupendous and relentless force to pulverize them for sponsoring and abetting terrorism.

In spite of the disparities in the Israeli and Indian models of counterterrorism at the strategic level, the bilateral tactical cooperation is bound to grow in response to rising threats posed by Islamist fundamentalists. A hard state and an assertive state can profit from focused bilateral give-and-take in the security sphere. Due to the classified and sensitive nature of Israel-India counterterrorism work, we only know bits and pieces of how deeply enmeshed the two partners are at the operational level in fighting the jihadist threat. One will not read banner headlines and hear bullhorn announcements in this area of the friendship, but it will remain a core ingredient and a perennial growth area of the strategic partnership.

[462]Rogers, Paul, 'Israel's Use of Disproportionate Force is a Long-Established Tactic—With a Clear Aim', *The Guardian*, 5 December 2023, https://tinyurl.com/3fd6uk7v. Accessed on 17 June 2024.
[463]Chaulia, Sreeram, *Crunch Time*, op. cit.

It must be acknowledged that significant non-military and non-intelligence-based legs of the friendship do exist, and have been highlighted in bilateral communiqués and discourses to compensate for the official secrecy of the defence and anti-terror cooperation. The 'Strategic Partnership in Water and Agriculture' focuses on 'water conservation, waste-water treatment and its reuse for agriculture, desalination, water utility reforms, and the cleaning of the Ganges and other rivers using advanced water technologies.'[464] The India-Israel Industrial R&D Technological Innovation Fund (I4F) promotes 'co-development and commercialization of innovative technologies' in sectors like energy, healthcare and IT services.[465] Stellar improvements in productivity and quality in farming, thanks to trainings in Israeli 'Centers of Excellence' in agriculture, across the states of India have increased respect for the Israeli genius that made the desert bloom in the biblical Promised Land. Tie-ups between India's upcoming young entrepreneurs and their Israeli counterparts have stirred aspirations in India to emulate the 'start-up nation' that is famous for brilliant innovations despite its small size and existential conflicts with hostile neighbours. All these civilian components provide depth to the 'strategic' element in the Israel-India friendship.

REGIONAL SYNERGY

If pragmatic bilateralism has served Israel and India well for decades, concerted multilateralism for pan-regional integration is an emerging field for the friendship to break new ground. The launch of the 'I2U2' grouping, comprising Israel, India,

---

[464]MEA, 'India-Israel Joint Statement During the Visit of Prime Minister to Israel', Ministry of External Affairs, Government of India, 5 July 2017, https://tinyurl.com/346d74uj. Accessed on 17 June 2024.
[465]INI, 'I4F-Israel-India', Innovation Israel, https://tinyurl.com/yf8s2m7b. Accessed on 17 June 2024.

the USA and the UAE, in 2021 was a notable step towards economically integrating West Asia/the Middle East with South Asia, and consolidating the process of normalization of relations between Arab countries and Israel. The UAE was the first in a wave of Arab nations that recognized the State of Israel, and established full diplomatic relations with it under the 2020 Abraham Accords brokered by the USA. Capitalizing on the strong strategic partnerships that India had with both Israel and the UAE, the idea behind I2U2 was to bring India in, keep the USA involved, and buttress Israel's diplomatic status in a region that used to shun it since its creation in 1948. With the mandate for joint investments and new initiatives in water, energy, transportation, space, health and food security, the I2U2 aimed to 'reaffirm our support for the Abraham Accords and other peace and normalization arrangements with Israel,' and tap into 'the economic opportunities that flow from these historic developments.'[466]

In Israel, I2U2 was lauded as a unique instrument through which India could 'help to enhance and expand the scope of [the] Abraham Accords [by] bringing in new countries' and to 'push others by saying that it is in the interest of the world' to integrate with Israel.[467] Whatever remnants of isolating Israel remained in West Asia/the Middle East were expected to be blown away by the virtuous cycle of economic gains that I2U2 would engender. For India, I2U2 was billed as an opportunity to 'increase its regional influence and to strengthen its cooperation with the US,' and to extend its pre-existing bilateral partnership with Israel in water

---

[466]PTI, 'I2U2 Grouping of India, Israel, UAE, US Expresses Commitment to Deepen Economic Partnership', *The Times of India*, 21 September 2022, https://tinyurl.com/2cna8c7f. Accessed on 17 June 2024.
[467]PTI, 'India's Partnership Can Be "Game Changer" in I2U2 Grouping: Former Israeli NSA', *The Economic Times*, 13 July 2022, https://tinyurl.com/enz4fery. Accessed on 17 June 2024.

management, energy and new technologies to the wider West Asia/the Middle East.[468] The Modi government's 'Look and Act West' policy could indeed get a major fillip if I2U2 yields tangible outcomes. It is worth recalling that Prime Minister Netanyahu had coined the term 'I2T2' in 2017, when Prime Minister Modi made history by eschewing past ideological and political hang-ups, and becoming the first Indian prime minister to set foot in Israel. Netanyahu explained I2T2 as 'Indian talent times Israeli technology,' and predicted that 'it equals Israel-India's ties for tomorrow.'[469] Presumably, I2U2 is an externalization of I2T2, and it will ensconce the bilateral strategic partnership in a web of regional friendships.

In 2023, I2U2 members expanded the circle of friends to include Saudi Arabia, France, Germany, Italy and the EU, and announced the formation of the multi-modal trans-continental India-Middle East-Europe Economic Corridor (IMEC) to connect South Asia with the Persian Gulf, the Levant and Europe. The boldest geoeconomic initiative the world had seen since China's BRI, it gave Israel the coveted position of a transit country for trade and transportation flows between East and West. The groundwork for one of IMEC's routes was laid when Israel sold its strategically situated Mediterranean Sea Port of Haifa to India's Adani Group for $1.18 billion, terming it 'a very symbolic sign of deep trust in depositing [...our] strategic assets in the hands of Indian companies.'[470] The takeover of the Port of Haifa by the Indian conglomerate

[468]Afterman, Gedaliah, 'Israel-India Strategic Partnership Could be Game-Changer for Both', *The Jerusalem Post*, 23 January 2023, https://tinyurl.com/yckney65. Accessed on 17 June 2024.

[469]GOVIL, 'Statements by PM Netanyahu and Indian PM Narendra Modi', op. cit.

[470]Laskar, Rezaul, 'Adani Group Paid in Full for Haifa Port, Eyes Other Projects, Says Israeli Envoy', *Hindustan Times*, 22 February 2023, https://tinyurl.com/2e4hj4pw. Accessed on 17 June 2024.

happened in the context of Israel responding to American concerns about China, and 'taking more systematic steps to scale back potentially risky Chinese critical infrastructure and hi-tech investments.'[471] The attraction of IMEC for India is that China has been deliberately excluded from it. India is painfully aware that China tends to take centre-stage, set the rules and standards, and dominate the economic exchanges wherever it is present, be it the BRI or the RCEP. The USA's endorsement that the IMEC is attractive 'because it is transparent, high standard and not coercive,'[472] i.e. it is an alternative model of globalization and connectivity, with no threat of Chinese hegemony, appeals to India.

It is unrealistic to expect that Israel and the Gulf monarchies will totally spurn China and conduct business exclusively with the West and India. Popular representations of I2U2 as the 'West Asian Quad' or an alliance to roll back Chinese influence rest on assumptions that Israel, India and the Gulf countries are functioning under a grand USA-orchestrated plan to counterbalance or dislodge China from West Asia/the Middle East. But India's separate strategic partnership with Iran and the determined pursuit of strategic autonomy by Saudi Arabia and the UAE (*see* Chapter 7) make countering China in West Asia/the Middle East a complex proposition.

I2U2 and IMEC are also not immune from periodic wars and outbreaks of violence between Israel and the Palestinians, which make it politically uneasy for Gulf countries to be seen in a coalition with the Arab street's much-hated 'Zionist enemy'. The remark by Isaac Herzog, President of Israel, that

---

[471]Millner, Sam, 'Israel Looks to India, not China, for Haifa Port', The Jewish Institute for National Security of America', 5 August 2022, https://tinyurl.com/2nmt7c2h. Accessed on 17 June 2024.

[472]HT, 'Stamp on New Trade Corridor to Counter China's BRI Push', *Hindustan Times*, 10 September 2023, https://tinyurl.com/3savens5. Accessed on 17 June 2024.

the 7 October 2023 terror attacks were launched by the 'empire of evil Iran' to derail IMEC and 'to undermine any inclusion of Israel in the region'[473] was a reminder about the fragility of regionalism in a West Asia/the Middle East that sits on a perpetual powder keg.

Nonetheless, we can be certain that the Israel-India bilateral friendship will be nested in regional and global synergies that are structurally enduring. India's closeness to Israel has created positive spin-offs for the USA-India strategic partnership. And New Delhi's alignment with Washington has enhanced Jerusalem's keenness to partner with the former. In Chapter 3, we mentioned that the Jewish lobby in the USA made common cause with the Indian diaspora as it pushed Washington to act against Pakistan-sponsored jihadist terrorism. There were other accomplishments of the lobbying duo, which reconfirmed the USA's role as a site and as a catalyst in the Israel-India friendship. In the 2000s, 'the Jews and the Indians worked together to gain the Bush administration's approval for Israel to sell Phalcon AWACS to India,' and 'Jewish support was important in passing in [the] US Congress, the Indo-US nuclear deal that allowed India access to nuclear technology for civilian uses.'[474] The American Jewish Committee (AJC), an influential global advocacy organization headquartered in New York, champions a 'trilateral India-Israel-U.S. nexus,' and networks with Indian Americans on the bases of 'attachment to a distant ancestral homeland, and concerns about extremism.'[475]

---

[473]ANI, 'Iran Orchestrated October 7 Attacks to Derail India-Middle East-Economic Corridor: Israel', *Hindustan Times*, https://tinyurl.com/y6386y7u. Accessed on 17 June 2024.

[474]Inbar, Efraim, 'Israel and India: Looking Back and Ahead', in Prasad, Jayant, and Samuel Rajiv, eds., *India and Israel: The Making of a Strategic Partnership*, 2020, Routledge, Abingdon, p. 35–36.

[475]AJC, 'India: Building on Cultural Affinities and Strengthening Trilateral Ties', American Jewish Committee, https://tinyurl.com/2p977v6r. Accessed on 17 June 2024.

Apart from the two fraternal diasporas in the USA lending a hand to the Israel-India friendship, India's diaspora in Israel itself could become a key variable. As of 2023, Israel had about 85,000 Jewish citizens of Indian origin, but only 18,000 Indian citizens worked as nurses, caregivers, diamond traders and IT professionals there. The acute labour shortage which struck Israel's construction industry after the 7 October 2023 terrorist attacks and the war created openings for tens of thousands more Indians to fill the vacuum. Crisis-hit Israeli builders reached out to 'engage 50,000 to 100,000 workers from India to be able to run the whole sector and bring it back to normal.'[476] In the medium to long term, if I2U2 and IMEC progress and regional stability holds, hundreds of thousands of Indians might be required to move in and out of Israel and the neighbouring countries for execution of projects. Such a human bridge would add a people-to-people layer of reinsurance to a most consequential strategic partnership on which there is no going back.

---

[476]LM, 'Israel to Hire 1 Lakh Indian Workers Amid War with Hamas? MEA Says...', *Mint*, 9 November 2023, https://tinyurl.com/2xbcerch. Accessed on 17 June 2024.

7

I TOO, YOU TOO: THE UAE AND INDIA IN A TRANSFORMATIVE EMBRACE

Our strategic relationship with India is above all since India is one of the most important countries on the globe. So, it has nothing to do with India-Pakistan relations. India is important because it is India. It has opportunity, potential, science and population.[477]

—Anwar Gargash, Minister of State for Foreign Affairs of the UAE, 2017

In August 2019, the Narendra Modi government ushered in a landmark structural reform to fortify India's national security. It announced a radical reorganization of the Jammu and Kashmir (J&K) region by revoking its seven-decade-long separate autonomous status under Article 370 of the Indian Constitution, and by converting it into a centrally administered territory. For decades, autonomy in J&K had become a slippery slope for separatism, jihadist extremism,

---

[477]GN, 'Strategic Partnership with India is Above All, UAE Minister Says', *Gulf News*, 23 January 2017, https://tinyurl.com/mr2ymu2d. Accessed on 19 June 2024.

and alienation of Kashmiri Muslims from the rest of India. The special status had been a gift for neighbouring Pakistan to exploit and fan alienation of Kashmiri Muslims against India. By capitalizing on Article 370, which allowed J&K to have a half-hearted existence in India, Islamabad sponsored wave after wave of cross-border terrorism, with the goal of wresting Kashmir from India and annexing it to Pakistan. The abrogation of Article 370 shut the door to separatism, and to Pakistan-sponsored secessionist designs, making it a game-changing decision that altered the nature and contours of politics not only in J&K but across South Asia. It sent out a clear signal that India would no longer be in a defensive mode in protecting its core territorial integrity and sovereignty.

Sensing that India had moved decisively to fully integrate Kashmir into its national mainstream, and fearing a new era of Indian consolidation over the contested Himalayan region, Pakistan reacted with threats that it would 'exercise all possible options to counter the illegal steps' by India.[478] Its options included authorizing banned proxy jihadist terrorist groups to carry out major attacks, internationalizing Kashmir as a dangerous flashpoint or hotspot that could explode in war and nuclear holocaust, appealing to the USA to intervene immediately and prevent Kashmir from blowing up into 'a regional crisis'[479], and knocking on the doors of the UN and the Islamic world by alleging deterioration in human rights conditions of Muslims in J&K. Although Donald Trump, the then President of the USA, reiterated whimsical talk of mediating between India and Pakistan, those were typical

---

[478]Ameer, Hamza, 'Will Exercise All Possible Options to Counter "Illegal" Steps: Pakistan on Article 370', *India Today*, 5 August 2019, https://tinyurl.com/2kwnc9ad. Accessed on 19 June 2024.
[479]Bhattacharjee, Kallol, 'Regional Crisis Possible Over Kashmir, Says Imran Khan', *The Hindu*, 4 August 2019, https://tinyurl.com/4k3jrt37. Accessed on 19 June 2024.

off-the-cuff offers with no substance or real intent. He soon backtracked and brushed off the whole issue by quoting Prime Minister Modi that the situation was 'under control'.[480]

European countries joined the USA to block repeated efforts by Pakistan and China to issue a statement in the UN Security Council, condemning India's 'unilateral' measures in J&K. India's main strategic partner in Europe and ever-reliable friend in the UN Security Council, France, said it had learnt from Modi that the scrapping of Article 370 was 'in their sovereignty', and warned that 'no third party should interfere or incite violence.'[481] With the exception of Pakistan's 'all-weather strategic partner' China, hardly any major power stood up for it in that moment of reckoning. A visibly frustrated and deflated Imran Khan, the then Prime Minister of Pakistan, admitted that Islamabad's narrative on Kashmir had fallen on deaf ears because 'people look upon India as a market of 1.2 billion people [...] Some are appalled by it but by the end of it, they think of it as a market.'[482]

A STRATEGIC TURNAROUND

What particularly hurt and shocked Pakistan was that this 'market' power or global influence of India had swayed even the traditionally pro-Pakistan corners in the Islamic world. Since Islamabad viewed the Kashmir issue, and Pakistan's decades-long conflict with India, through the religious prism

---

[480]AFP, 'Trump Says India's Modi Feels He Has "It Under Control in Kashmir"', *Voice of America*, https://tinyurl.com/4sz924dp. Accessed on 19 June 2024.
[481]DNA, '"Their Sovereignty": France's Macron Backs India's Article 370 Move on Kashmir in Meeting with PM Modi', *Daily News and Analysis*, https://tinyurl.com/33zfbbje. Accessed on 19 June 2024.
[482]TOI, '"No Pressure on Modi": Imran Khan Disappointed with World Community on Kashmir', *The Times of India*, 25 September 2019, https://tinyurl.com/mv9mb26r. Accessed on 19 June 2024.

as a 'self-determination struggle' of oppressed Muslims against a Hindu-majority adversary, it nursed high hopes about rallying the *Ummah* (community) to support its claims and to pressurize India. When foreign ministers of two leading Islamic countries, Saudi Arabia and the UAE, arrived in Islamabad for consultations a month after India put Article 370 to rest, Pakistan expected it to be a big show of pan-Islamic solidarity. Instead, the two Gulf powerhouses blandly committed to 'remain engaged to help address the current challenges, defuse tensions, and promote an environment of peace and security.'[483] To some extent, Saudi Arabia humoured Pakistan by joining Azerbaijan, Niger and Turkey to issue a statement on behalf of a 'Kashmir Contact Group' at the Organisation of Islamic Cooperation (OIC) that India must 'rescind its unilateral illegal actions'.[484] Shortly thereafter though, Saudi Arabia hosted Prime Minister Modi, announced a \$15 billion investment in India's oil giant, Reliance, launched a bilateral 'Strategic Partnership Council' with India, and 'told Pakistan that what India is doing in Kashmir is New Delhi's internal matter.'[485] As the orthodox custodian of the two holiest shrines of Islam and the self-described leader of the Muslim world, Saudi Arabia lent lip service to Pakistan on Kashmir, but pragmatically advanced its strategic partnership with India.

The sternest setback to Pakistan actually came from the multicultural and cosmopolitan UAE, which was quoted as saying that 'Kashmir is not an issue concerning Muslim

[483]PTI, 'Imran Khan Discusses Kashmir Situation with Saudi, UAE Foreign Ministers', *India Today*, 5 September 2019, https://tinyurl.com/296a7d3y. Accessed on 19 June 2024.

[484]Haidar, Suhasini, 'Kashmir Issue: Rescind Action on Article 370, Organisation of Islamic Cooperation Tells India', *The Hindu*, 26 September 2019, https://tinyurl.com/mseup9y4. Accessed on 19 June 2024.

[485]Basu, Nayanima, 'Saudi Arabia "Backs India" Against Pakistan on Kashmir and Article 370', *The Print*, 31 October 2019, https://tinyurl.com/5etc3d2x. Accessed on 19 June 2024.

Ummah but rather a dispute between Islamabad and New Delhi, and that revocation of Article 370 was an "internal matter" of India aimed at "reducing regional disparity and improving efficiency".[486] To rub it in for Pakistan, within days of the abrogation of Article 370, Abu Dhabi's Crown Prince and the UAE's de facto ruler, Mohamed bin Zayed Al Nahyan (MBZ), personally bestowed on Modi the Order of Zayed medal, the UAE's highest civilian honour, addressed him as 'my dear friend', and credited him for boosting the UAE's 'comprehensive strategic ties with India'.[487] Earlier in 2019, much to Pakistan's chagrin, the UAE pulled off a diplomatic coup by inviting 'the friendly country of India' as Guest of Honour at the OIC foreign ministers meeting in Abu Dhabi, and justified that unprecedented choice on the grounds of India's 'great global political stature as well as its time-honoured and deeply rooted cultural and historical legacy, and its important Islamic component.'[488] Pakistan was so outraged and isolated that it boycotted the ministerial where the then Indian External Affairs Minister Sushma Swaraj held forth about the need to dismantle terrorist infrastructure in states that harbour and shelter extremists. Further proof that the UAE had swung around to India came just prior to the OIC meeting in February 2019, when a tense military stand-off after the capture of an Indian Air Force pilot, Abhinandan Varthaman, by Pakistan was averted due to a constructive behind-the-scenes role played by the UAE 'in

---

[486]ANI, 'Kashmir Issue Does Not Concern Muslim Community: UAE Snubs Pak', *Business Standard*, 5 September 2019, https://tinyurl.com/r34fc2c4. Accessed on 19 June 2024.

[487]AJ, 'India's Narendra Modi Gets Top UAE Honour Amid Kashmir Crisis', *Al Jazeera*, 24 August 2019, https://tinyurl.com/yzxurnmf. Accessed on 19 June 2024.

[488]Chaudhury, Dipanjan, 'India Invited as Guest of Honour for 1st Time Ever by OIC; Delhi's Big Pitch in Islamic World', *The Economic Times*, 23 February 2019, https://tinyurl.com/j4buewzw. Accessed on 19 June 2024.

reducing tension', and helping 'sort out differences between the two sides in a peaceful manner through negotiations.'[489] Abu Dhabi apparently teamed up with Riyadh and Washington to apply pressure on Islamabad to defuse the crisis.

Over the years, the UAE has not only banned many India-designated terrorist groups and aligned with India in seeking to curb the threat of the Taliban and other jihadists in Afghanistan, but also reacted to Pakistan-sponsored jihadist violence in J&K by expressing 'solidarity with India and support to all actions it may take to confront and eradicate terrorism.'[490]

That the UAE was India's best friend in the Muslim world for blunting Pakistan's rallying cry of Islam being in danger in Kashmir, became more evident after the Dubai-based Emaar Group, the builder of the world's tallest skyscraper Burj Khalifa, turned out to be the first foreign company to make an investment worth $60 million in J&K in 2023 for constructing a mega mall and other infrastructure works. Expecting that it would generate thousands of jobs for local Kashmiris, India hailed 'the Mall of Srinagar and allied projects with the government of Dubai,' and predicted they would fuel 'the economic growth of J&K, and bring the region closer to achieving the shared vision of strengthening bilateral trade and investment ties between UAE and India.'[491]

Many more investments from the UAE in hotels, residential and commercial complexes, hypermarkets and tourism in

---

[489]Mohan, Geeta, 'UAE Played Important Role in De-Escalating Tensions Between India, Pakistan: UAE Envoy to India', *India Today*, 18 March 2019, https://tinyurl.com/rpyafbye. Accessed on 19 June 2024.

[490]KT, 'UAE Condemns Terror Attack on Indian Army Base', *Khaleej Times*, 18 September 2016, https://tinyurl.com/ymdkyh4h. Accessed on 19 June 2024.

[491]ANI, 'UAE's EMAAR Makes First-Ever FDI in a Srinagar Mall', *Asian News International*, 9 March 2023, https://tinyurl.com/yeywduy8. Accessed on 19 June 2024.

J&K are on the anvil, spurred especially by Indian diaspora businesspersons operating out of the Emirates. With the UAE acting as a torchbearer, Saudi Arabia and other wealthy Gulf nations could follow suit, and help anchor stability in J&K, accomplishing a fundamental strategic goal of India.[492] In Chapter 1, we saw how Japan was entrusted with the role of modernization of infrastructure in sensitive parts of Northeast India which faced territorial claims and military threats from China. The UAE, a Muslim country, has the potential to perform a similar strategic role in J&K to check Pakistan-inspired Islamist separatism and assist India in ending the so-called 'Kashmir problem'.

UNITED AGAINST TERROR

The big switch in the UAE's foreign policy away from Pakistan is not driven solely by the allure of India's fast-growing market and immense commercial opportunities, which outshine Pakistan's sinking and debt-dependent economy. It is also the product of an internal reassessment in Abu Dhabi about the grave dangers posed by Islamist terrorism. In 1999, when an Indian Airlines flight was hijacked by Pakistani jihadists and landed in Dubai, the UAE did not assist India. New Delhi believed that the Emiratis were 'reluctant to get embroiled in a hijacking involving a so-called Islamic cause,' and let the plane depart to Kandahar in Taliban-ruled Afghanistan.[493] Today, the India-UAE comprehensive strategic partnership is so robust that Abu Dhabi takes New Delhi's side during crises over Islamabad-sponsored terrorism.

---

[492]Ehsan, Mir, 'Kashmir: India's Ambassador to Saudi Arabia for Promotion of Trade', *Hindustan Times*, 3 June 2023, https://tinyurl.com/bdfwsepm. Accessed on 19 June 2024.
[493]IT, 'Why Didn't the Hijack Drama End in Dubai?' *India Today*, 13 September 2012, https://tinyurl.com/2p9thck6. Accessed on 19 June 2024.

Since the 9/11 attacks, in which two of the nineteen Al Qaeda hijackers were Emiratis, the UAE set out to demonstrate to the world that it would have a zero-tolerance policy towards jihadist extremism and fundamentalism through visible actions. Aware that the mastermind, Khalid Sheikh Mohammed, was a Pakistani, and knowing that India had been a long-time sufferer of jihadist terror originating from Pakistan, the UAE moved to arrest and extradite at least seven wanted terrorists to India between 2002 and 2013, including those involved in the 1993 Mumbai serial bomb blasts.[494] The illicit financial operations of India's most wanted terrorist Dawood Ibrahim were broken up in Dubai. Pakistan-based terror groups today find it 'harder to raise money in the UAE due to the increased scrutiny on money transfers.'[495] Following the 2008 Mumbai attacks that were carried out by Pakistan's Lashkar-e-Taiba (LeT), India's intelligence-sharing and information gathering with the UAE and other Gulf states increased and yielded prize catches of wanted fugitive terrorists.

In the second decade of the 21st century, a new avatar of jihadist trouble brewed and proved to be deeply detrimental to the cause of stability in West Asia/the Middle East, affecting countries in the region and having a ripple effect far beyond it. The ISIS monster reared its head as a result of a complex historical turn of events, and morphed from a sectarian Islamist insurgency aiming for regime change in Iraq and Syria, to threaten regional and global security. The UAE moved swiftly against this hateful force and focused on busting India-focused radical expatriate cells and modules of

[494]MEA, 'List of Fugitives Extradited/Deported by Foreign Governments to India', Ministry of External Affairs, Government of India, 2015, https://tinyurl.com/muswadfe. Accessed on 19 June 2024.
[495]Siyech, Mohammed Sinan, 'The India-UAE. Strategic Partnership in Regional Context: A Zero-Sum Game?' Middle East Institute, 16 May 2017, https://tinyurl.com/52jzjmmf. Accessed on 19 June 2024.

ISIS based in the Emirates, and organizing deportations of suspects to Indian custody. Indian agencies credited the UAE for having 'one of the most sophisticated security systems in the region, including state-of-the-art cyber capabilities that have helped it to catch terrorists and criminals,' and touted the bilateral comprehensive strategic partnership's emphasis on a 'holistic approach, which includes disrupting the use of the internet and social media for promotion of extremist and violent ideologies; preventing the use of religious centres to radicalize youth and recruit terrorist cadres, and promoting tolerance.'[496]

Between 2012 and 2018, of the more than two dozen terror suspects sent to India from the Gulf, 18 were from the UAE and Saudi Arabia alone, proving how strategic partnerships with leading Muslim countries yield tangible results for India's national security, and help reinforce the idea of an indivisible global security against transnational religious fundamentalism.[497]

Compared to Saudi Arabia, which had a history of financing and spreading ultra-conservative and hard-line Wahhabi ideology worldwide, the UAE has less Islamist baggage of its own to shed and has, hence, been more forthcoming to team up with India on strategic initiatives to promote moderate and tolerant variants of Islam. It is a rare distinction that the UAE government set up a full-fledged Ministry of Tolerance and Coexistence, dedicated to officially promoting diversity, dialogue and peace within the country

---

[496]Chaudhury, Dipanjan, 'UAE Quietly Deporting IS Sympathizers of Indian Origin', *The Economic Times*, 6 December 2018, https://tinyurl.com/44sk54jm. Accessed on 19 June 2024.
[497]Ahuja, Rajesh, and Jayanth Jacob, 'Of 24 Terror Suspects Turned in by Gulf Countries to India Since 2012, 18 are from UAE and Saudi', *Hindustan Times*, 24 August 2018, https://tinyurl.com/3m7xk55u. Accessed on 19 June 2024.

and with foreign counterparts. By hosting Pope Francis, the head of the Roman Catholic Church, approving the building of Hindu temples and Sikh gurudwaras, and opening the Abrahamic Family House which contains a mosque, church and synagogue, the UAE burnished its soft power and appealed to Indian sensibilities.

During Modi's historic visit to the UAE in 2015, the first by an Indian prime minister in 34 years, the two sides affirmed that 'the UAE is a shining example of a multi-cultural society' while 'India is a nation of unparalleled diversity, religious pluralism and a composite culture,' and condemned 'efforts, including by states, to use religion to justify, support and sponsor terrorism against other countries.'[498]

The running theme of a common moderate identity has been a values-based cement in the UAE-India friendship, with both countries committing 'to the fight against extremism and terrorism, including cross-border terrorism' and to 'promoting the values of peace, moderation, coexistence, and tolerance among peoples.'[499] The domestic security threat perceptions of the UAE's secular authoritarian regime about Islamism, and its manifestations like the Muslim Brotherhood in West Asia/ the Middle East and the Tablighi Jamaat in South Asia, have helped bring Abu Dhabi closer to New Delhi in ideological terms.

The not-so-subtle jabs against the radical Islamist approach of Pakistan in jointly worded UAE-India statements have been unmissable. They convey that apart from nuts-and-

---

[498]MEA, 'Joint Statement Between the United Arab Emirates and the Republic of India', Ministry of External Affairs, Government of India, 17 August 2015, https://tinyurl.com/bde2tnwf. Accessed on 19 June 2024.

[499]MEA, 'India-UAE Joint Statement During the Visit of Prime Minister, Shri Narendra Modi to UAE', Ministry of External Affairs, Government of India, 15 July 2023, https://tinyurl.com/5ezczdyx. Accessed on 19 June 2024.

bolts counterterrorism cooperation, there is a larger spiritual struggle for the soul of Islam in which Abu Dhabi and New Delhi are together in one corner. This tag-teaming came to light dramatically in 2022, when a controversy had been raked up in the Islamic world about supposed threats being faced by Muslim minorities in India, following unfortunate derogatory remarks made by a BJP spokesperson. MBZ, who had recently become president of the UAE, brushed aside the fracas and personally received Modi with a warm embrace in the Abu Dhabi airport. The Indian leader declared, 'I am touched by the special gesture of my brother.'[500] The Modi-MBZ personal chemistry, which has driven the bilateral friendship to the level of a 'comprehensive strategic partnership', is underpinned as much by shared worldviews as shrewd pragmatism. It is thanks to the Modi-MBZ duo's signalling from the topmost echelons that the 'fourth pillar' of security and defence ties—over and above the traditional pillars, the 'three Es' of economy, expatriates and energy—has been elevated in the bilateral friendship.[501]

THE FOURTH PILLAR

Besides counterterrorism, defence cooperation has grown in salience in the UAE-India friendship in light of the two countries upping their respective games to be regional security providers and leaders. Despite its relatively small size, and a post-independence history of maintaining a low and

---

[500]ND, 'UAE President's Surprise Special Gesture, Receives PM Modi at Abu Dhabi Airport', *CNN-News18*, 28 June 2022, https://tinyurl.com/mvf47ej9. Accessed on 19 June 2024.
[501]Singh, Manjari, 'India's Strategic Partnerships in the Gulf: Context, Objective and Components', in Pant, Harsh, and Hasan Alhasan, eds., *India and the Gulf: Theoretical Perspectives and Policy Shifts*, 2023, Cambridge University Press, Cambridge, pp. 86–87.

unassertive profile, under MBZ, the UAE set the ambitious goal of becoming 'a regional power with an international reach.'[502] One pathway chosen for greatness was military modernization and self-reliance. In a span of less than two decades, massive state spending on defence, harnessing of defence diplomacy with friendly countries, skilful deployment of expatriate military professionals, and a willingness to send troops for operational missions abroad to sustain combat-readiness, enabled the UAE to build up what defence expert Athol Yates has called 'the Arab region's most capable military,' that 'is described admiringly as a "little Sparta".'[503]

Security analyst Karam Shahrour has argued that the acquisition of military heft was part and parcel of the UAE's shift 'from mildness, Arabness and bandwagoning to assertiveness and increasing self-reliance,' which was propelled by 'a slow, yet structural, US withdrawal from the Middle East' as evidenced by Washington's 'pivot' to Asia, its unwillingness to protect allied regional regimes during the Arab Spring uprisings, and its unreliability in containing the UAE's main regional adversary, Iran.[504]

The UAE's old assumption used to be that, as a small state content with survival, staying under the Western security umbrella of the UK or the USA would be sufficient to guarantee its internal and external security. But the viability of such a bandwagoning strategy faded amidst perceived American

---

[502]Sherwood, Leah, 'Risk Diversification and UAE Foreign Policy', in Almezaini, Khaled, and Jean-Marc Rickli, eds., *The Small Gulf States: Foreign and Security Policies Before and After the Arab Spring*, 2017, Routledge, London, p. 11.

[503]Yates, Athol, *The Evolution of the Armed Forces of the United Arab Emirates*, 2020, Helion & Company, Warwick, Back Cover.

[504]Shahrour, Karam, 'The Evolution of Emirati Foreign Policy (1971–2020): The Unexpected Rise of a Small State with Boundless Ambitions', Sciences Po, Kuwait Programme, 2020, pp. 1,7, https://tinyurl.com/mr45wtwr. Accessed on 19 June 2024.

abandonment, and increasing threats of attacks from Iran and its range of proxy Islamist militias. It is in the backdrop of this mounting insecurity that 'little Sparta' arose, and began to assert itself in the region with a willingness to use hard power and intervene militarily in strategically crucial theatres. By acquiring a string of overseas military bases in Yemen, Somalia and Eritrea, and positioning itself as a guarantor of the safety of the sea lines of communication (SLOC) around the chokepoint of the Bab-al-Mandab Strait, Abu Dhabi sought to 'play a more active role in ensuring the security of the international trade routes in the Gulf of Aden and the Indian Ocean.'[505] Although Emirati hyper-activeness and involvement in proxy wars in Syria, Yemen and Libya eventually backfired and forced Abu Dhabi (as well as Riyadh) to pursue a rapprochement with their archenemy Tehran by 2023, the conversion of the UAE into a formidable regional power is a fait accompli, and it has opened up mutually beneficial avenues for geopolitical coordination with India in the Western Indian Ocean.

The UAE was the first Gulf country to sign a defence cooperation agreement with India in 2003. It focused on weapons sales, joint trainings and military coordination, and was inked just as the UAE was embarking on its self-reliance strategy in light of the USA's invasion and toppling of the Saddam Hussein regime in Iraq, and the geopolitical advantage which that seminal event had handed over to Iran. The value of India to the UAE in the defence sector lay in it being one of the alternative power centres which could help Abu Dhabi diversify its security partnerships and reduce overreliance on Washington. India fit into a larger long-term Emirati strategy of spreading its risks by signing agreements to host France's Indian

---

[505]Telci, Ismail, and Tuba Horoz, 'Military Bases in the Foreign Policy of the United Arab Emirates', *Insight Turkey*, Vol. 20, No. 2, 2018, p. 157.

Ocean Regional Command, entering into a formal military alliance with Saudi Arabia, attempting to create a Unified Military Command for all the Gulf Cooperation Council (GCC) members, and purchasing weaponry from a range of countries like the UK, China, Russia, South Africa and Turkey. Foreign mercenaries from South Asia, East Africa and South America have also served as force multipliers for the UAE's expeditionary missions. One specialist in politics of the Gulf countries, Robert Mason, has observed that although enhanced military coordination with the USA and bandwagoning with Saudi Arabia have been bedrocks of the UAE's security, 'the greatest potential for the UAE to address ideological issues (i.e. violent Islamism) in the Middle East and worldwide is through working with a diverse range of partners.'[506]

India has gradually moved up from being one among many in the UAE's bouquet of friends to an indispensable defence partner. The 2017 upgrade of the bilateral strategic partnership by adding the prefix 'comprehensive' came with a pledge to ramp up 'joint exercises, training of naval, air and land forces, as also in the area of coastal defence' and to 'exchange experiences in maritime security, including joint anti-piracy training and exercises' in the Gulf and the IOR.[507] The UAE's 100 billion barrels of proven oil reserves, its status as the world's sixth largest oil exporter, and the fact that the primary destinations of its petroleum exports lay to the east in India, China, Japan, Singapore and Thailand, mean that SLOC protection and keeping the entrances to the Indian Ocean,

[506]Mason, Robert, 'Breaking the Mould of Small State Classification? The Broadening Influence of United Arab Emirates Foreign Policy Through Effective Military and Bandwagoning Strategies', *Canadian Foreign Policy Journal*, Vol. 24, No. 1, 2018, p. 102.

[507]MEA, 'India-UAE Joint Statement During State Visit of Crown Prince of Abu Dhabi to India', Ministry of External Affairs, Government of India, 26 January 2017, https://tinyurl.com/5n8ez3fz. Accessed on 19 June 2024.

such as the Bab-al-Mandab Strait and the Strait of Hormuz, free from attacks and blockades are existential necessities for Abu Dhabi.

Since India and France have significant naval power projection and asset deployment in the Western Indian Ocean, the UAE has been keen to engage these two friends and benefit from their experience in naval patrolling and MDA. From 2021, the UAE's navy joined the France-India Varuna naval exercises in the Western Indian Ocean, converting these hitherto bilateral war games into a trilateral. Unlike the Emirati Air Force, Land Forces and the Presidential Guard, the UAE's navy has been rated as 'the least capable', and lacking in sufficient firepower and know-how to have a strategic impact.[508] The combined naval endeavours under the IFU trilateral are of high value for the UAE to scale up capabilities and hone skills. Indian strategists have suggested roping in Egypt, with whom India announced a 'strategic partnership' in 2023 (*see* Annexure, Table III), and expanding the IFU into a quadrilateral maritime axis that could be more potent as Egypt boasts of 'a modernized blue water fleet in the Red Sea'.[509] The UAE's active membership of the IORA and IONS, and its support for a 'joint Indian Ocean strategy in terms of security and economics, rather than a focus on separate national strategies for development,'[510] carry the potential for going beyond trilaterals and drawing in more

[508]Pollack, Kenneth, 'Sizing Up Little Sparta: Understanding UAE Military Effectiveness', American Enterprise Institute, October 2020, p. 5, https://tinyurl.com/yck5ac2x. Accessed on 19 June 2024.

[509]Malpekar, Aditya, 'Egypt-France-India-UAE Quadrilateral: An Axis in the Strategic Waters', Vivekananda International Foundation, 25 August 2023, https://tinyurl.com/37us27rr. Accessed on 19 June 2024.

[510]MOFA, 'UAE Sees the Strengthening of Cooperation Between Indian Ocean Rim Countries as a Priority', United Arab Emirates Ministry of Foreign Affairs, 4 February 2021, https://tinyurl.com/yze3weak. Accessed on 19 June 2024.

partners, using India's facilitation as the lead convener and security provider in the IOR.

For India, whose 90 per cent trade and 80 per cent energy come and go by sea, attacks on commercial shipping in the Red Sea and the Arabian Sea by Somali pirates, and the Iran-allied Houthis have been worrisome reminders that the security of the Western Indian Ocean is inextricably linked to security and partnerships in West Asia/the Middle East. Among the GCC nations, Oman is an intimate friend of India and an enabler of India's maritime strategy in the IOR. In 2018, Oman gave access to its strategically located Duqm Port, overlooking the Arabian Sea, to the Indian Navy and it has been credited with 'enabling New Delhi to maintain its role of net security provider in the Western Indian Ocean Region where China has embarked on a plan to boost its strategic presence.'[511] Since the UAE is Oman's direct neighbour and a fellow GCC member country with whom Muscat has repaired relations, coordinating with these two countries together as a pair will be of high value for India's maritime security goals in the IOR. The UAE's establishment of a military base on Yemen's Socotra Island at the mouth of the Gulf of Aden in the Western Indian Ocean Region could also be leveraged by India. Indian analysts consider Socotra Island valuable for protecting Indian commercial vessels from pirates and militias, keeping an eye on the busiest trade routes, and preparing for 'future maritime events to counter the Chinese naval presence in Djibouti.'[512]

Averting a potential wartime Chinese blockade of the Western Indian Ocean through Beijing's 'string of pearls'

[511]Chaudhury, Dipanjan, 'NSA Visits Oman's Duqm Port Where Indian Navy has Strategic Access', *The Economic Times*, 29 June 2023, https://tinyurl.com/ymnffr46. Accessed on 19 June 2024.
[512]Pandey, Devvrat, 'What UAE's Control Over Socotra Island Means for India, Rest of the World?' *India Today*, 7 April 2023, https://tinyurl.com/57rub7nz. Accessed on 19 June 2024.

via the Doraleh Port in Djibouti and the Gwadar Port in Pakistan remains a military priority for India. Here, India's Gulf friendships, as well as its strategic partnership with Iran, can come in handy. The USA and Israel, both of which are said to have set up intelligence and military presence on Socotra Island, are seen to be backing the UAE's proactive actions abroad 'as part of a balancing act against China's growing influence in Africa.'[513] Yet, as a small state whose number one trade partner has been China (with India and the USA placed second and third), it is unlikely that the UAE will want to be seen as part of any counterbalancing coalition against China on the left flank of the Indo-Pacific.

In the context of the IFU trilateral, it has been pointed out that by teaming up, Abu Dhabi, Paris and New Delhi can 'strengthen their strategic autonomy and secure their interests,' but with the caveat that 'while China may seem as the dominant security threat for India and France, it is not so for the UAE.'[514] The UAE-based Indian scholar Narayanappa Janardhan has argued that 'Asianisation' and 'Look East' outlooks of Gulf countries involve a diversification of economic relations and foreign policies towards all major Asian power centres—China, India, Japan and South Korea—and imply 'a policy of "omni-balancing" that has helped the bloc see beyond the "exclusive" GCC-US framework of the past.'[515]

Just as India will not oblige Gulf countries and Israel in their anti-Iran agenda, and forego its strategic partnership with Tehran, where New Delhi has invested vast sums to develop the Chabahar Port as a counter to Beijing's Gwadar Port

---

[513]Telci, Ismail, and Tuba Horoz, op. cit., p. 156.
[514]Lawale S., and T. Ahmad, 'UAE-India-France Trilateral: A Mechanism to Advance Strategic Autonomy in the Indo-Pacific?' *Asian Journal of Middle Eastern and Islamic Studies*, Vol. 15, No. 4, 2021, pp. 488, 486.
[515]Janardhan, Narayanappa, ed., *The Arab Gulf's Pivot to Asia: From Transactional to Strategic Partnerships*, 2020, Gerlach Press, Berlin, p. 31.

next door in Pakistan, the UAE is not going to drop China to suit Indian or American interests. Friction between Abu Dhabi and Washington over a possible secret military base of the Chinese PLA in the UAE's Khalifa Port, and over the UAE's interest in China's Huawei for its 5G telecom network, suggests that the UAE would be reluctant to join any alliance-like formation against China. Abu Dhabi's 'string of ports' will not be available for New Delhi to counter Beijing's string of pearls, at least not explicitly. Still, there are roundabout ways in which the UAE has helped India to deter China. In 2021 and 2022, the UAE provided mid-air refuelling services to France's Rafale jets so that they could fly non-stop and get delivered to India quickly. This allowed India to activate military bases close to the tri-junction of Sikkim, Bhutan and Chinese-occupied Tibet on a timely basis and strengthen its air capability in the eastern sector[516] amid a tense military stand-off with China (see Chapter 5). The informal name of the IFU trilateral—'Rafale Forum'—conveys a lot.

Both the I2U2 and the IMEC, of which the UAE and India are founding members, also carry shades of soft balancing of China. Abu Dhabi wants these trans-regional initiatives to succeed regardless of the roadblocks posed by the 2023 Israel-Hamas war, and the denial of a political solution to the festering Palestinian problem. The UAE had been the first Gulf nation to open a secret diplomatic channel with Israel, and enjoyed the reputation in Jerusalem as a country with 'the most guts' that was 'way ahead of everyone else in the region' in clandestinely cooperating with Israel.[517] India may

---

[516]Gupta, Shishir, 'Deepening India-UAE Defence Cooperation Enlarges India's Footprint in West Asia', *Hindustan Times*, 15 March 2021, https://tinyurl.com/y4z4cprr. Accessed on 19 June 2024.
[517]Bob, Yonah Jeremy, and Ilan Evyatar, *Target Tehran: How Israel is Using Sabotage, Cyberwarfare, Assassination—and Secret Diplomacy—to Stop a Nuclear Iran and Create a New Middle East*, 2023, Simon & Schuster, New York, p. 46.

have indirectly spurred the covert tryst between Israel and Gulf states to come out of the shadows. In 2022, Naor Gilon, the Israeli Ambassador to India, remarked that 'the Modi government's successful compartmentalization of its Palestine and Israel policies was an inspiration and example for Gulf countries to take similar policy positions and pursue overt, beneficial relations with Israel.'[518] Neither India nor the UAE was the inventor of the I2U2 concept, but both were ready for it due to their openness to Israel.

The formation of I2U2 and IMEC can be traced to Egyptian writer Mohammed Soliman's idea that an 'Indo-Abrahamic alliance' of India, Israel and the UAE existed for 'countering Islamist extremism, defending state sovereignty, and pushing back against the growing influence of the [Pakistan-supportive] Turkey-led Muslim order.'[519] The pace, scale and geographical breadth of the 'new Cold War' between the USA and China will determine how far these plurilateral concepts can venture out to tackle the challenge of China's lengthening shadow in West Asia/the Middle East. One must wait to see the logical denouement of the Indian External Affairs Minister Subrahmanyam Jaishankar's observation that the UAE-India friendship is 'fitting into transformations which are independently underway in this region [West Asia/the Middle East], and often helping to take that transformation forward.'[520]

---

[518]Rajiv, Samuel, *The India-Israel Strategic Partnership: Contours, Opportunities and Challenges*, 2023, Pentagon Press, New Delhi, p. 132.
[519]Soliman, Mohammed, 'An Indo-Abrahamic Alliance on the Rise: How India, Israel and the UAE are Creating a New Transregional Order', Middle East Institute, 28 July 2021, https://tinyurl.com/mrxjrhfe. Accessed on 19 June 2024.
[520]ANI, 'S. Jaishankar Addresses at India Global Forum in UAE', *Asian News International*, 12 December 2022, https://tinyurl.com/3dtvkn3u. Accessed on 19 June 2024.

THE BURJ KHALIFA DREAM

As mutual trust between the state apparatuses of the UAE and India reached unparalleled levels in the domains of security, defence and geopolitics, it has reinforced and redoubled momentum in the old pillars of the 'three Es'—economy, expatriates and energy. In Chapter 2, we noted that India had been shedding old hesitations about FTAs and moving towards signing them with trusted friends and like-minded nations as part of a new outward-looking strategy where economics and geopolitics are inseparable. Thanks to top-level guidance from the Modi-MBZ duo, and Abu Dhabi's alignment with New Delhi in security and global outlooks, the UAE became the first mover in India's shift of gears by signing a Comprehensive Economic Partnership Agreement (CEPA) with it in 2022. Negotiated and inked in a shortened timeframe of merely 88 days, the CEPA was projected to more than double bilateral trade beyond $100 billion, generate over one million jobs in India, and add 1.7 per cent to the UAE's GDP.

Piyush Goyal, India's Commerce Minister, highlighted the CEPA's 'strategic advantages to India' and emphasized that because the 'UAE functions as a trading hub, the Agreement will help provide us market entry points to Africa, Middle East and Europe.'[521] Thani bin Ahmed Al Zeyoudi, the UAE's Minister of State for Foreign Trade, concurred that the CEPA was 'a plan designed to spark holistic, broad-based growth' and that 'by opening up new high-growth markets, we will spark a new era of industrial output, create new opportunities for services exports, particularly finance, professional services, tourism and consulting, and catalyse growth across many

---

[521]PIB, 'India-UAE Economic Partnership Agreement to Open Up New Markets for Indian Goods and Services', Press Information Bureau, 20 February 2022, https://tinyurl.com/33cxdrdn. Accessed on 19 June 2024.

other sectors.'[522] Such was the booster dose of the CEPA that within one year of its signing, the UAE became India's second-largest export destination, and third-largest trading partner, behind only the USA and China.

In 2023, the UAE also leapfrogged from the seventh-largest foreign investor in India to the fourth largest. In 2024, the signing of the UAE-India Bilateral Investment Treaty (BIT) sped up this process and enthused big Emirati investors to bankroll domestic manufacturing and generate employment in India. For a small-sized country like the UAE to reach a stage where it is decisively impacting the economic fortunes of a leading power or a would-be great power such as India, is no mean feat.

Since the 3rd millennium BC, civilizations along India's coastline and their contemporaries in the Arab world had been linked through travel and trade via the Western Indian Ocean. Mercantile connections grew more pronounced when the Trucial States—territories comprising the current-day UAE—were administered by the British operating out of their colony in India in the 19th and 20th centuries. Given the long historical patterns of economic exchanges, the present-day commercial dynamism between the UAE and India brings with it a sense of the wheel of history coming full circle.[523]

In 2023, economic ties received another shot in the arm with an element of nostalgia when Abu Dhabi and New Delhi implemented a Dirham-Rupee settlement system that would permit exporters and importers on both sides to bypass the American dollar, and issue invoices and payments in their respective domestic currencies. The move brought

---

[522]BW, 'India-UAE Economic Partnership is Major Milestone in History of Both Nations: UAE Minister for Foreign Trade', *Business World*, 15 July 2023, https://tinyurl.com/25e75ffh. Accessed on 24 June 2024.
[523]Lentin, Sifra, 'India-UAE Trade Comes Full Circle', Gateway House, 21 April 2022, https://tinyurl.com/3n8m79cd. Accessed on 19 June 2024.

'tangible benefits including easier cross-border trade payments with lower transaction costs' and opened 'a broad range of opportunities that provides more choice to businesses.'[524] For the Indian Rupee, which had been the official currency of the Trucial States under British colonialism, there could be no better brand ambassador than the fiercely independent UAE to gain greater acceptability as an international currency. The UAE's decision in 2023 to invite India's pioneering RuPay card network to 'construct, deploy, and operationalize the UAE's national domestic card scheme, which aims to accelerate the growth of e-commerce and digital transactions, advance financial inclusion, and align with the UAE's ambitious digitization agenda,'[525] was another marquee moment in the friendship as it demonstrated to the world that India could be a provider of DPI not only to poor nations but also to rich ones. The resultant Jaywan RuPay cards were rolled out in the UAE by all banks in 2024, and sought to be co-badged with Mastercard and Visa to 'extend the reach to the rest of the world.'[526] For an Indian Fintech innovation to go global through the channelling of the UAE is exactly what this transformative embrace is all about.

Likewise, in 2023, the announcement that the prestigious Indian Institute of Technology (IIT) Delhi would establish a campus in Abu Dhabi to offer degree programmes and promote research in sustainable energy, climate studies, computing, and data sciences was a major endorsement of India's potential

---

[524]Sayegh, Ahmed Ali Al, 'Trade is at the Heart of the India-UAE Relations', *Hindustan Times*, 5 September 2023, https://tinyurl.com/355w97tu. Accessed on 19 June 2024.
[525]AIR, 'India and UAE Forge Historic Partnership for RuPay Domestic Card Scheme Implementation', *All India Radio*, 5 October 2023, https://tinyurl.com/6n6ksjuc. Accessed on 24 June 2024.
[526]Abbas, Waheed, '"All UAE Banks have to Launch Jaywan Debit Cards": Rollout to Happen in Phases', *Khaleej Times*, 14 May 2024, https://tinyurl.com/27ybkbn3. Accessed on 19 June 2024.

for global leadership in the higher education sector. It also fit into the UAE's long-term plans like the Economic Vision 2030 and the Centennial Plan 2071, which prioritize reducing dependence on oil, teaching advanced sciences and technology, and building a diversified knowledge economy in the UAE by the time it reaches its 100th anniversary.[527] As the Indian security analyst P.N. Khushnam put it, 'the Emirates' plans to develop a diversified, knowledge-based 21st century economy have dovetailed with the Modi administration's blueprint for unleashing India's economic potential.'[528]

The 2022 UAE-India agreement to set up a Food Security Corridor worth $7 billion 'to connect Indian farms directly to the UAE ports throughout the food production value chain'[529] is another strategic initiative to meet Abu Dhabi's priorities of expanding non-oil trade and making IMEC a multidimensional project. If two countries set respective long-term goals and these are fulfilled by means of the bilateral friendship, it is literally making the best of both worlds.

Even in the conventional sphere of fossil fuels, the UAE-India friendship has gone strategic and transcended the traditional buyer-seller relationship. In 2018, the UAE became the first foreign partner to invest $400 million in India's Strategic Petroleum Reserves Programme, wherein the Abu Dhabi National Oil Company (ADNOC) stored millions of barrels of oil in an underground rock cavern in Mangalore, and helped India build a storage of liquid gold that it could tap into during emergencies and protect itself 'from serious disruptions

[527]UC, 'UAE Centennial Plan 2071', United Arab Emirates Cabinet, https://tinyurl.com/5xnsbz4c. Accessed on 19 June 2024.
[528]Khushnam, P.N., 'India-UAE Relations: Poised to Climb to New Heights', Middle East Institute, 23 March 2021, https://tinyurl.com/28uyfx4c. Accessed on 19 June 2024.
[529]EPC, 'UAE-India Food Security Corridor: A Global Supply Chain Alternative', Emirates Policy Center, 1 December 2023, https://tinyurl.com/yc6uwfw2. Accessed on 19 June 2024.

in [the] global crude oil supply chain.'[530] The special utility of the UAE to India lies in it being a bellwether country that sets a precedent whose example is followed by other GCC nations. After the UAE launched Phase I of India's strategic reserve and got the ball rolling, Saudi Arabia inked a 'comprehensive cooperation agreement' in energy with India in 2023, whose remit included renewable energy, energy efficiency, hydrogen and strategic petroleum reserves. Internal competitive dynamics within the GCC are such that once the UAE-India FTA was signed and implemented, Saudi Arabia engaged with India for expediting the broader GCC-India FTA and for trading in local currencies with all GCC member countries.

That the UAE is the harbinger of India's 'Link West' policy, which aims to improve relationships in the Gulf and the rest of West Asia/the Middle East, is also apparent from the way it has been a regional leader in absorbing enormous waves of Indian migrant workers into its economy and nation-building endeavours. A unique 'national minority state' where 'nationals [native Arabs holding citizenship] are a minority among the population'[531] and expatriates constitute 90 per cent of the society, the UAE made a clear choice that it preferred and trusted Indians over any other group of foreigners to form the bulk of its labour force. As of 2023, the UAE hosted more than 3.5 million Indians, making it 'the most popular destination for Indian citizens seeking work overseas.'[532] That meant Indians made up around one-third of the UAE's total

[530]MPNG, 'Indian Strategic Petroleum Reserve Limited', Ministry of Petroleum and Natural Gas, Government of India, https://tinyurl.com/y2224n3f. Accessed on 19 June 2024.

[531]Horinuki, Koji, 'Controversies Over Labor Naturalisation Policy and its Dilemmas: 40 Years of Emiratisation in the United Arab Emirates', *Kyoto Bulletin of Islamic Area Studies*, Vol. 4, Nos. 1–2, 2011, p. 41.

[532]TN, 'Indian Population in UAE Crosses 3.5 Million, Minister Says', *The National*, 13 August 2023, https://tinyurl.com/5n7nwx7b. Accessed on 19 June 2024.

population, and were larger in number than the combined total of the next four biggest groups of expatriates from Pakistan, Bangladesh, the Philippines and Iran.

In Chapter 3, we referred to the American Dream and how a slice of America beats in India's heart due to the huge diaspora presence there. For states of India which send the maximum expats to the UAE, 'a very close heart-to-heart relationship' with the Emirates is a central fact of life and a determining aspect of their local societies and economies.[533] However, unlike the *Desi*s in the USA, the Indian diaspora in the UAE lacks a pathway to naturalization and citizenship, and approximately 60 per cent of it is employed in manual blue-collar work. Given the tightly controlled monarchical regime in the UAE, and the non-permanent residence permits issued to expats, Indians there are politically disenfranchised and not an organized lobby. Still, the remittances sent by the expats from the UAE accounted for 18 per cent of India's total inward remittances in 2023, second only to the money flows received from the *Desi*s in the USA. Two writers on West Asia/the Middle East, Omar Bortolazzi and Noor Khan, have studied 'transnational diaspora entrepreneurs' among white-collar Indians based in the UAE, and argued that they generate 'capital gain' for India. These skilled Indian expats are 'more willing to engage in high-risk business activities in emerging markets, owing to their expanded knowledge of the local, political, economic, and cultural environment, their individual connections and linguistic abilities, and their use of global networks.' They have 'created opportunities for investment, trade, and outsourcing, fostering strategic partnerships, leveraging access to relatively cheap labor and large talent

[533]GN, 'UAE, Kerala Have Heart-To-Heart Relationship: Chief Minister Pinarayi Vijayan', *Gulf News*, 3 February 2022, https://tinyurl.com/2rzvzk66. Accessed on 19 June 2024.

pools, and utilizing sources of political and financial capital in facilitating the transfer of knowledge and technology.'[534]

The trailblazing success of expatriate Indian business conglomerates in the UAE like the LuLu Group, Landmark Group, Varkey Group, the Ravi Pillai Group and Alukkas has not been limited to accumulating wealth and living the Burj Khalifa dream of unfettered capitalism in the desert. Their wealth circulates between the UAE and India and across the Gulf region through networks. The Indian diaspora is the lynchpin, driving the burgeoning bilateral trade and FDI flows and is the living and breathing champion of the UAE-India friendship. It has also been a medium through which India's soft power has spread throughout West Asia/the Middle East.

Much of the international recognition of India's films, music, books, TV shows and yoga is thanks to the choice of the glitzy heights of Dubai and Sharjah as launchpads by India's creative class, which has a home away from home in the UAE because of the vector-like role played by the Indian migrant community there. MBZ acknowledged this when he credited Indian expats in the UAE for 'deepening popular links between the two countries, and strengthening the basis of common interests which open up bigger prospects for the future of bilateral relations.'[535] With the UAE and India venturing into triangular development cooperation in Africa, the expansion of UAE-based Indian business empires which are investing large sums in the African continent has the potential to hoist the bilateral friendship into wider terrain.

---

[534]Bortolazzi, Omar, and Noor Khan, 'From "Brain Drain" to "Capital Gain": Indian Skilled Migration to the UAE', in Rahman, Md Mizanur, and Amr Al Azm, eds., *Social Change in the Gulf Region*, 2023, Springer, Singapore, p. 235.

[535]UC, 'Mohamed Bin Zayed: UAE-India Bilateral Relations are Solid; Both Sides Keen on Strengthening Strategic Partnership', United Arab Emirates Cabinet, https://tinyurl.com/mryjmhx4. Accessed on 19 June 2024.

The vibrant diaspora could well ensure that in India's list of comprehensive strategic partnerships (*see* Annexure, Table III), one country that has to get an upgrade by insertion of the word 'global' will be the UAE.

EPILOGUE:
THE PATH OF A LEADING POWER

The Vijigishu [conqueror] should cultivate the alliance
of monarchs stationed far off, of those who constitute
his Mandala [concentric circle], of local governors and
also of the Foresters [those who hold forts and castles].
It is those monarchs well-supported by their allies that
can consolidate their empire.[536]

—Kamandaka, Indian strategist,
circa AD 6th or 7th century

In 2006, India's Ministry of External Affairs (MEA) reportedly prepared a list of countries ranked according to their importance in the coming decades. Dubbed as the 'Relevance for India Index', it assigned a numerical score on the basis of each nation's political and strategic significance, cultural affinity and hosting of the Indian diaspora, and economic and commercial promise. The USA came out on top in this index, with 92 points, followed by the UK at 86 points, and then France, Japan and Russia, all of which were rated equally at 79 points. Given the flavour of that era, when China was perceived as a benign player, a fellow emerging power and a strategic partner of India (*see* Annexure, Table III), it was assigned the sixth position with 77 points.

---

[536]Dutt, Manmatha Nath, *Kamandakiya Nitisara or The Elements of Polity* (Translated), 1896, Elysium Press, Calcutta, p. 95.

The debate surrounding it apparently was that some Indian officials had been 'at a loss to understand why Japan should be more important than China' despite the latter's 'proximity and strategic importance'.[537]

Looking back at this index from a contemporary lens, expectations that the USA, France, Japan and Russia would be most relevant to India in the future turned out to be absolutely accurate. The UK may also catch up with these four as it would not want to be seen as lagging behind its European competitor France in shaping a rules-based Indo-Pacific. India upgraded its friendship with the UK to a 'comprehensive strategic partnership' in 2021, and there are indications that trade and defence ties between them will scale up in the coming years.

However, it is fascinating that three of India's friends—Australia, Israel and the UAE—whose strategic value we have demonstrated in this book, were not ranked highly in the 2006 index. The other change from today's perspective is that China cannot, by any stretch of imagination, be considered a friend of India. Due to its acknowledged great power status and hegemonic conduct, China does remain relevant to India but in a negative sense—as an adversary or threat and not as a partner or opportunity.

The journey of India's strategic evolution over the past two decades is thus as much of change as of continuity, with Australia, Israel and the UAE entering India's orbit of most consequential friends, and the 800-pound dragon China falling out of the orbit. The former British Prime Minister Lord Palmerston's oft-quoted 19th-century maxim that a country 'has no permanent friends; she has only permanent interests'[538]

---

[537]Chaudhury, Nilova Roy, 'India Maps its Equation with the World', *Hindustan Times*, 22 October 2006, https://tinyurl.com/y4x43nw9. Accessed on 24 June 2024.
[538]Cited in Walt, Stephen, *The Origins of Alliances*, 2013, Cornell University Press, Ithaca, p. 33.

is only partially borne out by the Indian experience. Some of the friends covered in this book have been permanent friends or anchors of stability despite the international order undergoing pronounced shifts from bipolar to unipolar, and then back to bipolar and thence to an emerging multipolar structure. On the other hand, the advent of new friends in the past two decades, and the recalibration of old friendships to suit contemporary needs, attests to the altered reality of India rising from the ranks of middle powers and heading towards the status of a leading power or a would-be great power. The composition, functions and operational content of India's friendships have undergone adjustments in keeping with the kind of power that India has become.

Throughout this book, we have shown that there is an inseparable link between India's upward movement in the global power configuration and the type of friends it hangs out with and the range of activities it does with these friends. To quote External Affairs Minister Subrahmanyam Jaishankar, as India 'rises up the global hierarchy of power, the requirement for reliable friends will grow, not lessen.'[539] The equation between India and its seven friends chronicled in this book rests not just on the basis of what India gives and takes in economic or military domains from them, but also on where India stands alongside each of them in the international power hierarchy. If some old friends have stuck to India despite monumental modifications in regional and global orders, it is because their own long-term foreign policy goals are being fulfilled by associating with India. As to the new friends of the past few decades, they see in India a partner which can assist in achieving their revised regional and global ambitions. Friends are fundamental to making India a leading power, and India in turn is fundamental to the aspirations of its friends.

---

[539]Jaishankar, Subrahmanyam, *Why Bharat Matters*, 2024, Rupa Publications, New Delhi, p. 85.

A common pattern among most of the friends analysed in this book is that India is valued by them due to its unshakeable faith in strategic autonomy vis-à-vis great powers. Since birds of a feather flock together, India's independent approach to foreign policy attracts middle and small powers like Australia, France, Japan, Israel, Russia and the UAE—all of whom have been striving to carve out their own respective zones of strategic autonomy from the USA or China. We saw in this book that even the 'quasi-friends' who are drawn to India by virtue of its friendship with their treaty ally USA, have subtly relied on India to fill the vacuum left by a declining, distracted or disappointing USA. India is not a substitute for the USA, but it certainly has picked up the slack left by perceived failures or lacunae of the USA as a trustworthy ally or strategic partner. As to the other great power, China, how strongly and steadfastly India counterbalances it will mean much to its friends as they despair about losing their traditional spheres of influence to an expansionist China. How willingly and boldly India stands up to China is also going to be the defining parameter in the USA-India friendship.

To sum up, India cannot make do without friends as it assumes its destiny as a leading power in the world. The kind of power that India is today and will be tomorrow is reflected in its choice of friends, and the forms of cooperation it engages in with these friends. Very much in line with ancient Indian strategic wisdom, there is a clear-cut role for enemies in crafting India's core friendships and determining their depth and breadth. In return, India's strategic partners leverage their friendship with it for soft balancing or hard balancing their respective enemies or threats. Thus far, India has managed to juggle its strategic partnerships with countries such as Russia and the USA, which consider each other enemies and find themselves in opposite camps in a highly divided world.

But as polarization in international relations intensifies, will India be forced to prioritize some friendships over others and abandon the flexible formula of multi-alignment? Will strategic partnerships be sufficient for India or will circumstances compel it to convert them into formal alliances?

The answer to whether varied friendships have to give way to one or a select few marriages depends on how much hard economic and military power India accumulates, how bellicosely China behaves, and whether Russia can find a modus vivendi with the West. With so many unknowns and imponderables out there, the safest path for a leading power is to converge and coordinate ever more closely with the assets it can count upon—its best friends.

ANNEXURE

Table I
Strategic and Other Partnerships of the United States of America[540]

Region/ Sub-Region	Country	Year of Establishment/ Upgrade	Form of Partnership
Indo-Pacific	China	1997	Constructive Strategic Partnership
		2011	Cooperative Partnership Based on Mutual Respect and Mutual Benefit

---

[540]There is no single publicly available official list of all the strategic partnerships of the USA. This table is compiled from various joint statements and declarations issued by the government of the USA, and partner countries, as well as commentaries and analyses of the USA's ties with each of these partners. The data provided here is not necessarily exhaustive, comprehensive or updated, as the naming and upgrading of partners is a dynamic process.

Region/ Sub-Region	Country	Year of Establishment/ Upgrade	Form of Partnership
	India	2004	Strategic Partnership
		2009	Global Strategic Partnership
		2016	Major Defence Partnership
		2020	Comprehensive Global and Strategic Partnership
	Indonesia	2010	Comprehensive Partnership
		2015	Strategic Partnership
		2023	Comprehensive Strategic Partnership
	Pakistan	2006	Long-Term Strategic Partnership (besides formal Major Non-NATO Ally status)
	Malaysia	2014	Comprehensive Partnership
		2015	Enhanced Strategic Partnership
	Singapore	2005	Strategic Framework Agreement
		2012	Strategic Partnership
	Vietnam	2013	Comprehensive Partnership
		2023	Comprehensive Strategic Partnership

Region/ Sub-Region	Country	Year of Establishment/ Upgrade	Form of Partnership
Europe	Czech Republic	2022	Strategic Dialogue Partnership (besides formal Ally status in NATO)
	Poland	2018	Strategic Partnership (besides formal Ally status in NATO)
	Romania	1997	Strategic Partnership (besides formal Ally status in NATO)
	Slovenia	2020	Strategic Dialogue Partnership (besides formal Ally status in NATO)
West Asia/ Middle East	Egypt	1979	Strategic Partnership (besides formal Major Non-NATO Ally status)
	Israel	2014	Strategic Partnership (besides formal Major Non-NATO Ally status)
	Jordan	2022	Strategic Partnership (besides formal Major Non-NATO Ally status)
	Qatar	2018	Strategic Dialogue Partnership (besides formal Major Non-NATO Ally status)

Region/ Sub-Region	Country	Year of Establishment/ Upgrade	Form of Partnership
	Saudi Arabia	2023	Strategic Partnership (besides formal Ally status through a Mutual Defence Assistance Agreement)
	Turkey	2021	Strategic Mechanism (besides formal Ally status in NATO)
	UAE	2020	Strategic Dialogue Partnership
Africa	Kenya	2022	Strategic Trade and Investment Partnership
	Nigeria	2021	Strategic Partnership
Latin America	Brazil	2019	Strategic Dialogue Partnership (besides formal Major Non-NATO Ally status)

Table II
Strategic and Other Partnerships of the
People's Republic of China[541]

Country/Institution	Year of Establishment/ Upgrade	Form of Partnership
Afghanistan	2012	Strategic and Cooperative Partnership
Algeria	2014	Comprehensive Strategic Partnership
Angola	2010	Strategic Partnership
Argentina	2001	21st-Century-Oriented Comprehensive Cooperative Partnership
	2004	Strategic Partnership
	2014	Comprehensive Strategic Partnership
Australia	2013	Strategic Partnership of Mutual Trust and Mutual Benefit
	2014	Comprehensive Strategic Partnership
Bangladesh	2016	Strategic Cooperative Partnership

---

[541]As with the USA, China does not provide any single publicly available official list of all its strategic partnerships. This table is compiled from joint statements and declarations issued by the Chinese government and its foreign counterparts, websites of Chinese embassies, as well as news media and scholarly publications on China's diplomatic strategies. The data given here is not necessarily exhaustive, comprehensive or updated, as the naming and upgrading of partners is a dynamic process.

Country/Institution	Year of Establishment/ Upgrade	Form of Partnership
Belarus	2013	Comprehensive Strategic Cooperative Partnership
Belgium	2014	All-Round Partnership of Friendship and Cooperation
Brazil	1993	Strategic Partnership
	2012	Comprehensive Strategic Partnership
Bulgaria	2014	Comprehensive Friendly Cooperative Partnership
	2019	Strategic Partnership
Cambodia	2006 2010	Comprehensive Cooperative Partnership Comprehensive Strategic Partnership of Cooperation
Canada	1997 2005	21st-Century-Oriented Comprehensive Cooperative Partnership Strategic Partnership
Chile	2004 2012	Comprehensive Cooperative Partnership Strategic Partnership
Costa Rica	2015	Strategic Partnership
Croatia	2005	Comprehensive Cooperative Partnership
Czech Republic	2016	Strategic Partnership

Country/Institution	Year of Establishment/ Upgrade	Form of Partnership
Democratic Republic of the Congo	2015	Strategic Partnership of Win-Win Cooperation
	2023	Comprehensive Strategic Cooperative Partnership
Denmark	2008	Comprehensive Strategic Partnership
Ecuador	2016	Comprehensive Strategic Partnership
Egypt	2014	Comprehensive Strategic Partnership
Ethiopia	2017	Comprehensive Cooperative Partnership
European Union	1998	Comprehensive Partnership
	2003	Comprehensive Strategic Partnership
Fiji	2006	Important Cooperative Partnership
	2014	Strategic Partnership of Mutual Respect and Common Development
France	1997	Comprehensive Partnership
	2004	Comprehensive Strategic Partnership
	2010	New, Mature and Stable Comprehensive Strategic Partnership

Country/Institution	Year of Establishment/ Upgrade	Form of Partnership
	2014	Close and Lasting Comprehensive Strategic Partnership
Gabon	2016	Comprehensive Cooperative Partnership
	2023	Comprehensive Cooperative Strategic Partnership
Germany	2014	All-Round Strategic Partnership
Greece	2006	Comprehensive Strategic Partnership
Guinea	2016	Comprehensive Strategic Partnership
Hungary	2004	Friendly Cooperative Partnership
	2017	Comprehensive Strategic Partnership
India	2003	Constructive Partnership
	2005	Strategic and Cooperative Partnership for Peace and Prosperity
Indonesia	2005	Strategic Partnership
	2013	Comprehensive Strategic Partnership
Iran	2021	25-Year Comprehensive Strategic Partnership

Country/Institution	Year of Establishment/ Upgrade	Form of Partnership
Ireland	2012	Strategic Partnership of Mutual Benefit
Israel	2017	Innovative Comprehensive Partnership
Italy	1998	Comprehensive Partnership
	2004	Comprehensive Strategic Partnership
Jamaica	2005	Friendly Partnership for Common Development
	2019	Strategic Partnership
Jordan	2015	Strategic Partnership
Kazakhstan	2005	Strategic Partnership
	2011	Comprehensive Strategic Partnership
	2019	Permanent Comprehensive Strategic Partnership
Kenya	2013	Comprehensive Cooperative Partnership
Kyrgyzstan	2013	Strategic Partnership
	2023	Comprehensive Strategic Partnership
Laos	2009	Comprehensive Strategic Partnership of Cooperation

Country/Institution	Year of Establishment/ Upgrade	Form of Partnership
Liberia	2015	All-Round Cooperative Partnership
Madagascar	2017	Comprehensive Cooperative Partnership
Malaysia	2013	Comprehensive Strategic Partnership
Maldives	2014	Comprehensive Friendly Partnership
Mexico	1997	Cross-Century Comprehensive Cooperative Partnership
	2003	Strategic Partnership
	2013	Comprehensive Strategic Partnership
Mongolia	2003	Good-Neighbourly and Mutual Trust Partnership
	2011	Strategic Partnership
	2014	Comprehensive Strategic Partnership
Morocco	2016	Strategic Partnership
Mozambique	2016	Comprehensive Strategic Partnership
Myanmar	2011	Comprehensive Strategic Cooperative Partnership

Country/Institution	Year of Establishment/ Upgrade	Form of Partnership
Namibia	2018	Comprehensive Strategic Partnership of Cooperation
Nepal	2019	Strategic Partnership of Cooperation Featuring Ever-Lasting Friendship for Development and Prosperity
Netherlands	2014	Open and Pragmatic Partnership for Comprehensive Cooperation
New Zealand	2014	Comprehensive Strategic Partnership
Nigeria	2005	Strategic Partnership
Pakistan	1999	Partnership of Comprehensive Cooperation
	2005	All-Weather Strategic Partnership
State of Palestine	2023	Strategic Partnership
Papua New Guinea	2018	Comprehensive Strategic Partnership Featuring Mutual Respect and Common Development
Peru	2004	Comprehensive Partnership
	2008	Strategic Partnership
	2013	Comprehensive Strategic Partnership

Country/Institution	Year of Establishment/ Upgrade	Form of Partnership
Poland	2004	Friendly Cooperative Partnership
	2011	Strategic Partnership
	2016	Comprehensive Strategic Partnership
Portugal	2005	Comprehensive Strategic Partnership
Qatar	2014	Strategic Partnership
Russia	1994	Constructive Partnership Featuring Good Neighbourliness and Mutually Beneficial Cooperation
	1996	
	2001	Partnership of Strategic Coordination Based on Equality and Mutual Benefit and Oriented Towards the 21st Century
	2019	Comprehensive Strategic Partnership of Coordination
		Comprehensive Strategic Partnership of Coordination for a New Era
Saudi Arabia	2022	Strategic Partnership

Country/Institution	Year of Establishment/ Upgrade	Form of Partnership
Serbia	2009	Strategic Partnership
	2013	Deepening Strategic Partnership
	2016	Comprehensive Strategic Partnership
Sierra Leone	2016	Comprehensive Strategic Cooperative Partnership
Solomon Islands	2023	Comprehensive Strategic Partnership Featuring Mutual Respect and Common Development for a New Era
South Africa	2004	Strategic Partnership Featuring Equality, Mutual Benefit and Common Development
	2010	Comprehensive Strategic Partnership
South Korea	1998	Collaborative Partnership for the 21st Century
	2003	Comprehensive Partnership
	2008	Strategic Partnership
Spain	2005	Comprehensive Strategic Partnership

Country/Institution	Year of Establishment/ Upgrade	Form of Partnership
Sri Lanka	2005	Comprehensive Partnership
	2013	Strategic Cooperative Partnership
Sudan	2015	Strategic Partnership
Syria	2023	Strategic Partnership
Tajikistan	2013	Strategic Partnership
Tanzania	2022	Comprehensive Strategic Cooperative Partnership
Thailand	2012	Comprehensive Strategic Cooperative Partnership
Timor-Leste	2023	Comprehensive Strategic Partnership
Turkey	2002	Enhanced Partnership
	2010	Strategic Partnership
Turkmenistan	2013	Strategic Partnership
	2023	Comprehensive Strategic Partnership
Ukraine	2011	Strategic Partnership
UAE	2012	Strategic Partnership
UK	1998	Comprehensive Partnership
	2004	Comprehensive Strategic Partnership

Country/Institution	Year of Establishment/ Upgrade	Form of Partnership
USA	1997	Constructive Strategic Partnership
	2011	Cooperative Partnership Based on Mutual Respect and Mutual Benefit
Uruguay	2016	Strategic Partnership
Uzbekistan	2005	Friendly and Cooperative Partnership
	2012	Strategic Partnership
Vietnam	2008	Comprehensive Strategic Cooperative Partnership
Venezuela	2001	Strategic Partnership for Common Development
	2023	All-Weather Strategic Partnership
Zambia	2023	Comprehensive Strategic Cooperative Partnership
Zimbabwe	2018	Comprehensive Strategic Partnership of Cooperation

Table III
Strategic and Other Partnerships of India[542]

Region/Sub-Region	Country/Institution	Year of Establishment/Upgrade	Form of Partnership
Indo-Pacific	ASEAN	2012	Strategic Partnership
		2022	Comprehensive Strategic Partnership
	Australia	2009	Strategic Partnership
		2020	Comprehensive Strategic Partnership
	China	2005	Strategic and Cooperative Partnership for Peace and Prosperity
	Japan	2000	Global Partnership in the Twenty-First Century
		2006	Global and Strategic Partnership
		2014	Special Strategic and Global Partnership

[542]Like in the cases of the USA and China, India has not released any single official list of all its strategic partnerships. This table has been prepared by collating joint statements and declarations issued by the Indian government and its foreign counterparts, websites of Indian embassies and high commissions, as well as news media and scholarly publications on India's diplomacy. The same disclaimer applies here that the data given is not necessarily exhaustive, comprehensive or updated, as the naming and upgrading of partners is a dynamic process and keeps evolving.

Region/Sub-Region	Country/Institution	Year of Establishment/Upgrade	Form of Partnership
	Indonesia	2005	Strategic Partnership
		2018	Comprehensive Strategic Partnership
	Malaysia	2010	Strategic Partnership
		2024	Comprehensive Strategic Partnership
	Mongolia	2015	Strategic Partnership
	Seychelles	2015	Strategic Partnership
	Singapore	2015	Strategic Partnership
	South Korea	2010	Strategic Partnership
		2015	Special Strategic Partnership
	Vietnam	2007	Strategic Partnership
		2016	Comprehensive Strategic Partnership
West Asia/the Middle East	Egypt	2023	Strategic Partnership
	Iran	2003	Strategic Partnership
	Israel	2017	Strategic Partnership
	Oman	2008	Strategic Partnership
	Saudi Arabia	2010	Strategic Partnership
		2019	Strategic Partnership Council
	UAE	2015	Strategic Partnership
		2017	Comprehensive Strategic Partnership
Central Asia/South Asia	Afghanistan	2011	Strategic Partnership

Region/Sub-Region	Country/Institution	Year of Establishment/Upgrade	Form of Partnership
	Kazakhstan	2009	Strategic Partnership
	Tajikistan	2012	Strategic Partnership
	Uzbekistan	2011	Strategic Partnership
Europe/Eurasia	Czech Republic	2024	Strategic Partnership on Innovation
	Denmark	2019	Green Strategic Partnership
	EU	2004	Strategic Partnership
	France	1998	Strategic Partnership
	Germany	2001	Strategic Partnership
	Greece	2023	Strategic Partnership
	Italy	2023	Strategic Partnership
	Netherlands	2022	Strategic Water Partnership
	Poland	2024	Strategic Partnership
	Russia	2000	Strategic Partnership
		2010	Special and Privileged Strategic Partnership
	UK	2004	Strategic Partnership
		2021	Comprehensive Strategic Partnership
Africa	Rwanda	2017	Strategic Partnership
	South Africa	1997	Strategic Partnership
		2019	Strategic Programme of Cooperation
	Tanzania	2023	Strategic Partnership
South America	Argentina	2019	Strategic Partnership

Region/Sub-Region	Country/Institution	Year of Establishment/Upgrade	Form of Partnership
	Brazil	2006	Strategic Partnership
North America	USA	2004	Strategic Partnership
		2009	Global Strategic Partnership
		2016	Major Defence Partnership
		2020	Comprehensive Global and Strategic Partnership

ACKNOWLEDGEMENTS

Although my previous book, *Crunch Time: Narendra Modi's National Security Crises* (Rupa Publications, 2022), focused on India's two principal adversaries, China and Pakistan, its narrative briefly touched upon several crucial friends of India. Like the Shiva and Shakti of Indian philosophy, and the Yin and Yang of Chinese philosophy, enemies and friends, conflict and cooperation, competition and coordination, are two sides of the same coin. The idea of *Friends: India's Closest Strategic Partners* emanated from the realization that having extensively covered India's opponents in a full-length volume, it was time to take an in-depth look at India's strategic partners.

As I started my preparatory readings, and began collecting material for this book, the themes of existing literature in the domain only served to reconfirm the validity of this project. No one had yet covered all of India's closest friends in a single book. This lacuna could possibly be put down to the practice of area or regional studies, wherein institutions and individual scholars are encouraged to specialize in a single country, or a set of countries within a geographical space, and stick to writing about India's relations with only that specific country or area. Entire books focus, for instance, only on the Japan-India partnership, or on the USA-India friendship. They dive deep into the nitty-gritty of one bilateral dyad, and offer dense details on it.

While such works are necessary from a specialist's point of view, for general readers of non-fiction who are curious about India's foreign policy, and the role of its varied friends in its rise, a single work that profiles all the top strategic partners of India, using a broad comparative lens, has been long overdue. *Friends,* hopefully, shall plug that gap, and help readers appreciate the unique and beneficial role of India's varied friendships in its overall grand strategy.

For the six singly authored books that I have published at regular intervals since 2011, and that have earned me the tag of a 'prolific writer', I am beholden to my institutional home over the past 15 years, O.P. Jindal Global University (JGU). Under the dynamic leadership of Vice Chancellor C. Raj Kumar, JGU has become the quintessential abode for intellectual pursuits, where there is absolute and unconditional freedom of thought and academic openness.

The plethora of resources that JGU provides to a writer is second to none. No matter which book, journal, report, magazine or newspaper I needed, JGU's library staff would go out of their way to get these for me as hard or soft copies almost immediately. My senior manager Lalit Kumar is a dream worker whose incessant efforts and efficient handling of my schedule ensured timely completion of this book. Swarnima Singh and Tanu Singh, my administrative colleagues, diligently handled the daily tasks so that I could concentrate for long spells on finishing the manuscript. My faculty colleagues, particularly those manning administrative positions, also eased my task as a writer through their diligence and willingness to take on infinite commitments. I thank them all, especially the late Pankaj Jha, whose loss is irreplaceable.

Among JGU's biggest assets is its vast pool of young talent—brilliant bachelor's, master's and doctoral students. As with all my previous books, I could count on a large team of background researchers and fact-finders from among our top students to provide me empirical and conceptual inputs. Special thanks to Seerat Arora and Raghav Dua for spearheading the student research team, and for delivering specific answer sets to questions that I would prepare for them. I have little doubt that, in years to come, Seerat and Raghav will make waves in the academic field of International Relations.

The following team members took time out from classes, exams, extra-curriculars and socials to assist me with this project: Anayaah, Ananya Purohit, Krishangi Kathotia, Nandini Bhatnagar, Nikita Anand, Rishabh Sachdeva, Sarthak Mukherjee, Shatakshi Tyagi, Uttara Iyer, Vanshika Sirohi and Vartika Sharma. These outstanding young minds are India's future.

Friends is my second successive book with Rupa Publications. The intense editorial involvement, professional development of the manuscript, post-publication marketing and retail visibility that Rupa offers are unmatched in India. A special word of thanks to Executive Editor Yamini Chowdhury and her colleagues for getting me into the habit of publishing with the 'House of Bestsellers'.

It takes a strong personal support system to make an author. I am no exception. The intellectual motivation and inclination of my father, Prafulla Kumar Chaulia, and the infinite love of my mother, Chandrakala Chaulia, have formed my very core as a writer. Gratitude is an inadequate word to use for both of them.

Looking out for my best interests, my partner Usha Rani Damerla has been my greatest support for decades in building my career in writing, academia and the news media. I thank her for her giving and forgiving nature, which made one more book possible yet again.

I am thankful to my two children, Debarchan Vishnu Chaulia and Ahaana Kranti Chaulia, for putting up with my periodic absences and chronic absent-mindedness. They are now old enough to know why Dad the writer needed his space and time to write these books. A special shout-out to my high school-going son Deb, who was the first person to diligently proofread the complete manuscript. His suggestions and corrections helped me edit and make this book simpler and reader-friendly.

In the final analysis, *Friends* is the result of my earnest desire to see India attain the status of what Prime Minister Narendra Modi calls a 'leading power' in world affairs. If I were to work my way backwards, had there been no patriotic Indian heart beating inside me, this book would never have even been conceived. I sincerely hope that through *Friends*, readers will gain a deeper understanding of the kind of power India is, and is destined to be.

INDEX